CHINESE COOKING

KNACK®

CHINESE COOKING

A Step-by-Step Guide to Authentic Dishes Made Easy

BELINDA HULIN

WITH KIAN LAM KHO

Photographs by Liesa Cole

KNACK®
MAKE IT EASY

Guilford, Connecticut
An imprint of Globe Pequot Press

Copyright © 2010 by Morris Book Publishing, LLC

Editor in Chief: Maureen Graney
Editor: Katie Benoit
Cover Design: Paul Beatrice, Bret Kerr
Text Design: Paul Beatrice
Layout: Melissa Evarts
Cover photos by Liesa Cole
Interior photos by Liesa Cole

Library of Congress Cataloging-in-Publication Data
Hulin, Belinda.
  Knack Chinese cooking : a step-by-step guide to authentic dishes made easy / Belinda Hulin and Kian Lam Kho ; photographs by Liesa Cole.
     p. cm.
 ISBN 978-1-59921-616-4
 1. Cookery, Chinese. I. Kho, Kian Lam. II. Title. III. Title: Chinese cooking.
 TX724.5.C5H855 2009
 641.5951—dc22
                        2009025978

The following manufacturers/names appearing in *Knack Chinese Cooking* are trademarks:
Crock-Pot®, Stilton™, Tsingtao®

Printed in China

10 9 8 7 6 5 4 3 2 1

Dedication

To Sophie: My inspiration and one of China's treasured gifts

Acknowledgments

Cookbooks are, by nature, collaborative efforts. Each recipe pays homage to the generations of cooks who came before. My thanks to those sung and unsung who have added to the great body of culinary knowledge. Deepest appreciation also goes to Kian Lam Kho of www.redcook.net, my creative, insightful, and ever-patient collaborator. Thanks to Maureen Graney, Globe Pequot Press's editor extraordinaire and Knack series guru, and especially to my tenacious, resourceful agent Bob Diforio. Finally, love and gratitude to my husband Jim Crissman and children Dylan and Sophie, who taste test my recipes without complaining (much).

Photographer Acknowledgments

The Omni was awash in the most wonderful exotic aromas while we worked on this project; we could hardly wait to sample the dishes before we photographed them! Belinda Hulin has done a remarkable job of making traditional Chinese cooking accessible to anyone. Thank you Maureen Graney, Katie Benoit, and all the wonderful professionals at Knack. Thanks also to Jonathan Schnoer who kept the delicious recipes flowing from the studio kitchen. Tony Rodio, our production manager, performed the role of "Supreme Taster" with eager panache. Thank you all for making our work on this project a genuine pleasure.

"Kai wei" everyone! (Happy eating)
Liesa Cole
Photographer, Omni Studio

CONTENTS

INTRODUCTION

I tried to remember every detail as I traveled through the country. I took in the smartly dressed career women on the streets of Beijing and the masses of bicyclists filling city streets and nonchalantly playing chicken with cabs and buses. In Guangzhou, there were elderly men strolling through the flower-lined parks and thoroughly modern Gen-Y entrepreneurs packing cell phones and laptops and happily offering greetings in English. In Foshan, whole families seemed able to lash themselves to a single motor scooter and zip through the intersections.

Away from the hazy cities, I felt the quiet embrace of the lush, mountainous countryside, where villagers still carry goods to market in mule-driven carts. And everywhere the juxtaposition of ancient and modern gave a comforting sense of continuity and persistence.

I tried to imprint all these things on my brain so someday I could share them with my daughter Sophie. My husband and I had traveled to China to adopt our baby, and I wanted to make sure I could tell her everything we saw and appreciated about her homeland.

And over the years I have tried. Recently Sophie and I pulled out a collection of China photos and, as often happens, I began talking about the Forbidden City, the Great Wall, and the hilarious Halloween celebration at the Hard Rock Café Guangzhou. This time, however, my now nine-year-old daughter grew impatient.

"But Mom," she said, "what did you eat while you were there? Were the noodles and shrimp good? Dad said they gave you a whole fish—did it still have the eyes on? Did they have snacks? What did you do without chocolate?"

And therein lies a tale of nature versus nurture.

My Huazhou-born daughter has the most adventurous palate of any child I've ever known. She can down a spicy bowl of Cajun gumbo, happily eat a fish she personally

But even as I told the stories of the wonderful things I'd eaten in China, I couldn't help thinking about some equally delicious meals I'd enjoyed that were prepared by Chinese expatriates in New York, Vancouver, Philadelphia, San Francisco, Boston, Boca Raton, New Orleans, and even Rome. Were these not authentic Chinese experiences?

The truth is there is no singular, isolated Chinese cuisine. Instead the Chinese culinary palette emerges from a vibrant mosaic that includes the Eight Great Traditions (or regional cuisines) of Chinese cooking, as well as the sophisticated Imperial cuisine of Beijing and the culinary contributions of the Chinese diaspora.

caught, twirl noodles, and expertly crack the top of a crème brûlée. At the same time, she knows the Hulin-Crissman clan goes nowhere without spending an inordinate amount of time eating. For better or worse, we define our travels by the meals we've had. In order to really know about her homeland, Sophie reasoned, she had to know about the food.

Fortunately there are plenty of food memories to share— an elegant and amazing twelve-course banquet (with a whole fish); pan-fried noodles and eggs for breakfast; delicious pork buns and lo mein from a storefront eatery; pizza topped with corn and Chinese sausage; the most beautiful fruit and cold foods buffet I've ever seen; and a fascinating stroll through a wet market, where all edibles that cluck, crawl, hop, and swim can be purchased "on the hoof," so to speak.

Centuries-old dishes share table space with world cuisine accents and modern innovations in a culinary tradition that is both ancient and evolving.

Although purists love to discount dishes served at Chinese restaurants outside mainland China, these well-loved treats often represent honest adaptations of traditional Chinese fare. First- and second-generation émigrés take old family recipes and cooking techniques, adapt them to the ingredients at hand, and throw in a bit of personal creativity. Depending on the cook, the long noodles of Shanxi, the sweet prawns of Shandong, the soups of Fujian, the sauces of Guangdong, and the chiles of Hunan are all still in evidence.

At the same time, Chinese cooking is being influenced by the expanding, worldwide exchange of ingredients, equipment, and ideas. The exchange of ingredients, in particular, has made it possible for more cooks to have the pleasure of cooking dishes true to the spirit of Chinese cuisine.

The opportunity to spread the word and encourage home cooks to dabble in delicious Chinese fare made me jump at the chance to write this cookbook. Long before I visited China and became enchanted by the land, I loved the food. When I was a child, my family would visit the House of Lee in Metairie, Louisiana, and I can still recall being captivated by the perfume of that lovely white-tablecloth restaurant. As a young adult, I tried to capture that essence by buying a wok and stir-frying everything I could get my hands on. Some of it tasted good, but none of it tasted Chinese.

It wasn't until I stumbled into the "store" at the back of a Chinese restaurant in Houston that I discovered toasted sesame oil—the perfume of the House of Lee—as well as

good soy sauce, hoisin sauce, fermented black beans, and real Chinese noodles.

Now all those things, as well as hot chile sauce, sesame paste, fresh ginger root, oyster sauce, and premade wonton wrappers, can be found at ordinary supermarkets in small to large cities around the world. In addition, well-made woks, electric woks, electric hot pots, rice cookers, and steamers are as close as the nearest mall or discount store.

Knack Chinese Cooking will show you how to use these readily available ingredients and equipment to create authentic dishes pulled from the great cuisines of China, as well as from the best Chinese kitchens outside China. Favorites—like Beef with Broccoli, Shredded Pork in Garlic Sauce, and Wonton Soup—are in here, as well things you never thought you'd be able to make at home (Easy Moon Cakes, anyone?).

Each recipe includes adaptations that show how to add variety, make the dish using a different technique, or make the dish more quickly. A guide to the best equipment and shopping lists for fresh and shelf-stable ingredients will allow you to begin your Chinese cooking odyssey. Full-color photos will help identify, explain, and simplify.

For the record, Sophie has already started developing her cooking skills . . . and her discerning palate. She's proclaimed the Pork Lo Mein and Almond Cookies in this book excellent, but says she'll wait to pass judgment on the tofu dishes until she "learns to like it." Whether she ever embraces bean curd or not, I hope that over time the book will give her a sampling of the culinary bounty of her birth country.

I hope this book gives you a taste of China, as well. There's no way to cover the vast Chinese repertoire—from in and outside the country—in one cookbook. But with knowledge of authentic techniques and essential flavors, the spirit of China can emerge from any kitchen.

WOKS & STEAMERS

Years of wonderful Chinese meals begin with these sturdy vessels

If you have a skillet, you can begin experimenting with Chinese recipes. But be warned: The flavors, freshness, and textures are addictive. And once you get a hint of the culinary possibilities, you'll want to expand your repertoire. Once that happens, you'll both want and need the equipment that makes Chinese cooking unique and relatively simple to prepare.

Woks and steamers form the core of the Chinese cooking armory. The curving sides of the wok conduct heat and allow liquids to pool in the center well, keeping meats and vegetables from stewing in the sauce. Steamers raise dumplings, fish, and fruit above simmering water, creating a closed system that gently cooks delicate ingredients and intensifies flavors.

You can re-create the effects of these vessels with ordinary pots and makeshift steaming appliances, but once you get

Woks and Lids

- A sturdy wok with a lid is essential to preparing authentic Chinese stir-fries. The sloping sides allow heat to reach the greatest surface area, so dishes cook quickly and evenly.

- Traditional round-bottom steel woks work best on gas-fired stoves. The stabili-

- zation ring keeps the wok in place, while flames cup the curved bottom of the wok.

- Flat-bottom woks are fine for both electric and gas-fired stoves, plus they're easier to handle.

- For a single-wok kitchen, use a flat-bottom style.

Metal Rack Insert

- A metal steaming rack fits snuggly into the wok, usually about two-thirds of the way down.

- This leaves room for water beneath the rack, while a plate or bowl of ingredients can be positioned above the liquid.

- The rack turns the wok itself—assuming the wok has a tight-fitting lid—into a steamer.

- Using a rack with a solid plate or bowl allows juices from the steamed ingredients to be captured. The rack also can support a shallow bamboo steamer.

started you'll want equipment designed to make the job easy.

Happily, woks and steamers are both inexpensive and versatile. A clean wok on the stove can be used for everything from stir-frying to boiling eggs to heating soup. Steaming racks and steamers, when not being used to create Chinese specialties, can be used for ordinary steamed vegetables or for reheating grains and pilafs.

Bamboo Steamer

- The woven bamboo steamer is a traditional piece of Chinese cooking equipment that is inexpensive, effective, and attractive.

- Buy a strong, woven-bamboo steamer with a domed lid and as many steamer baskets as can be layered in your pan or wok.

- Unlike metal steamers, bamboo steamers absorb condensation, keeping the condensed steam from dripping back onto the food.

- Bamboo steamers are especially handy for moist dumplings and steamed breads.

Metal Steamer

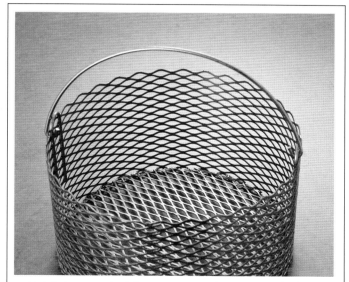

- Metal steamers don't have the folk-art aesthetic of bamboo steamers, and they're more expensive.

- They also last longer and are easier to clean. A stainless steel or aluminum steamer is a great investment if you plan to steam whole fish or thick cuts of poultry on a regular basis.

- If possible shop for a stockpot or saucepan that comes with a fitted steamer insert.

- You'll be able to use the pot with the steamer for steamed dishes as well as for reheating pasta, rice, and other grains.

PROPER POTS
Best practices in any culinary genre begin with the right pots

Here are two pots all cooks should have, as well as two pots you'll be absolutely grateful to have.

No kitchen is complete without a good-quality, cast-aluminum or stainless steel stockpot. Aside from the obvious use—making stocks and soups—you can use it for anything that has to be boiled or simmered on the stove. In addition to a stockpot, a Dutch oven with a tight-fitting lid should be on hand for cooking foods slowly on the stove or in the oven.

For Chinese slow cooking, the preferred vessel is a covered ceramic pot or sand pot.

Chinese hot pot dishes require either an authentic Asian hot pot or an easy-to-find electric fondue pot. The electric versions make it easy to maintain cooking broths at safe, high temperatures.

An electric rice cooker can save time and aggravation for anyone with a love of Asian cuisines, or even Caribbean or

Stockpot

Dutch Oven or Clay Sand Pot

- Shop for a 4- to 6-quart stockpot, which should ensure that you can easily simmer a whole chicken or boil wontons without crowding the pan.

- With luck you can find a stockpot with a metal steamer attachment, or one designed to accommodate

- a perforated metal steamer basket from the same manufacturer.

- It isn't necessary to spend hundreds of dollars on a stockpot, but do splurge a little for a well-made, heavy-gauge steel or cast-aluminum pot.

- The tight seal and domed lid of a Dutch oven allows food to cook slowly.

- Modern Dutch ovens are made from cast iron, enamel-coated cast iron, or aluminum.

- Chinese cooks opt for a closed ceramic sand pot,

- rather than metal, when preparing braised or slow-cooked dishes.

- Sand pots have a rough exterior and smooth, glazed interior. They can be used on the stove or in the oven. Never place a hot sand pot on a cold or wet surface.

American Cajun, Creole, or Low-Country dishes. Just add the correct proportion of grains to liquid, and the rice cooker cooks the food at the proper temperature and switches to a warming setting when the rice is done.

Electric Fondue and Chinese Fire Pots

- Chinese hot pots have a metal chimney surrounded by a well. Boiling broth is poured in the well; hot coals or canned fuel keeps everything bubbly.

- Authentic hot pots can be fashioned from any number of materials.

- All hot pots have one problem: keeping the broth in the ring hot enough to maintain a safe cooking temperature. Hot coals aren't safe to use indoors; canned fuel may have to be replaced over lengthy meals.

- An electric fondue pot may give you better results.

Electric Rice Cooker

- Rice is the backbone of Asian cuisine. It's almost impossible to create an authentic Chinese meal without it.

- Electric rice cookers produce perfect steamed rice, without sticking or burning. The appliances don't require monitoring, which is a huge convenience when preparing a multi-step stir-fry.

- Cooks can choose from very basic models to elaborate multiprogram machines.

- Decide how you'll use your rice cooker and shop accordingly.

THE CUTTING EDGE
The right knife makes food preparation easier

Chinese cooking calls for advance ingredient preparation and knife work. Well-balanced, sharp knives will make the job easier and the results more satisfying. You may already have one or two good paring knives on hand, but as your interest in Chinese food grows, consider shopping for a good Chinese-style cleaver. A sharp cleaver can make short work of slicing through poultry and mincing meats.

For both paring knives and cleavers, consider whether you prefer a wood, hard plastic, or metal handle. Wood tends to be easier to grip, but degrades over time. Full-tang knives are forged in one piece, with a metal strip that extends into the handle. These usually last longer and are more balanced tools.

Likewise, you'll need a firm, nonslip work surface to support your slicing and dicing. Although wood-block cutting boards are attractive, you'd be better off buying boards made

Chinese Cleavers

- Chinese cleavers look imposing but have multiple uses in the kitchen.

- Aside from the obvious chopping and carving, wide-blade cleavers can easily scoop up a mound of minced cilantro or separate pork matchsticks from trimmings.

- Buy a cleaver with a 7- or 8-inch-long forged-steel blade. Choose one that feels comfortable and well balanced in your hand.

- Handles can be blunt nosed (to be used for pounding ingredients) or curved. Pick the one that feels best.

Paring Knives

- The best utensil for most peeling and close work is the utilitarian paring knife.

- Keep one or two pointed, sharpened paring knives on hand and learn to wield them with confidence.

- Buy forged-steel paring knives with 3- or 4-inch

- blades and handles that fit comfortably in your hand. The handle should be bigger than the knife blade.

- One reason many cooks eschew peeling and paring duty is the scourge of cheap paring knives with tiny handles that become uncomfortable to use.

from nonporous, engineered material or silicone. These can be thrown in the dishwasher or scrubbed down with anti-bacterial soap.

Finally, Chinese recipes call for a lot of fresh garlic. A garlic press is an indispensable kitchen aid, instantly creating a fine puree of garlic that can be added directly to sauces, soups, and stir-fries.

Cutting Boards

- Butcher-block cutting boards are beautiful. Prop them on the counter as kitchen art and buy fully washable nonporous cutting boards.

- Cutting boards in solid-surface materials like Corian and Silestone have heft and are easy to clean.

- For lighter weight cutting boards, molded synthetic materials can be found in decorative shapes and colors.

- For tight spaces, shop for a package of multicolored flexible silicone cutting mats that can be washed and rolled up for storage.

Garlic Press

- Pressed garlic instantly blends into cooking ingredients, disperses garlic flavor, and solves the problem of crunchy bits of garlic in sauces.

- These handy devices also separate garlic peels from garlic cloves, eliminating the task of peeling the cloves.

- That said, having no garlic press is better than having a cheap plastic press, which will clog up and quickly break.

- Shop for a stainless or cast-aluminum garlic press with a metal plunger.

CHOPSTICKS & MORE

Grab-and-go cooking utensils make handling hot food simple

The right cooking utensils can mean the difference between properly, evenly cooked victuals and burned or gummy food. More to the point, the right utensils can mean the difference between burning your hands and not.

When shopping for stirrers, turners, and tongs, always find items that are the right length for your grip and your pots. All metal utensils last a long time and are easy to clean, but if you often forget to grab a potholder before working with hot ingredients, you may be better off buying heat-safe plastic or wood-handled tools. Look for utensils weighted toward the business end so a spoon or spatula temporarily rested inside a wok is more likely to stay put than flip out.

You'll need at least one good metal spatula to turn scallion pancakes and dislodge some ingredients, but coated or hard nylon utensils will preserve nonstick surfaces.

Tongs let you remove large items from woks and pans while

Cooking Chopsticks

- You'll need several pairs of long, heat-safe cooking chopsticks to use when serving hot pot recipes.

- Guests should be able to comfortably hold the chopsticks, loaded with meat or vegetables, in the hot pot broth without the risk of burnt fingers.

- Chopsticks also make wonderful stirrers for blending eggs into soups or tossing noodles.

- Use long chopsticks at the table for serving cooked foods.

Tongs

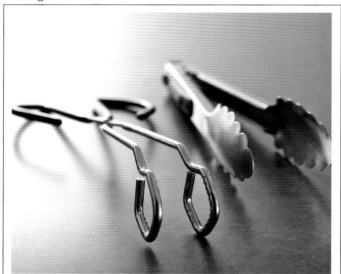

- Practiced cooks can deftly pluck a spring roll from hot oil with chopsticks, but the key word is practiced.

- For the rest of us, there are tongs.

- Spring-hinged metal tongs or scissor-grip tongs help you remove frying wontons and rolls from oil without scooping up a ladle full of hot fat.

- Tongs also can be used to move boiled dumplings or steamed vegetables from wok to serving plate without piercing or cutting the food.

allowing hot oil and cooking liquids to stay put. In a pinch, they can also be used to toss greens and mix noodles.

Of course Chinese cooks use long wooden or heat-safe plastic chopsticks for many cooking duties, including plucking ingredients from a steamer basket or stirring soups.

Spatulas

- If you've cooked an egg or a pancake, chances are you already have one or two of these kitchen essentials on hand.

- Chinese cooks use solid metal spatulas to turn sauce-coated, meaty stir-fries in woks.

- Slotted metal spatulas are used to dislodge reluctant seared meats, pot stickers, and egg dishes from woks and skillets without removing all the oil.

- Of course a slotted spatula is a must-have for turning scallion pancakes.

Wood and Plastic Stirring Spoons

- Some cooks believe metal utensils give foods a metallic taste.

- Whether that's true or not, it is true that wood, coated metal spoons, and hard plastic spoons are better for your pots.

- If you'll be using a wok or stockpot with a nonstick surface, invest in a set of nonmetal spoons to avoid scratching the nonstick coating.

- You'll also need wood or plastic spoons to mix and serve ingredients from a sand pot or ceramic Dutch oven.

STRAINERS & LADLES
Scoop it out or sauce it up with the right strainer or ladle

In cooking, timing is everything. Draining pasta before it gets gummy, removing battered meats before the coatings burn, getting the soup to the table while it's still hot . . . these things can significantly affect the dining experience.

Having properly made, properly shaped strainers and ladles can mean the difference between a watery wonton in tepid broth and an excellent soup course.

Chances are you already have a few ladles, strainers, and

slotted spoons sitting around the kitchen. And chances are your utensils have either seen better days or were never the right size to begin with.

Before taking up Chinese cooking—with its myriad soups, sauces, and noodle and rice dishes—take a minute to assess your equipment. You'll need a Chinese-style basket strainer to use in cooking, fine-mesh and medium-mesh strainers for clarifying broths and draining noodles, an all-purpose slotted

Cooking Skimmers and Strainers

- Few ingredients are as useful, or as underused, as the basket strainer.

- Available in different sizes, with different depths, these utensils can be used to skim floating dumplings from a broth or frying pork cubes from oil.

- Small basket strainers make hot pot cooking quicker. Traditional basket strainers have wooden handles, making them an easy-grip, stay-cool option.

- Find basket strainers at kitchen stores. In a pinch you can use a large, long-handled slotted spoon.

Strainers

- Keep a long-handled fine-mesh strainer handy for removing solids from broths and clear sauces.

- You'll need a medium-mesh strainer, preferably one that can balance over a pot or sink, to drain water from noodles and for straining large bones from stock.

- For the longest wear, look for stainless steel, enamel-coated, or rust-resistant strainers.

- To keep particles from drying in the mesh, clean strainers with a brush or nylon scrubber immediately after use.

spoon, and rice paddles for serving steamed rice. Wood, plastic, and silicone rice paddles can be used for serving other steamed grains and pilafs, as well. Just remember to rinse after each use. Stuck-on grains dry out quickly.

Long-Handled Ladles

- Smallish ladles are great for family suppers and serving soup from the stove.

- But to transfer large quantities of broth from a stockpot to a hot pot, or to move wonton soup to a tureen, you need something bigger.

- Shop for a long-handled metal ladle with a wide, shallow bowl. This will allow you to transfer soup quickly and see what you're adding to the hot pot or tureen.

- A hooked handle will keep the ladle from sliding into the stockpot.

Rice Paddles

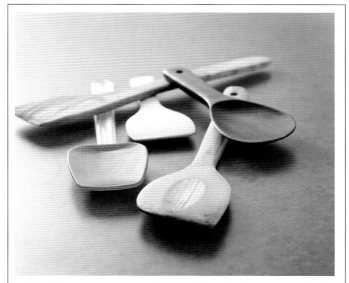

- Electric rice cookers usually come with a plastic rice paddle.

- You'll want more than one. These traditional, aesthetically pleasing little spades lift cooked rice without smashing or cutting the grains.

- They also have a practical purpose: Curved plastic or wood rice paddles allow you to serve rice directly from your rice cooker or a ceramic rice pot without fear of scratching or cracking the pot.

- Rinse rice paddles in cold water after using.

TABLETOP IDEAS
Add stylish touches to your table setting just for the fun of it

You can prepare good, authentic Chinese dishes even if you don't have an electric spice mill, an artist's palette of beautiful bowls and sauce dishes, or a cloisonné teapot. But such trappings, while not absolutely necessary, certainly add to the festivities.

Peruse stores that specialize in an eclectic mix of imported housewares. Often you can find bowls, tea sets, and accessories at modest prices at such retail venues. Asian markets carry Chinese soup spoons and tea sets, while any kitchenware store will have spice mills or a stone mortar and pestle set.

Thrift stores and consignment shops often have barely used tea sets and pretty table trappings that fell victim to redecorating or downsizing.

Spice Mill or Mortar and Pestle

- Chinese spices, star anise and Szechwan peppercorns especially, benefit from being ground just before using.

- Food processors grind spices and chop dried hot chiles, but they aren't efficient. Consider investing in an electric spice mill.

- Electric spice mills work like small electric coffee grinders. In fact, if you have a spare coffee grinder, you can use it for grinding spices.

- If you prefer to go old school and manually grind spices, buy a mortar and pestle.

A Bevy of Bowls

- Individual portions of rice, dipping sauces, soups . . . Chinese cuisine is full of excuses to buy beautiful bowls.

- Invest in a variety of simple, rimless ceramic bowls that complement one another, but don't necessarily match.

- Tiny bowls can be found in markets that sell sushi supplies. Or, individual clear or white ramekins can do double-duty.

- For a multicourse Chinese meal, Western-style soup or cereal bowls are too large. If you must use them, watch serving sizes.

GREEN ● LIGHT

Buy inexpensive bamboo placemats and napkin rings and bright, solid-color linens to offset multihued floral teapots or bowls. Remember: Red is a lucky color in Chinese homes.

RED ● LIGHT

If your kitchen shopping takes you to garage sales and flea markets, make sure anything you buy is safe for table use. Avoid putting foods inside vessels that have cracked glazes or glazes that contain lead. If you aren't sure about the glaze, but love the design of a pot or bowl, buy it and use it for a centerpiece.

Soup Spoons

- In China, most diners would rather eat soup with inexpensive plastic spoons than with sterling silver.

- Eating with metal utensils is seen as less than aesthetically pleasing.

- That tradition isn't rigidly observed outside China, but it is common enough that Chinese soup spoons can be found in Asian markets and specialty shops.

- To give your meal an authentic touch, buy molded-plastic or ceramic Chinese spoons with decorative designs.

Tea for Two, or Four or More

- Tea is as much a part of the Chinese culinary tradition as rice.

- Selecting the proper tea, brewing the leaves perfectly, and maintaining the tea at the perfect temperature are all part of a revered art form.

- Invest in a Chinese tea set with a ceramic pot and handleless cups. Heat the pot with boiling water before brewing, then brew loose tea leaves with fresh boiling water.

- Your tea set can be simple or ornate.

SAUCES
Well-chosen sauces give Chinese dishes their unique character and flavors

In Chinese cuisine, sauces are used to enhance and enrich the flavors of the food, never to mask or overwhelm them. Simple ingredients—beans, garlic, fish and seafood, fruit, peppers—are transformed through fermentation; blending; long, slow cooking; and distillation into elixirs that can add spicy, tart, sweet, and savory essences to a variety of dishes.

Certain Chinese regional cuisines favor one or more combinations of sauces over another. Cantonese cooks have a particular fondness for deep brown oyster sauce, while chile and garlic sauces frequently show up in Szechwan and Hunan dishes. In Shanghai, sweet and peppery sauces and peanut-laced sauces appear. Hoisin sauce is a favorite in both Beijing-

Soy Sauce

- Authentic soy sauce is made from soybeans, roasted grains (typically wheat), water, and salt. These ingredients are mixed with yeast, fermented, and strained.

- Chinese soy sauce usually contains a high proportion of soybeans to grain and may contain a bit of sugar or molasses.

- First-pressed "light" soy sauce is rare and highly valued. "Dark" soy sauce is more widely used.

- Japanese-style tamari sauce is lighter and has a higher proportion of wheat.

Oyster Sauce

- Oyster sauce is made from oysters, yet tastes nothing like oysters.

- Cooking the mollusks in water over low heat for long periods extracts salty, sweet essences from the oysters and turns the oyster broth a caramel color.

- Bottled oyster sauce may or may not have added seasonings or soy sauce.

- Vegetarian oyster sauce can be made by slow cooking oyster mushrooms into a sauce with characteristics similar to true oyster sauce.

style dishes as well as some Cantonese fare.

The Chinese invented soy sauce, and it has appeared in the kitchens of all Chinese regions for more than two millennia. But not all Chinese dishes contain soy sauce. Indeed, one of the complaints Chinese people voice about Western Chinese–style food is that it's all drowned in soy sauce, making everything taste the same. Soy sauce forms the basis for other Chinese sauces, and often supermarkets carry soy sauce flavored with ingredients like ginger, sesame, and mushrooms.

Plum Sauce

- Plum sauce contains plums or plum preserves, vinegar, sugar, and ginger, plus occasionally a bit of onion, garlic, and dried chile pepper.

- The best homemade versions resemble a smooth-textured chutney. Plum sauce may range in color from dark brown to golden.

- Use plum sauce as a condiment for egg rolls, spring rolls, and fried wontons.

- Plum sauce is sometimes called duck sauce, which comes from its mistaken use with Peking duck.

Hoisin Sauce

- This Chinese classic can be used as a condiment and dipping sauce or as a cooking sauce.

- Made from soybean paste, sugar, chile peppers, and a variety of seasonings, hoisin is the usual accompaniment for Peking duck and mu shu pork.

- Like many Chinese sauces, hoisin has sweet-and-sour aspects.

- Hoisin is a reddish brown, thick sauce that can be used to glaze roasted or barbecued meats. The strong flavor of soy paste may be an acquired taste for some.

OILS, VINEGAR, & WINE
These simple ingredients add complex flavors to Chinese dishes

Stir-frying and frying play such a large role in Chinese cuisine that it makes sense to spend time focusing on oils and marinade ingredients like vinegar and wine.

Unlike their European counterparts, Chinese cooks rarely use butter in recipes. The preferred fat for stir-frying and frying is peanut oil, which can withstand high heat without breaking down or burning. Peanut oil brings out the natural flavor of foods, rather than masking or adding to it. Good quality canola or vegetable oil are fine substitutes, especially if you're concerned about peanut allergies.

Chinese cooks do turn to other oils to flavor dishes, however. Dark sesame oil, extracted from toasted sesame seeds, is one of the essential flavors of Chinese cuisine. Used in dipping sauces and marinades and as a seasoning for steamed and stir-fried dishes, dark sesame oil is irreplaceable. It's also high in omega-3 fatty acids and antioxidants.

Dark Sesame Oil

- Sesame oil, such as the Korean variety shown here, is extracted from sesame seeds. This is an expensive process.

- Raw sesame seed oil is clear to pale amber in color. It has a subtle flavor.

- Dark or toasted sesame oil is pressed from toasted sesame seeds and retains the rich flavor of the caramelized seeds.

- That wonderful flavor is volatile and dissipates during long cooking. Use in marinades, as a condiment, or add at the end of cooking.

Hot Chile Oil

- Hot chile oil is an infusion, with crushed dried chiles steeped in cold or warmed oil (usually peanut or soybean oil), then strained.

- Commercial brands may use additional seasonings, such as Szechwan peppercorns.

- To make your own, chop dried chiles in a food processor to make 4 to 6 tablespoons flakes. Place in a heat-safe jar. Pour hot oil over flakes. Let stand 1 to 2 hours. Strain and refrigerate.

- Or, pour cold oil over chiles and refrigerate for a month.

The fire of hot chile oil, of course, can be replaced with crushed dried chiles or fresh chiles. But the oil blends smoothly into sauces and coats ingredients uniformly, making it very useful.

The element that gives Chinese sweet-and-sour sauces a tart kick is rice wine vinegar, which is milder and slightly sweeter than ordinary white vinegar. Rice wine, also known as yellow wine, is an aged wine made from fermented glutinous rice and sometimes millet. In some marinades, rice wine can be used instead of rice wine vinegar.

················· RED ● LIGHT ··············
Japanese sake should not be substituted for Chinese rice wine. Sake has a sweeter, lighter flavor. If you can't find or don't have Chinese rice wine available, use a dry sherry in its place.

Rice Wine Vinegar

- Mild, sweet rice wine vinegar turns up in most Chinese sweet-and-sour and hot-and-sour sauces, as well as marinades.

- The acids in the vinegar break down fibers in proteins, tenderizing less-tender cuts of meat.

- Regular white vinegar isn't a good substitute for rice wine vinegar, although apple cider vinegar will do in a pinch.

- Chinese cooks also use red and black rice vinegars, which have stronger flavors. These most often appear as accents or condiments.

Rice Wine

- Chinese rice wine, also known as Shaoxing wine for the city reputed to produce the best rice wine, is made from fermented grain and aged at least ten years.

- This produces a golden, full-bodied liquid with an alcohol content of 17 percent or more.

- Chinese manufacturers produce rice wine used primarily for cooking, as well as more expensive, longer-aged wine meant for drinking.

- Drinking-quality rice wine is available at some liquor stores and Chinese markets.

SAVORY & SWEET PASTES
Purees and pastes flavor sauces and fill pastries in Chinese cuisine

Who knew that beans could be so versatile? In Chinese cuisine, legumes can be preserved in salt and mashed into sauces, or sweetened and cooked into a pastry filling. In fact beans in China exist largely to be transformed—very rarely does one find a simple boiled or stewed legume on a plate.

Sesame paste brings one of China's oldest seasonings (and favorite flavors) to the table as a coating or sauce base, while chile paste adds heat to dips and stir-fries.

Generally, pastes are thicker and more intensely flavored than sauces. Some are an acquired taste. Fermented black beans have an earthy flavor, while sesame paste carries a strong roasted essence. Adzuki fillings—that is, sweet red bean paste—may come as a surprise to someone expecting the texture of a custard or fruit-based pastry filling.

Experiment with cooking pastes by sampling a bit from the jar or adding small amounts to recipes until you reach your

KNACK CHINESE COOKING

Fermented Black Beans and Black Bean Paste

- Salted, preserved black soybeans have an intense, earthy flavor. They're added sparingly to sauces and are usually rinsed to reduce saltiness.

- The beans form the backbone of black bean paste, a thick puree seasoned with soy sauce and garlic.

- Black bean paste mixed with chiles or other ingredients can be found in supermarkets.

- Fermented black beans and black bean paste appear in several classic Cantonese dishes.

Sweet Red Bean Paste

- Red adzuki beans, cooked and sweetened with sugar or honey, find their way into many Chinese sweets.

- Sweet red bean paste forms the center of glutinous rice balls, rice puddings, and the Autumn Moon Festival's signature pastry, moon cakes.

- Some cooks make their own paste by simply cooking adzuki beans to a soft consistency and adding sugar to taste.

- Jarred sweet red bean paste comes in a thick mashed version and a finer strained puree.

16

comfort level. Prepared pastes add richness and complexity to Chinese dishes without adding a lot of work or expense.

········· GREEN●LIGHT ·············

When cooking with whole fermented black beans, soak the beans briefly in cool water to soften and remove more salt (after rinsing). After adding the beans to stir-fries and stews, use a spoon to mash the beans against the side of the wok. This spreads the flavor of the beans and adds body to the sauce.

Sesame Paste

- Chinese sesame paste is rich and aromatic. Unlike Middle Eastern tahini, Chinese sesame paste begins with toasted, not raw, sesame seeds.

- Buy Chinese sesame paste in the Asian foods section of supermarkets and some specialty food stores.

- If sesame paste isn't available, substitute natural-style smooth peanut butter.

- Sesame paste often separates in the jar, with the oil rising to the top. Simply stir the oil back into the paste before using.

Hot Chile Paste

- Many Chinese cooks consider hot chile paste to be a sauce or condiment, rather than a paste.

- The readily available ingredient begins with soaked and ground dried chile peppers, salt, and oil.

- Sometimes fresh chiles, vinegar, garlic, and black beans may be added.

- Hot chile paste can be used as a dipping sauce or added to stir-fries and other sauces.

A TOUCH OF SPICE

For a quick infusion of authentic Chinese flavor, grab a shaker

Ground, flaked, or powdered spices provide convenience that can't be matched by other flavor enhancers.

Buy whole Szechwan peppercorns and whole star anise at Asian markets and gourmet shops. Five-spice powder and dried red peppers are available at most supermarkets. Sometimes you'll have to browse a few sections—Asian foods, spices, produce—to find them.

Keep spices in a cool, dark place, but don't forget to use

them! Whole spices keep for three to four years, while ground spices last two years, and dried herbs one to two years. As long as the spices remain dry, they won't turn rancid, but they will lose potency.

Buying spices in large quantities from specialty stores sometimes makes sense from an economic and convenience standpoint. If you find yourself buying more dried red peppers or star anise pods than you're likely to use, consider split-

Dried Chile Peppers

- Any hot dried capsicum adds heat to dishes. Most Chinese cooks use narrow red chiles cultivated in southern China.

- Buy dried chiles by the bag and keep in a dark, dry place. You can also buy dried chile flakes, or make them in a food processor.

- Remove the woody stem of dried chile peppers before using. Dried chiles should be soaked in water before they are added to stir-fries.

- Dried red chiles add a dark red color to oils and vinegars.

Szechwan Peppercorns

- Szechwan peppercorns aren't really peppercorns. They are dried flower buds from a type of ash tree that grows in Asia.

- Cooks toast and grind the husks of the tiny reddish brown buds to use directly in spicy dishes and as part of spice mixes. A favorite

- mix is a simple blend of ground Szechwan pepper and sea salt.

- Devotees note that Szechwan pepper isn't so much fiery as it is numbing, giving foods another taste sensation.

ting the find and sharing the cost with one or two friends.

Star Anise

- Star anise adds a bold licorice flavor to Chinese dishes. Although not related to anise, which is a sweeter, milder, fennel-like herb, star anise does have a similar taste profile.

- The hard, star-shaped seedpods come from Asian evergreen shrubs.

- Whole star anise may be added to slow-simmered soups and stews, while ground star anise may be sprinkled into quick-cooking dishes.

- Star anise sometimes substitutes for anise in the production of licorice-flavored liqueurs.

Five-Spice Powder

- Five-spice powder represents the Chinese pantheon of ground spice favorites—but exactly which spices that pantheon includes is up for debate.

- Purists insist the mixture should include ground star anise, Szechwan peppercorns, cassia bark, cloves, and fennel.

- However, cinnamon, ginger, or cardamom sometimes steps in for one of the ingredients.

- Shop for a brand that appeals to you, or make your own.

NOODLES & RICE

Keep these building blocks of Chinese cuisine in the pantry

It would be simple—and somewhat true—to say that Northern Chinese cooks rely on wheat noodles, while in Southern China, the preferred starch is rice.

But wheat noodles show up in Cantonese lo mein and other favorites, while rice certainly plays a role in the menus of Beijing and other northern cities. And in all of China, mung bean starch noodles, aka cellophane or glass noodles, are used in soups and cold platters.

Truth is, the Chinese have made an art form of grains and starches, giving these inexpensive meal stretchers the important roll of carrying and balancing the vibrant flavors of a typical Chinese meal.

In addition, cornstarch, with its smooth texture and quick-acting thickening power, is the binding agent of choice.

Note that cornstarch is called corn flour in some countries. However, the white powdered starch should not be

Noodles

- Most Chinese wheat noodle recipes call for egg noodles.

- Dried Chinese-style egg noodles can be found in various widths in most supermarkets. Refrigerated fresh or vacuum-packed soft noodles may be available.

- Rice flour noodles come in a variety of widths. These noodles are brittle and must be softened in warm water before cooking.

- Likewise, cellophane noodles must be softened before adding to dishes, although they can be thrown into soups or hot pots as is.

Long-Grain Rice

- China produces most of the world's rice exports, and its citizens consume 135 million tons each year.

- Rice is a significant part of the culture; many ancient sayings associate rice with health and well-being.

- Long-grain white rice

appears at most Chinese tables. Fragrant jasmine and basmati rice—popular in other Asian countries—are served occasionally.

- Forbidden rice and red rice are heirloom varieties. These nutty-tasting whole grains cook to a dark purple or red when steamed.

confused with the American version of corn flour, which is a finely milled cornmeal used as a breading for seafood.

Glutinous Rice

- Glutinous rice, also called "sticky rice" or "sweet rice," is a short, fat-grained rice bred for its propensity to stick together.

- In some Southeast Asian countries, glutinous rice is the dominant rice produced and served.

- Chinese cooks usually turn to glutinous rice for special appetizers or desserts, and glutinous rice flour is used in cakes and pastries.

- Polished white glutinous rice is most commonly used, although black- and red-hulled varieties can be found.

Cornstarch

- Cornstarch, a powdered white starch produced from the endosperm of corn kernels, has twice the thickening power of flour.

- Cornstarch works best when added to sauces at the end of the cooking process. The starch loses its raw flavor quickly and instantly begins to thicken and bind ingredients. This makes it perfect for stir-fries.

- Cornstarch can also be used as a coating.

- Always dissolve cornstarch in cold water before adding to hot sauces to prevent lumps.

A FEW EXTRAS

For instant authenticity, keep these shelf-stable items on hand

The fresh-food revolution of the past quarter century has, for the most part, been a great blessing, weaning consumers away from processed foods and toward just-picked victuals.

That said, some things just aren't readily available in fresh form and aren't easily replaced by just-picked substitutes.

For example, water chestnuts and bamboo shoots must be grown in tropical climates, harvested properly, and handled promptly. Both vegetables can be found fresh in Asian markets in some cities. If you're inclined to peel fresh water chestnuts and store in daily changes of cold water in the refrigerator for no more than a week, you'll find them to be far superior to canned varieties. Likewise, peeling and blanching (to remove bitterness) fresh bamboo shoots is a worthwhile endeavor.

But for those times and places when fresh isn't practical, a few cans in the pantry can give your dishes the variety and

Wood Ear Mushrooms

- Wood ear mushrooms grow wild on hardwood trees and rotting tree trunks throughout China and in other parts of the world.

- Fresh, the ear-shaped fungus is somewhat gelatinous and can range from reddish brown to black.

- Since the flavor and texture of soaked, dried wood ears and fresh wood ears is similar, most cooks keep dried on hand.

- After soaking in hot water for 30 minutes, wood ears grow four or five times in size and become flexible with a slight bite.

Dried Tiger Lily Buds

- You've seen dried tiger lily buds—thick gold threads also known as golden needles—in bowls of hot and sour soup.

- Although called tiger lily buds, the buds actually come from orange day lilies, which originated in China.

- The buds are inexpensive and sold at Asian specialty stores and some supermarkets.

- Soak lily buds in hot water for 30 minutes to soften. Cut off the hard woody end before adding to dishes. Some cooks like to tie the soaked buds in knots.

crunch required, and often streamline the cooking process.

Dried mushrooms are much easier to store and much less perishable than their fresh counterparts. Wood ear mushrooms lose very little character when dried, and the convenience factor is enormous.

Long, golden tiger lily buds—dried, unopened flowers—add a woodsy flavor to hot-and-sour soup and some stir-fries.

Bamboo Shoots

- The biggest problem with canned bamboo shoots is a slight tinny taste that can seep into the shoots.

- Buy canned bamboo shoots from a store that has a good turnover, and try to use the shoots within six months of purchase.

- Before using bamboo shoots, drain and rinse with hot water, then soak in ice water for a few minutes.

- Bamboo shoots are available sliced in different widths, as well as whole.

Water Chestnuts

- Water chestnuts aren't nuts. They're actually an aquatic vegetable that has a thin brown skin and looks a bit like a chestnut.

- Water chestnuts add a crunchy texture and a mild, slightly sweet texture to stir-fries, egg roll fillings, and some Chinese soups.

- Buy canned water chestnuts whole, sliced, or slivered at most supermarkets.

- As with bamboo shoots, drain and rinse water chestnuts, then refresh in ice water to remove any metallic taste.

GREENS & SPROUTS

Getting your daily greens is a pleasure with these options

Westerners often feel virtuous when eating Chinese stir-fries, patting themselves on the back for getting "all those vegetables." What they may not realize is that in China, most meals also include a wok or steamer basket full of beautiful, healthful greens.Lightly cooked greens retain their natural flavor and vibrant color and add disease-fighting nutrients to the menu.

Chinese cooks have access to a wide range of tender greens, including several varieties of spinach, kale, cabbage,

chard, and broccoli. These perishable fresh vegetables can occasionally be found in Asian markets and in specialty produce stores in large cities around the world.

Bok choy can be found in most supermarkets. More unusual greens, such as baby bok choy, Chinese broccoli, and Chinese mustard greens occasionally turn up in specialty produce markets and farmers' markets, as well as Asian grocery stores. But lack of access to authentic Chinese mustard

Chinese Broccoli

- This tender, slightly bitter green also goes by the name Chinese kale and kai-lan or gai-lan.

- It's long and leafy, with thick stems and a flower head that looks like a broccoli floret. Chinese cooks serve it lightly stir-fried.

- Although Chinese broccoli comes from the same family as ordinary broccoli, the flavor is sweeter.

- Chinese broccoli can be hard to find. Check Asian markets and specialty produce counters. In a pinch, use broccoli rabe or regular broccoli.

Bok Choy

- Bok choy and baby bok choy are different cultivars of the same vegetable—the "baby" version has smaller heads.

- Also known as Chinese cabbage and bok choi or pak choi, this green has long, mild-tasting leaves with a white center spine.

- Chopped bok choy is used in stir-fries and soups. Steamed baby bok choy, drizzled with sesame oil, is a healthful treat.

- Choy sum or bok choy sum is a small, very tender variety of the vegetable. Buy it when you can.

greens shouldn't deter you from following the spirit of the Chinese dinner palette. Select your favorite greens from a local market and pick a recipe to adapt.

Washed and coarsely chopped kale, mustard greens, and collard greens are often available in supermarket produce aisles. These healthful convenience foods make it extremely easy to expand your greens savvy. Shop for bags filled with blemish-free, crisp-looking leaves and always check the sell-by date.

Use any greens within a day or two of purchase.

Napa Cabbage

- Napa cabbage originated in Asia and is now grown throughout the world.

- The long, slender heads have either slightly crinkled or very crinkled leaves and a pale green color.

- The leaves have a mild flavor, making them a favored vegetable for salads, stir-fries, soups, and dumpling or egg roll fillings. The leaves are flexible enough to be used as wraps.

- As with all produce, shop for crisp, unblemished napa cabbages with good color.

Mung Bean Sprouts

- Health food fanatics grow their own mung bean sprouts, using containers that allow for daily moistening and rinsing of the sprouting beans.

- Satisfying as that effort may be, it's completely unnecessary. Fresh mung bean sprouts are available at most supermarkets.

- Buy crisp, long, silver-stemmed sprouts and store in fresh water in the refrigerator, changing water daily, for up to five days.

- To use within a day or two, refrigerate in a resealable plastic bag.

FRESH INGREDIENTS

AROMATICS

Unlock the flavors of China with these easy-to-find ingredients

Green onion, garlic, and fresh ginger root make up the flavor trinity of Chinese cuisine. Stock those three ingredients, a bottle of good soy sauce, and maybe a bottle of sesame oil or chile pepper flakes, and you're well on your way to creating stir-fries with an authentic Chinese taste print.

Of course not all dishes get equal amounts of all aromatics. In fact Chinese cooks fault Western adaptations of their culinary favorites for "all tasting alike" by virtue of applying

the same seasoning formula to different meats. While personal preferences might lead a cook to use a heavy hand with garlic, for example, it's important not to treat every dish the same.

Interestingly, Chinese aromatics include two ingredients—garlic and ginger—regularly touted as natural remedies for cardiovascular, bronchial, and gastrointestinal complaints. Garlic, in particular, has been shown to kill various strains of

Leeks

- Chinese recipes rarely call for onions—the flavor is considered too strong.

- But sometimes a dish needs something a little more substantial than green onions or chives. That's where leeks come in.

- Leeks have a crisp texture that withstands cooking and a slightly sweet onion flavor.

- Depending on the recipe, the edible white portion of leeks can be sliced horizontally or diagonally or cut vertically into shreds.

Green Onions

- Green onions, also called scallions, are used whole in hot pots, shredded into stir-fries, and minced for garnishes.

- Green onions are the immature shoots of regular onions, pulled from the ground before a large bulb develops.

- Buy green onions with firm, bright green tops. The smaller and thinner the onion, the milder the flavor.

- The Chinese use all parts of the green onion—white and green—in cooking. Very tough tops should be trimmed or finely minced.

bacteria, and ginger can soothe the digestive system.

The Chinese fervently believe in the medicinal value of foods and herbs; however, as with culinarians everywhere, the first concern is flavor. The aesthetic and aromatic contributions of pungent garlic, sweet ginger, mild green onions—and by extension, leeks—can't be denied.

Garlic

- China produces more garlic than any other country and twice as much as the next highest producer.

- The Chinese use this onion relative in marinades, prepared sauces, and recipes. Mostly, garlic is served cooked, which sweetens the flavor.

- Add whole, peeled cloves of garlic to dishes that simmer for long periods, while minced or slivered garlic works for most quick-cooking dishes.

- To dissipate fresh garlic flavor quickly in a sauce or dressing, push the cloves through a garlic press.

Ginger Root

- Fresh ginger root—a knobby brown rhizome—contains volatile oils that are released by cutting into the fibrous root.

- Finely mince the peeled root before adding to dishes, or add large slices that can be removed before serving.

- Buy young, small roots, wrap well, and keep refrigerated. Handled properly, ginger root should remain fresh for two weeks or more.

- Use spicy, sweet-scented ginger in savory and sweet dishes. In a pinch, use preserved or pickled ginger.

VEGETABLES
Fresh produce brings color, texture, and flavor to Chinese cuisine

The entire world of fresh vegetables is fodder for stir-fried and steamed Chinese-style dishes. That said, a few favorites stand out of the market basket.

In particular, Chinese cooks favor Asian-style eggplants for both meat-based stir-fries and vegetarian main dishes. Although there are many different cultivars lumped into the category "Asian" eggplant, the things most have in common are a long, slender profile and sweeter flavor than the large

European-style eggplants found in supermarkets.

Asparagus is a fairly recent addition to the wok, gaining popularity in the last century, although China is now one of the world's largest producers of green asparagus.

Snow peas, and sometimes the new hybrid sugar snap peas, are favored for their delicate flavor and ability to add sweetness to a savory dish. Likewise, baby corn makes a beautiful show in a wok full of ingredients.

Asian Eggplant

- All eggplants originated in Asia, but certain varieties gained favor in China and Japan; others were encouraged in Europe.

- Asian eggplants are long and thin, with skins ranging from white to purple. The flesh is denser, less seedy, and less bitter than the

- flesh of European eggplants.

- All eggplants discharge a lot of liquid when cooked.

- To draw out some of the liquid, cut and salt the eggplant. Let it drain in a colander for 30 minutes, then rinse.

Asparagus

- Asparagus first appeared in the Mediterranean; the Chinese have long embraced the delicate vegetable.

- Buy fat, firm asparagus spears with tightly packed tips. Most Chinese dishes use green asparagus, but you can use slightly sweeter white spears, too.

- Asparagus toughens when overcooked, making it perfect for a quick stir-fry or dunk in a hot pot.

- Discard the woody ends, then slice diagonally into 1-inch pieces, leaving the tips intact. Stir-fry briefly.

Happily, you can find all these vegetables at produce counters around the globe, as well as in freezer packs. If you live near an active farmers' market, check for local growers who specialize in fresh Asian vegetables.

Snow Peas and Sugar Snap Peas

- Edible pea pods are picked young, before they become tough. They carry all the sweetness of the peas and very little of the starch.

- Chinese cooks love snow pea pods for the textures and shapes they add to stir-fries. They complement chicken and seafood well.

- Before using snow peas, strip the stringy fiber from the side of the pod. The peas can be served raw as well as cooked.

- Sugar snap peas can be used in place of snow peas in most recipes.

Baby Corn Ears

- Baby corn, or miniature corn, is really ordinary sweet corn, plucked from the stalks within a few days after silks emerge.

- Until recently most baby corn in dishes prepared outside China came from cans. Now many supermarkets carry fresh baby corn.

- The little ears, eaten cob and all, can be served raw or cooked. Blanching in boiling water tenderizes fresh ears a bit.

- Use baby corn in stir-fries and soups to enhance color and texture.

MUSHROOMS, PEPPERS, & HERBS
Three categories of ingredients and unlimited possibilities

Throw sliced mushrooms, diced peppers, and a handful of chopped fresh herbs in a pan of hot oil, stir the mix for a few minutes, and your kitchen will smell like you've been slaving over gourmet fare. Few ingredients offer such high impact for such little effort as the families of edible fungi, capsaicins, and culinary herbs. Aside from the aromatic properties, mushrooms and peppers can change the appearance and texture of a dish, plus offer earthy, sweet, or hot flavors. Fresh

herbs are the grace notes of any recipe, adding a just-picked essence. Chinese cuisine shares a love of mushrooms and peppers with other strong world culinary capitals like Italy and Greece. And like those countries, China has only enjoyed hot and sweet chiles since the Columbian exchange of the 1500s. China's favorite herbs—cilantro and chives in particular—are homegrown affairs. In fact Marco Polo is credited with bringing chives to Italy from China.

Mushrooms

- Meaty, earthy shiitake mushrooms are the mushroom of choice in many Chinese dishes.

- Grown in China and Japan, fresh shiitakes can be found in most supermarkets. Rinse and slice or chop the caps and reserve the woody stems for flavoring stocks.

- Other favorite Chinese mushrooms are enokis, oyster mushrooms, and straw mushrooms. Of the three, straw mushrooms may be difficult to find fresh.

- Ordinary white button mushrooms can be used as a substitute for any variety of mushrooms.

Bell Peppers

- Is there a more perfect ingredient? Bell peppers are crisp, aromatic, and sweet and come in beautiful, bright colors.

- These plump fruits are used in many stir-fries and slow-simmered Chinese dishes, a gift of the Columbian exchange of ingredients

from the Americas.

- Bell peppers are the only capsicum fruit that does not contain capsaicin, which puts the heat in peppers.

- Always remove the seeds and inner ribs from bell peppers, which can be bitter, before adding to dishes.

Hot Chile Peppers

- Hot chiles come in a wide range of shapes, colors, and sizes.

- Most of the fresh hot peppers used in Chinese cooking are Arbol or Serrano-type chiles. In fact dried red Arbols are commonly called Chinese hot peppers.

- However, any chiles—jalapeños, habañeros, bird peppers—can be used in sauces and stir-fries.

- The important thing to remember is that Chinese cuisine emphasizes balance. Even spicy dishes should offer diners something besides heat.

Cilantro and Chives

- This native Asian herb plant produces fresh cilantro leaves, as well as coriander seeds. The dried seeds and fresh leaves have very different flavors.

- Cilantro wilts quickly and loses flavor when cooked for long periods. Buying cilantro with roots still attached helps the leaves withstand a few days in the refrigerator.

- Chives in Chinese cuisine refer to flat-leafed garlic chives, which have a mild flavor reminiscent of garlic. Regular chives can substitute, but always be sure they're fresh.

FRESH INGREDIENTS

TOFU, CITRUS, & WRAPS

In Chinese cuisine many ingredients play supporting roles

Depending on your menu plans and where you shop, you'll have a plethora of choices to make when considering what type of tofu to buy, which roll or dumpling wraps to select, and what citrus fruit will best accent your dish.

Starting with tofu, that Asian vegetarian staple, there are two broad categories from which to choose: silken and firm. However, within those categories there are several different grades of density, as well as tofu that has been flavored, fer-

mented, smoked, crumbled, and pickled. If you're a tofu neophyte, sample a little ordinary firm tofu in hot and sour soup or a stir-fry, then move on to sampling other varieties.

Citrus fruits play a role in Chinese savory dishes as well as desserts. While fewer Chinese recipes call for lime, than say, the recipes of Thailand or Vietnam, there are many opportunities to add mandarins, regular oranges, and lemons to beef and poultry dishes. Less common fruits such as large, thick-

Tofu

- Tofu, or bean curd, has virtually no flavor. The spongy product of coagulated soy milk takes on the flavors of the sauces and ingredients with which it's cooked.

- What tofu does have is texture. Depending on the type, you can completely change the look and ex-

perience of the dish you're preparing.

- Silken tofu can be used in desserts and pureed into drinks, while firm tofu holds up to deep-frying and stir-frying.

- Tofu is a great source of vegetarian protein.

Citrus Fruits

- Tangerines, satsumas, and other varieties of Mandarin oranges have been cultivated in China for three millennia and are among the country's top exports.

- In China these fruits, along with regular oranges, appear as desserts or snacks, as well as in savory dishes such as

Orange-Scented Beef.

- Giant pomelos and tiny kumquats also appear at the Chinese table.

- These fruits may be drizzled with sweet syrups or preserved. Candied citrus peel is used in special-occasion puddings and cakes.

rinded pomelos and diminutive kumquats appear as well.

As for wraps, you'll be amazed at how easy it is to make homemade rolls, dumplings, and wontons with these handy little preformed dough sheets. What's more, refrigerated dough sheets can be stuffed with a filling, wrapped, and frozen without suffering much quality loss.

Wonton and Egg Roll Wrappers

- Some purists prefer to make dough for egg rolls and wontons. For the rest of us, there are ready-made wrappers.

- You'll usually find two or three different types of wrappers in the produce or refrigerated-foods section.

- Hearty egg roll wrappers can be cut to fit most recipes. An all-purpose "pasta wrapper" will work as well.

- Wonton wrappers come in precut small squares or ready-to-cut sheets. The layers come apart easily and are sealed with dissolved cornstarch after filling.

Spring Roll Wrappers

- Asian markets generally stock all types of wrappers, including delicate spring roll wrappers and rice paper wrappers.

- In supermarkets, the selection may be more limited. "Pasta wrappers," or large wonton wrappers, work for spring rolls, although

they're a bit thick.

- Some markets carry frozen spring roll wrappers, next to frozen Asian appetizers.

- For superflaky spring rolls, you can always use frozen phyllo dough.

FRESH INGREDIENTS

FRUITS

Chinese cuisine's emphasis on fresh produce doesn't stop with vegetables

In China, at New Year and during the fall Harvest Festival, gifts and temple offerings are likely to consist of beautiful whole fruits, as well as sugared fruits, to symbolize a happy and sweet life and renewal.

The Chinese love and value fresh fruit, and China's vast size ensures that it offers hospitable climates for most of the world's fruit specimens. Apples, peaches, apricots, pomegranates, melons, and bananas grow in China, as do more unusual fruits such as lychees, loquats, and longans.

In addition to eating fruit raw and in desserts, Chinese cooks rely on certain fruits to contribute to the yin and yang—that is, the sweet-and-sour—of the dining experience. Sweet and

Pineapple

- Pineapple originated in Brazil, and many centuries passed before the fruit took root in Southeast Asia.

- Fresh pineapple puts the "sweet" in many sweet-and-sour dishes, including raw salads and stir-fries.

- Pineapple is a critical part

of the standard recipe for sweet-and-sour pork.

- Pineapple may appear to be a thorny customer, but it's really a delicate tropical fruit that should be kept at room temperature and eaten quickly after ripening.

Mango

- Mangoes are one of the world's oldest cultivated crops, originating in India and going back to the fifth century B.C.E. in China.

- This tropical fruit—the most widely consumed fresh fruit in the world—appears in several Chinese desserts, including gluti-

nous rice balls with mango and mango pudding.

- Mango slices may be added to fruit salads, some savory stir-fries, and occasionally to sweet-and-sour sauces.

- Buy smooth-skinned fruit that gives slightly to the touch.

tart fruit and vegetable salads, pickled and preserved fruit, and sweet-and-sour dishes and dips regularly appear on the menu.

A few fruits take a central role in the mix. Crisp Asian pears are a favorite for steaming alone or with savory meats, mangoes and coconuts are part of banquet and holiday desserts, and pineapple stars in the Cantonese-American classic sweet-and-sour pork.

· · · · · · · · · · · GREEN ● LIGHT · · · · · · · · · · ·

Pineapple corers do exist, but if you don't have one, don't panic. Just take a sharp knife and lop off the leafy crown of your pineapple. Cut the whole pineapple in quarters, then slice off the core section from the top of the wedges. Cut the fruit from the peel and slice, dice, or cut into spears as needed.

Asian Pears

- Asian pears look and feel like apples. They're round, golden, and crisp and, like apples, ripen on the tree.

- The flavor of these sweet, juicy orbs is distinctly pear, with all the aromatic grace notes this edible member of the rose family can produce.

- Since Asian pears are sturdier than their buttery European counterparts, they hold up well in steamed dishes, salads, and puddings.

- Shop for Asian pear varieties in the specialty produce section of your supermarket.

Coconut

- Coconut and coconut milk make critical contributions to many southern Asian cuisines, such as Thai, Vietnamese, and Indian.

- Chinese cooks also appreciate the value of snowy, tropical coconut meat.

- Fresh coconut coats sweet glutinous rice balls at celebrations and banquets, and both coconut and coconut milk star in coconut puddings.

- Occasionally, in dishes influenced by the traditions of Singapore and Thailand, coconut milk is used to cool a spicy curry.

35

SPRING ROLLS

Treat guests to these crispy, delicate pastry wrappers stuffed with a mélange of flavors

Chinese spring roll wrappers are made with wheat flour and water rolled into translucent sheets. Unlike the rice flour spring roll wrappers used in Thai cooking, they're designed to be cooked rather than served raw. Find ready-to-use spring roll wrappers in the refrigerated produce section of your supermarket. In a pinch you can substitute wonton wrappers,

which will be a little thicker. Or use buttered sheets of phyllo dough for baked spring rolls. The secret to crunchy, golden spring rolls is a finely chopped, well-drained filling. Deep-fry spring rolls in hot oil, drain well, and serve. Uncooked spring rolls freeze well, and can be cooked directly from the freezer. *Yield: Serves 6–9*

Ingredients

3 dried wood ear mushrooms

8 ounces minced or ground pork

1 teaspoon cornstarch

1 tablespoon dark sesame oil

1 tablespoon vegetable oil

1 clove garlic, minced

1 green onion, shredded

¹/₃ cup matchstick-cut bamboo shoots

¹/₃ cup matchstick-cut carrots

1 cup finely shredded napa cabbage

2 tablespoons soy sauce

Salt and pepper to taste

4 ounces raw shrimp, chopped

18 spring roll wrappers

1 egg, beaten

Vegetable oil for deep-frying

Spring Rolls

- Place dried mushrooms in a bowl of warm water. Soak for 30 minutes, then drain. Slice the mushrooms into thin strips.

- Toss pork with cornstarch. Heat wok over high heat. Add sesame oil and vegetable oil.

- When oil is hot, stir-fry filling ingredients as directed. Using a slotted spoon or strainer, transfer mixture to a bowl. Blot as much liquid as possible from the filling.

- Fill wrappers and fold as directed. Fry rolls for 2 minutes, turning once. Serve as is or with dipping sauces.

Vegetarian Spring Rolls: Substitute 4 ounces finely diced firm tofu and 8 ounces chopped portobello mushrooms for the pork and shrimp. Sauté the mushrooms in a small amount of oil, let cool, then press excess moisture from the mushrooms with a paper towel. Combine tofu and mushrooms with other ingredients and prepare spring rolls as directed.

Shredded Chicken or Beef Spring Rolls: Sauté vegetables as directed. Add 1 to 1¼ cups cooked, finely shredded roasted chicken or lean pot roast to the wok. Stir until mixture is well blended. Remove from heat and let stand until cooled. Press out excess moisture and prepare spring rolls as directed. This is a great way to use leftovers.

Prepare Filling

Fold the Spring Roll

- Add garlic, green onion, bamboo shoots, carrots, and cabbage to the hot oil. Stir-fry 1 minute.

- Add pork and stir-fry until no longer pink. Add soy sauce, salt, and pepper. Add shrimp; stir-fry until shrimp turns opaque.

- Transfer mixture to a bowl. Let stand 15 to 20 minutes. Using paper towels, blot as much liquid as possible.

- Place a spring roll wrapper on a work surface so wrapper forms a diamond shape. Place a heaping tablespoon of filling on the lower third of the diamond.

- Lift the bottom corner of the wrapper and fold over the filling. Fold the two side corners over the filling. The three corners should overlap.

- Brush beaten egg over the folded edges. Lift the top edge of the wrapper and fold over and around the filling, forming a tightly closed packet.

- Heat a wok over high heat. Add 2 inches vegetable oil. When oil is very hot, fry spring rolls, a few at a time.

- Remove spring rolls and drain on paper towels.

APPETIZERS

EGG ROLLS

Hearty, crisp-fried egg rolls have become a staple on Chinese restaurant menus

Egg rolls offer a thicker, more substantial crust than spring rolls. While seen less often in China than its crispier cousin, the egg roll became popular among Chinese immigrants who wanted a transportable lunch or snack. Restaurateurs embraced these packets, which turned out to be popular with Western customers. Buy ready-made egg roll wrappers in supermarket produce sections and Asian markets. Pork and cabbage are traditional fillings, but do experiment with other savory ingredients. This version uses sweet onion, a vegetable not often found in Chinese dishes. Deep-fry egg rolls in hot oil, drain well, and serve with hot mustard.

Yield: Serves 6–9

Ingredients

12 ounces cooked shredded pork

2 tablespoons soy sauce

2 teaspoons oyster sauce

2 tablespoons vegetable oil

1 clove garlic, minced

1 small sweet onion, halved and finely sliced

1 rib celery, cut into matchstick pieces

8 ounces mushrooms, halved and sliced

2 cups finely sliced napa cabbage

1$\frac{1}{2}$ cups mung bean sprouts

1 egg, beaten

$\frac{1}{2}$ teaspoon sugar

Salt and pepper to taste

1 tablespoon cornstarch

12 egg roll wrappers

Vegetable oil for deep-frying

Egg Rolls

- Place pork in a large bowl. Toss with soy sauce and oyster sauce.

- Heat wok over high heat. Add the oil. When hot, add garlic, onion, celery, and mushrooms. Stir-fry 2 minutes. With a slotted spoon, remove ingredients; add to pork.

- Add cabbage and bean sprouts to the wok. Stir-fry 2 minutes. Add beaten egg and toss until egg is cooked and blended with cabbage. Sprinkle with sugar, salt, and pepper.

- Add cabbage to pork. Cool to room temperature. Fill, wrap and fry egg rolls.

Vegetarian Egg Rolls: Substitute 1 cup broccoli slaw and ½ cup slivered radish for the pork. Combine with other filling ingredients and prepare egg rolls as directed.

Shredded Duck Egg Rolls: Substitute 1½ cups cooked, shredded duck meat for the shredded pork. In place of the oyster sauce, use 1 tablespoon hoisin sauce and stir in ¼ teaspoon grated ginger root with the soy and hoisin sauce mixture.

Leftover Pot Roast Egg Rolls: Substitute 1½ cups cooked, shredded beef for the pork. Continue as directed.

Wrap and Roll

- Dissolve cornstarch in 2 tablespoons cold water. Lay one wrapper on a work surface, short sides of the rectangle at the top and bottom.

- Place 2 tablespoons filling across the bottom third of the wrapper, leaving a half-inch margin on each side.

- Fold the two long sides inward, partially covering the filling.

- Working from the bottom, roll the wrapper forward, keeping edges tucked inside.

- Brush cornstarch along seams. Place rolls, seam side down, on a platter.

Fry the Egg Roll

- Wipe the wok clean and heat over high heat. Add 2 inches vegetable oil.

- When oil reaches 375°F, add 2 egg rolls at a time. Cook, turning once, until wrappers are golden, about 3 minutes.

- Remove egg rolls to a platter covered with paper towels. Repeat the process until all egg rolls are fried.

- Let rolls stand a few minutes before serving with hot mustard for dipping.

APPETIZERS

SCALLION PANCAKES

Savory, crisp scallion pancakes make a satisfying snack or enticing first course

Every culture has some version of fried bread. Scallion pancakes are more fried bread than pancakes, but for all their simplicity, they're full of flavor. Use both the white and green parts of tender green onions for the filling. Some cooks prefer thick slices of green onion, while others add only finely minced green onion to their pancakes.

These golden-brown disks of unleavened dough can be served as appetizers or included in dim sum selections. In China, street vendors sell them as snacks, served plain or with a simple dipping sauce. A sesame-scented soy sauce is a good choice, although chile heads might add a bit of hot chile paste.
Yield: Serves 6

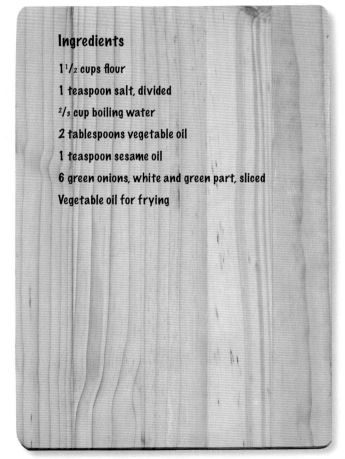

Ingredients

1¹/₂ cups flour

1 teaspoon salt, divided

²/₃ cup boiling water

2 tablespoons vegetable oil

1 teaspoon sesame oil

6 green onions, white and green part, sliced

Vegetable oil for frying

Scallion Pancakes

- In a bowl, combine flour and ½ teaspoon salt. Slowly add water, stirring to form a dough. With floured hands, shape into a ball. Let rest 15 minutes.

- Knead dough several minutes, until smooth and pliable. Divide dough in half. Shape each half into a long roll. Cut each roll into 6 even pieces.

- Roll pieces into rectangles. Brush with oils; cover with green onions and remaining salt.

- Roll dough to encase onions and create pancakes. Fry in hot oil. Keep warm.

Short-Dough Scallion Pancakes: Add 2 tablespoons shortening to flour and salt. Work shortening into flour with two knives or pastry blender until mixture resembles coarse meal. Add boiling water and continue as directed.

Mixed Herb Pancakes: Substitute 1 cup chopped mixed fresh herbs—basil, chives, tarragon, parsley—for green onions.

Garlic Butter Pancakes: Press 6 garlic cloves into 4 tablespoons melted butter. Brush garlic butter over dough in place of oil and green onions.

Add Green Onion Filling

- With smooth glass or rolling pin, roll one of the 12 dough pieces into thin rectangle about 6 to 8 inches long.

- Mix vegetable oil and sesame oil. Lightly brush top of rectangle with oil.

- Sprinkle green onions evenly over oil. Season with salt. Roll rectangle into a long tube, enclosing green onion filling.

- Pinch the ends closed to create a tube. Cover with damp cloth and repeat process with remaining dough.

Roll and Fry Filled Dough

- Place one dough tube on a work surface. Starting at one end, roll into a tight, flat coil. Tuck the exposed end of tube back into spiral.

- Press coil into a flat 4-inch pancake. Cover with damp cloth until all pancakes are assembled.

- Heat a flat-bottomed wok or skillet over high heat. Add oil to cover the bottom of pan. Add 2 or 3 pancakes.

- Cook pancakes, occasionally pressing to flatten, for 3 minutes on each side. Serve whole or cut into wedges.

APPETIZERS

SPARERIBS

These well-seasoned ribs are designed for sampling, rather than hunkering down

Have your butcher remove the chine bone at the top of the ribs, as well as the thick cartilage area. Save those pieces for flavoring sauces or stock. At home use a sharp knife to remove the tough connective membrane from the rack and discard. After trimming, you'll have a beautiful, uniform rack of ribs that will cook evenly.

Chinese spareribs are beloved for their sweet-savory sauce and succulent texture. But the sugary sauce means the ribs can burn easily. Check the ribs frequently and turn often while roasting. This recipe offers a taste of spareribs for each guest at a multicourse meal. For heartier portions, double the recipe. *Yield: Serves 6*

Chinese Spareribs

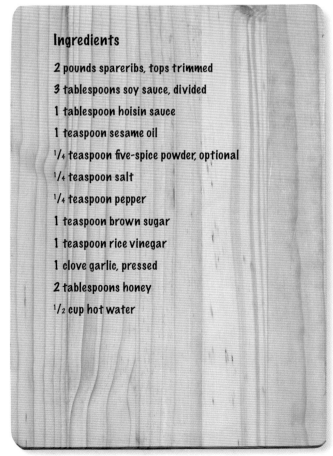

Ingredients

2 pounds spareribs, tops trimmed

3 tablespoons soy sauce, divided

1 tablespoon hoisin sauce

1 teaspoon sesame oil

$1/4$ teaspoon five-spice powder, optional

$1/4$ teaspoon salt

$1/4$ teaspoon pepper

1 teaspoon brown sugar

1 teaspoon rice vinegar

1 clove garlic, pressed

2 tablespoons honey

$1/2$ cup hot water

- Cut rack into two-rib sections. Line a baking dish with nonstick foil.

- Combine 2 tablespoons soy sauce, hoisin sauce, sesame oil, five-spice powder (if using), salt, pepper, brown sugar, and rice vinegar.

- Brush ribs with sauce. Place ribs on baking dish. Cover and refrigerate 6 to 8 hours. Remove and let stand 15 minutes.

- Roast ribs in 350°F oven 50 minutes, turning occasionally. Combine 1 tablespoon soy sauce and remaining ingredients; baste ribs and roast 10 minutes longer.

Hearty, Country-Style Ribs: Buy 2½ pounds thick, country-cut pork ribs. Double the recipe for the marinade and basting sauce. Follow instructions as noted, but increase cooking time by 10 minutes.

Chicken Wings in Rib Sauce: Cut 12 chicken wings at the joints. Discard tips. Prepare the rib marinade as directed, but add an additional tablespoon of soy sauce and a teaspoon of hot chile paste. Toss the 24 wing sections in the sauce, then follow instructions as for ribs. Add a dash of hot chile oil to the final honey glaze, if desired.

Coat Ribs with Sauce

- The initial sauce mixture serves as both a seasoning and a tenderizing marinade for the ribs.

- For best results, brush mixture liberally over each two-rib section.

- Once ribs have begun to marinate, the pork will release juices into the pan. Turn the ribs frequently, basting with seasoned juices.

- Before roasting, place rib sections in a clean roasting pan and discard marinade and juices.

Glaze the Ribs

- Glazing the ribs with a honey-based sauce gives the dish extra flavor and a beautiful finish.

- Combine remaining tablespoon soy sauce with garlic, honey, and hot water. Stir to blend.

- Lightly brush ribs with honey mixture after roasting 50 minutes. Cook ribs 10 minutes longer to set the glaze.

- Remove ribs from oven. Let stand a few minutes, then serve alone or as part of an appetizer assortment.

APPETIZERS

FRIED WONTONS

Children love these crispy little morsels, which often serve as their introduction to Chinese food

To make perfect, golden wontons, keep your filling cool and firm and your oil hot. The stuffed noodle pockets should cook quickly and evenly. In China, stuffed wontons may be served as well-folded packets or with the corners of the wrapper drawn together into a beggar's purse shape. Freeform wontons have just a dab of filling encased in a wide ruffle of crispy noodle.

Although wonton fillings have many regional variations, including an all-seafood blend and a minced beef and bok choy version, most purists prefer a pork and shrimp mixture. Likewise, strictly traditional cooks avoid adding soy sauce to the filling for fear that it will discolor the wrapper.

Yield: Serves 6

Ingredients

8 ounces finely ground pork

2 green onions, minced

1 teaspoon sesame oil

1 teaspoon soy sauce, optional

8 ounces small cooked shrimp, chopped

Pinch sugar

Salt and pepper to taste

24 wonton wrappers

1 tablespoon cornstarch

Vegetable oil for frying

Fried Wontons

- In a large bowl, combine pork, green onions, and sesame oil. Work with a spoon or your hands until mixture is well blended.

- Stir soy sauce, if using, into the pork. Fold shrimp into the pork mixture. Add sugar, salt, and pepper. Mix well.

- Cover bowl and refrigerate. Allow mixture to cool 15 minutes.

- Fill and fold wontons. Fry in hot oil until golden. Drain well and serve with your favorite dipping sauces.

Cream Cheese Wontons: Soften 12 ounces cream cheese. Mix with 3 tablespoons finely minced green onion, ½ teaspoon sugar, and white pepper to taste. Refrigerate until firm. Drop a scant tablespoon cream cheese filling onto wonton wrappers. Fold and fry as directed. For crab wontons, replace half the cream cheese with 1 cup of crabmeat and a dash of sesame oil.

Dessert Wontons: Place a scant tablespoon of ready-to-use cheesecake filling onto each wonton wrapper. Drop a drained, pitted cherry onto the filling. Fold and seal wontons and fry as directed. Drain wontons on a paper towel and dust with confectioner's sugar.

Fill the Wonton Wrappers

- Lay a wonton wrapper on a work surface. Place 1 teaspoon filling in the center.

- Fold one corner of the wrapper over the filling, forming a triangle.

- Dissolve cornstarch in 2 tablespoons cold water. Moisten the inside edges of the wrapper with cornstarch mixture and press to seal.

- Brush a little cornstarch mixture along the bottom fold of the triangle. Fold bottom edges of triangle over the top. Folded wonton should resemble a cap.

Fold Wonton Wrappers

- Repeat filling and folding technique until all 24 wonton wrappers have been filled.

- Place a wok over high heat. Add oil to a depth of 3 inches. Heat until oil is hot, about 350°F.

- Add wontons to the wok a few at a time. Fry 2 to 3 minutes, or until golden brown.

- With tongs or a slotted spoon, remove wontons and drain on paper towels.

APPETIZERS

45

LETTUCE WRAPS

Include this elegant appetizer in a multicourse meal, or serve a double portion for lunch

The word wrap might be an overstatement here, because ideally the open lettuce cups curl ever so slightly around the chicken filling, giving a hint at the delicious warm salad inside. The presentation is fresh and beautiful, making the search for perfectly cupped greens worthwhile. However, in a pinch the filling can be combined with shredded lettuce or cabbage and tucked into ready-to-use mandarin pancakes or flour tortillas. The filling also lends itself to substitutions, including any number of leftover shredded meats or browned ground chicken, beef, or pork. For hors d'oeuvres, spoon small amounts of the filling into firm endive or radicchio leaves.

Yield: Serves 8

Ingredients

1 pound boneless chicken breasts

Salt and white pepper to taste

1 tablespoon cornstarch

3 tablespoons vegetable oil

2 green onions, minced

1 teaspoon sesame oil

1 teaspoon rice vinegar

$1/2$ teaspoon sugar

2 tablespoons soy sauce

1 tablespoon hoisin sauce

$1/2$ cup diced celery

$1/2$ cup diced red bell pepper

$1/2$ cup diced carrots

2 tablespoons minced cilantro

Salt and pepper to taste

8 large Bibb or iceberg lettuce leaves or 16 radicchio or endive leaves, rinsed and blotted dry

Lettuce Wraps

- Dice chicken into cubes. Sprinkle with salt and pepper; coat with cornstarch.

- Place a wok over high heat and add vegetable oil. When oil is hot, stir-fry chicken. With a slotted spoon, remove chicken to a bowl.

- Sprinkle green onions over chicken. Mix together sesame oil, rice vinegar, sugar, soy sauce, and hoisin sauce. Pour over chicken to coat.

- Blanch vegetables. Toss with chicken, along with cilantro, salt, and pepper. Fill lettuce cups and serve.

• • • • RECIPE VARIATIONS • • • •

Pulled Pork Wraps: Buy or prepare a pound of barbe-cued pulled pork. Break up any large pieces and mix with sauce as directed. Spoon into lettuce cups and serve.

Turkey Breast Wraps: Substitute 1 pound raw, diced turkey breast for the chicken; prepare as directed. Or use

shredded leftover cooked turkey, add sauce, and place in lettuce cups as shown.

Vegetarian Wraps: Substitute 12 ounces diced firm tofu for the chicken. Add ½ cup sliced, blanched green beans or asparagus to the vegetable mixture.

Separate Chicken Cubes

- To get the best combina-tion of flavor and texture, the chicken cubes should be small but never clumped together.

- Add diced chicken to wok in small batches. While stir-frying, use a spoon or long chopsticks to break up the chicken.

- Remove each batch of chicken with a slotted spoon, allowing as much of the oil to remain in the wok as possible.

- Spoon cooked chicken into a large bowl. Once all chicken is cooked, add green onions and sauce.

Blanch Vegetables

- To prepare the vegetables, first drain oil from wok and wipe it clean. Add 2 cups water; bring to a rolling boil.

- Add celery, bell pepper, and carrots to water. Blanch vegetables 1 minute. Re-move wok from heat.

- Quickly pour vegetables into a strainer placed over a sink. Rinse vegetables with cold water. Drain well.

- Add drained, still-crisp veg-etables to chicken mixture and stir well to combine before filling lettuce cups.

HOT & SOUR SOUP

Simple ingredients make a bold statement in this fragrant, well-loved soup

Szechwan province usually gets credit for this sinus-clearing soup, but in fact versions of it are prepared in other parts of China and in other Asian countries. The classic soup gets its hot-and-sour components from white pepper and vinegar, added to a chicken, pork, or vegetable broth. Tofu slices absorb the seasonings and give the soup substance. In other cultures tofu is optional, while citrus fruits or tamarind provide tartness and chiles spice things up. Szechuan-style hot and sour soup served outside China is often thick with tofu, meat, mushrooms, and other ingredients. Chinese cooks prefer a more broth-heavy soup.

Yield: Serves 6

Ingredients

6 tiger lily buds, soaked

4 wood ear mushrooms, soaked

6 ounces boneless pork, matchstick sliced

1 tablespoon sesame oil, divided

$^1/_3$ cup soy sauce, divided

2 teaspoons cornstarch

4 ounces thinly sliced white or shiitake mushrooms

$^2/_3$ cup matchstick-cut carrots, optional

$^2/_3$ cup matchstick-cut bamboo shoots

10 cups chicken or pork broth

4 ounces firm tofu, cut into $^1/_2$-inch julienne slices

$^1/_3$ cup rice vinegar

2 teaspoons cornstarch dissolved in 1 tablespoon cold water

2 eggs, beaten

2 green onions, sliced

1 teaspoon white pepper

Salt to taste

Hot chile oil to taste

Hot and Sour Soup

- Drain and prepare tiger lily buds and wood ear mushrooms. Toss pork with half the sesame oil and 1 tablespoon soy sauce. Sprinkle with dry cornstarch.

- Bring mushrooms, carrots (if using), bamboo shoots, and broth to a boil in a large pot. Reduce heat. Add tofu, lily buds, and wood ears. Simmer 5 minutes.

- Add pork, remaining soy sauce, and sesame oil; simmer 5 minutes. Stir in vinegar and dissolved cornstarch. Add eggs, stirring constantly. Add green onions, white pepper, and salt. Serve with chile oil.

Seafood Hot and Sour Soup: Substitute 6 ounces peeled, diced shrimp and 2 ounces claw crabmeat or shredded crab legs for the pork. Prepare recipe as directed.

Vegetarian Hot and Sour Soup: Double the quantity of fresh mushrooms, using more than one variety. Substitute vegetable broth for the chicken or pork broth. Omit the pork and add all the soy sauce and sesame oil to the simmering broth. Add 1 tablespoon, total, dissolved cornstarch to the soup to thicken.

Prepare Wood Ears

- Dried tiger lily buds and wood ear mushrooms must be rehydrated before using.

- Place the two ingredients in separate, heat-safe bowls. Add enough hot water to cover. Let stand 30 minutes.

- Drain buds and mushrooms. Tiny lily buds can be used as is. Wood ears have a slightly chewy center. When thinly sliced, this adds an interesting texture to dishes.

- Thinly slice rehydrated wood ears. The result should be dark ribbons ready to use.

Thicken with Cornstarch

- Chinese cooks rarely use flour to thicken soups. They prefer cornstarch, which works quickly and cooks into a clear, glossy finish.

- Dry cornstarch absorbs moisture so quickly it cannot be added directly to soups and stews.

- To avoid gelatinous lumps, dissolve cornstarch in cold water, using 1 part cornstarch to 2 parts water.

- Pour mixture into a bubbling sauce or soup and stir to blend. Simmer until sauce is thick but no longer cloudy.

SOUPS

EGG DROP SOUP

This nourishing soup makes a great restorative when you need strength—or just something delicious

Egg drop soup is also called egg flower soup because the raw eggs "bloom" in the broth. Versions of this soup appear in other cuisines, including Italian stracciatella, made with "torn strips" of eggs and Parmesan cheese. German cooks add a touch of flour to the beaten eggs to make thin dumplings. In all versions it's important to start with a rich, flavorful chicken broth. To make broth with a Chinese flair, combine chicken backs and wings or a meaty chicken carcass with water, green onions, and several slices of ginger root. Simmer 3 hours, skimming any foam that rises to the top. Cool, strain, and refrigerate. Skim fat and use or freeze.

Yield: Serves 6

Ingredients

8 cups strong chicken stock

1 tablespoon rice wine

1 teaspoon sugar

4 large eggs

3 green onions, shredded

Salt and pepper to taste

Egg Drop Soup

- Combine chicken stock, wine, and sugar in a large soup pot; bring to a boil and cook 5 minutes.

- In a glass bowl or large cup with a handle, whisk eggs until thick and frothy. Hold bowl of beaten eggs in one hand and a large fork or whisk in the other.

- Slowly pour eggs into boiling chicken stock, whisking or stirring constantly while adding eggs.

- Add shredded green onions to soup, along with salt and pepper. Serve hot.

Main Dish Egg Drop Soup: Prepare soup as directed. Slice 4 poached chicken breast halves crosswise and stir into the soup along with 1 cup bok choy, sliced crosswise. Simmer just until bok choy is tender and chicken is heated through.

Egg Drop Soup with Meatballs: Prepare Meatballs (see Dim Sum Dishes), or use your own recipe. Add 12 cooked meatballs to prepared Egg Drop Soup and serve.

Whisk Eggs

- Beating eggs forces air into the whites and yolks. The air gets trapped in the protein-rich liquid, making the eggs fuller and lighter.

- Start with eggs at cool room temperature and use an electric mixer or, preferably, a whisk. Break eggs into bowl big enough to allow for expansion.

- Hold the bowl at a slight tilt. Whisk in a constant, even circular motion.

- Whisk until yolks and whites are completely blended. Then whisk rapidly for 30 seconds, until eggs increase in volume. Use immediately.

Add Eggs to Soup

- Adding eggs to hot liquid can be tricky. Upon contact with heat, eggs instantly want to "cook," a property that can result in lumpy sauces or poached eggs instead of egg ribbons.

- The eggs should blossom into ribbons in the simmering broth.

- To prevent them from cooking into heavy lumps, keep eggs and broth moving. Pour beaten eggs into broth in a slow, steady stream.

- While pouring with one hand, stir broth with the other. Keep stirring until all eggs have been added.

SOUPS

CHICKEN CORN SOUP

Savory chicken and sweet corn make an unbeatable combination in this homey soup

This version of chicken corn soup calls for cooked, shredded chicken. That means this great-tasting soup can be prepared quickly with leftover chicken or even cooked chicken from the supermarket deli.

If you prefer to make classic chicken corn soup, start with raw ground chicken mixed with the egg whites in the recipe.

Gently stir the chicken into the corn and broth. Allow the soup to simmer, without stirring, for 3 minutes. The chicken and egg whites will create little clouds that rise to the surface. The fluffy white appearance gives the soup its original Chinese name, which is chicken cotton corn soup.

Yield: Serves 6

Ingredients

8 cups strong chicken stock

1 tablespoon rice wine

1 shallot, finely chopped

2 cups cream-style corn

3 ears corn

1¹/₂ cups shredded cooked chicken

1 tablespoon cornstarch dissolved in 2 tablespoons cold water

2 egg whites

1 green onion, minced

¹/₄ cup minced cilantro

Salt and white pepper to taste

Chicken Corn Soup

- Combine chicken stock, rice wine, shallot, and cream-style corn in a large soup pot. Bring to a boil over high heat. Reduce heat to medium; simmer 10 minutes.

- Cut corn from cobs; stir into simmering stock. Continue to cook, stirring occasion-ally, 15 minutes. Add shredded chicken.

- Add dissolved cornstarch to soup. Simmer 2 minutes, stir, then add egg whites.

- Add green onion, cilantro, salt, and white pepper. Remove from heat. Let stand a few minutes, then serve.

Crab and Corn Soup: Substitute 12 ounces lump crab-meat for the chicken. Prepare the recipe as directed. Stir the crab into the soup gently and serve immediately.

Turkey, Cabbage, and Corn Soup: Substitute shredded cooked turkey for the chicken. Replace 1 cup of cream-style corn with 1 cup shredded cabbage. Prepare recipe as directed.

Cut Corn from the Cobs

- Remove husk and corn silk fibers from the corn ears; rinse well.

- Stand a corncob at a slight angle in a wide bowl. Using a sharp knife, slice corn kernels off the cob.

- Work in a downward motion, allowing the kernels to fall into the bowl.

- Some corn will remain on the cob. Scrape any corn pulp from the cob into the bowl. Repeat with remaining corn cobs.

Add Egg Whites

- Beat the egg whites with a fork until well blended, but still clear and liquid.

- Using the fork tines, slowly drizzle the egg whites into the soup.

- Gently stir the soup while adding the egg whites. The eggs should form faint ribbons in the broth.

- Simmer just until the egg whites are cooked; add remaining ingredients. Remove soup from heat.

SOUPS

DUCK & CABBAGE SOUP

Dark flavorful duck, salty ham, and crisp cabbage make this soup memorable

The secret ingredient in this assertive, but well-balanced soup is Smithfield ham. Authentic Smithfield hams—also known as country hams—are dry cured, hickory smoked, and aged. The result is ham that packs a lot of taste in a thin sliver. Smithfield ham comes close to the flavor and texture of Yunnan ham, a Chinese delicacy that's hard to find out-side the country. In this dish the minced ham simmers in the soup, so it doesn't matter if you use a fully cooked ham or one that's cured but uncooked.

Plan to cook the duck the day before. In a pinch, the duck meat can be pulled from ready-to-eat duck breasts.

Yield: Serves 6

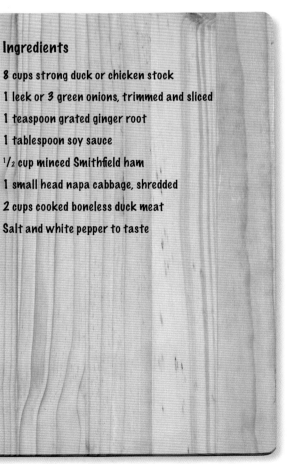

Ingredients

8 cups strong duck or chicken stock

1 leek or 3 green onions, trimmed and sliced

1 teaspoon grated ginger root

1 tablespoon soy sauce

$1/2$ cup minced Smithfield ham

1 small head napa cabbage, shredded

2 cups cooked boneless duck meat

Salt and white pepper to taste

Duck and Cabbage Soup

- Pour chicken or duck broth into a tall soup pot. Add leek or green onions, ginger, and soy sauce.

- Bring broth to a boil over high heat. Reduce heat to medium; stir ham into the broth and simmer 15 minutes.

- Add shredded cabbage and simmer 10 minutes longer.

- Shred duck meat and add to soup. Continue to simmer 10 minutes, then add salt and pepper to taste. Remove from heat and serve.

Chicken and Cabbage Soup: Substitute 2 cups cooked, shredded chicken thigh meat for the duck. Prepare recipe as directed.

Goose and Cabbage Soup: Substitute 1 cup cooked, shredded goose meat for the duck and double the amount of ham. Add a teaspoon of sugar to the broth. Prepare recipe as directed.

Shred the Cabbage

- Napa cabbage forms long, compact heads that look similar to tightly packed romaine lettuce.

- Napa cabbage is more expensive than regular cabbage, but the delicate flavor is worth the price.

- Rinse cabbage and shake dry. With sharp cleaver, remove stem end from cabbage and discard. Remove any discolored outer leaves.

- Cut cabbage lengthwise into quarters. Slice quarters crosswise into thin slices, then pull slices apart into shreds. Add cabbage to broth.

Shred the Duck Meat

- Prepare duck in advance.

- Preheat oven to 325°F. Rinse the duck and remove excess fat from the cavity; pat dry.

- Place duck on a rack in a roasting pan. Pierce skin all over with a fork; season with salt and pepper. Add 2 cups water to pan and roast 2 hours. Cool completely and separate drained fat.

- Remove duck meat from carcass in large pieces. Use carcass to make stock.

CRAB & ASPARAGUS SOUP

In the weeks when spring and summer meet, this soup celebrates the seasonal bounty

Delicate lumps of sweet blue crabmeat work best in this soup, although the shell-free meat of any edible crab can be used. The only absolute is this: Do not use any form of imitation crabmeat or surimi to make this soup. The texture will suffer, and the artificial taste of the surimi will overpower the fresh asparagus. If you're looking for a less-expensive substitute for the lump crabmeat, consider using claw crabmeat or a combination of claw crabmeat and a very mild-tasting white fish, such as tilapia or flounder. In place of the stirred egg in the broth, some cooks boil the egg separately, then slice it and garnish each bowl with a slice of egg.

Yield: Serves 6

Ingredients

¹/₂ pound fresh asparagus

1 tablespoon vegetable oil

¹/₂ teaspoon grated ginger root

1 leek, trimmed and sliced

6 cups chicken broth

1 tablespoon cornstarch dissolved in 2 tablespoons cold water

1 egg, beaten

¹/₂ pound lump crabmeat

Salt and white pepper to taste

Minced chives for garnish

Crab and Asparagus Soup

- Stir-fry asparagus in oil 15 seconds. Add ginger and leek; stir-fry 1 minute. Add broth; bring to a boil over high heat.

- Reduce heat to medium and simmer 8 minutes.

- Increase heat and, when soup is bubbling, add cornstarch mixture and stir. When soup begins to thicken, add beaten egg while stirring constantly.

- When egg forms white ribbons, remove from heat. Add crabmeat, salt, and pepper. Let stand 5 minutes. Garnish with chives and serve.

Shrimp, Scallops, and Asparagus Soup: Substitute 8 ounces small, peeled, deveined shrimp and 4 ounces bay scallops for the crab. Continue as directed.

Crab and Zucchini Soup: Substitute 4 small zucchini for the asparagus. Trim the ends off the zucchini, cut into quarters lengthwise, and remove the seeds. Slice remaining strips into 1-inch pieces. Follow recipe as directed.

Prepare Asparagus

- Asparagus stalks tend to get stringy and toughen as they cook, while the tips soften to the point of breaking.

- That's why, when asparagus is going to simmer in a sauce or soup, it's important to slice the stalks to break long fibers.

- Rinse asparagus well. Snap off the fibrous ends at the point where the green fades to beige.

- Slice spears diagonally into ½-inch pieces. Leave tips intact. Add to soup as directed.

Add Crabmeat

- Lump or giant lump crabmeat is the largest segment of muscle of the blue crab. The meat is sweet, cotton white, and delicate.

- "Back-fin" crabmeat, which includes lump and other white body meat, can be used in place of lump in this recipe, but check it carefully for shell bits.

- To keep crabmeat morsels from breaking up, add to the soup just before serving and stir gently.

- Fresh crabmeat should be kept in the coldest part of the refrigerator.

SOUPS

WONTON SOUP

Comfort food doesn't get any better than this chicken broth with meat-stuffed noodles

Cantonese wontons for soup usually boast a filling of ground pork and shrimp with a little green onion and no soy sauce. However, in Shanghai, cooks make wontons in a variety of shapes—some beggar's purses, some free-form—and the filling often includes finely chopped bok choy. This recipe pays homage to that version by adding cabbage to the meat filling.

For those who prefer an alternative to pork, there is the option of using ground chicken. Feel free to experiment with your own fillings, including ground duck or beef or a combination of minced fish, shrimp, and pork. For a classic Cantonese filling, use the recipe for Fried Wontons (see Appetizers).
Yield: Serves 6

Ingredients

¹/₂ cup napa cabbage

8 ounces ground chicken or pork

1 green onion, chopped

¹/₂ teaspoon sesame oil

1 teaspoon salt

¹/₄ teaspoon grated ginger root

Pinch sugar

Salt and white pepper to taste

18 wonton wrappers

10 cups strong chicken broth

4 leaves bok choy, washed

1 tablespoon cornstarch dissolved in 2 tablespoons cold water

Pepper to taste

Wonton Soup

- Place cabbage in a food processor; pulse to chop. Add meat and green onion; pulse to combine.

- Add sesame oil, salt, ginger, sugar, salt and pepper; pulse to combine. Cover mixture and refrigerate 30 minutes.

- Fill, fold, and boil wontons. Meanwhile, bring chicken stock to a boil in a soup pot.

- Slice bok choy horizontally into thick ribbons. Add to broth; simmer 5 minutes. Place cooked wontons in bowls or a soup tureen. Ladle broth over wontons and serve.

Quick-Fix Wonton Soup: No time to make wontons? Substitute 24 to 30 fresh or frozen meat-filled tortellini for the wontons. Boil the tortellini in a separate pot of water until just tender. Use a basket strainer or slotted spoon to transfer the tortellini to the prepared wonton soup broth. Simmer 10 minutes; serve.

Inside-Out Wonton Soup: Add 18 small, cooked meatballs to the simmering chicken broth. Simmer 10 minutes (20 if meatballs are frozen). Cut each wonton wrapper into four squares. Drop wrappers into separate pot of boiling water. Cook until just tender, about 2 minutes. With a slotted spoon, drop noodle squares into soup; serve.

Prepare Wontons

- Position a wonton wrapper on a work surface. Place a heaping teaspoon of chilled meat mixture at the center of the wrapper.

- Pull one point of the wrapper over the filling, forming a triangle.

- Using a brush or a finger, moisten the inside edges of the triangle with dissolved cornstarch and press together.

- Fold one side of the triangle over the top of the filling, then fold the other side over, and pinch the two corners together. Seal with cornstarch, if needed.

Boil Wontons

- It might be tempting to boil wontons or noodles directly in the soup. Convenient yes, but this is generally ill-advised.

- Cooking wontons and noodles separately allows excess starch to dissolve in the boiling water, without discoloring or clouding the soup broth.

- Bring a large pot of water to a rolling boil. Reduce heat to medium and boil wontons, a few at a time, 3 to 5 minutes.

- When wontons float to the top of the water, use a slotted spoon to remove them.

SOUPS

KUNG PAO CHICKEN

Fiery peppers and crunchy peanuts characterize this Szechwan palate teaser

Kung pao chicken is a fairly recent creation, as Chinese cuisine goes, dating back to the late 1800s in Szechwan province. Legend has it the dish was created in honor of a provincial official whose title (which means "palace guardian") gave the dish its name. Authentic kung pao uses Szechwan peppercorns, hot chile peppers, garlic, and ginger to spice

and flavor the oil that will ultimately be used to stir-fry the mouth-numbing chicken. Diced chicken thighs traditionally star in this spicy favorite, because dark meat stands up to the assertive sauce. However, if you prefer a lighter flavor, use boneless chicken breasts instead.

Yield: Serves 4–6

Ingredients

1 pound boneless, skinless chicken thighs, cut into ¹/₂-inch cubes

3 tablespoons soy sauce, divided

3 tablespoons rice wine, divided

1 teaspoon sesame oil

1 tablespoon cornstarch

¹/₂ cup vegetable oil

1 cup raw, shelled peanuts

4 garlic cloves, 2 whole and 2 minced

3 slices ginger root

6 dried red chile peppers, 4 whole and 2 chopped

1 teaspoon Szechwan peppercorns

2 green onions, sliced

1 teaspoon sugar

Kung Pao Chicken

- Combine chicken, 1 tablespoon soy sauce, 1 tablespoon rice wine, and sesame oil. Add cornstarch. Refrigerate 30 minutes.

- Flavor the oil with peanuts, whole garlic cloves, ginger, whole peppers, and Szechwan peppercorns. Stir-fry chicken; remove to a bowl.

- Remove all but 1 tablespoon oil. Add green onions, minced garlic, and chopped chiles to wok. Stir-fry briefly. Return chicken and peanuts. Stir sugar into remaining soy sauce and rice wine. Add to chicken and vegetables and stir-fry 1 minute. Serve.

• • • • RECIPE VARIATIONS • • • •

Kung Pao Shrimp: Substitute 1 pound shrimp—peeled, deveined, and diced—for the chicken. Prepare as directed. Cashews can replace the peanuts.

Kung Pao Tofu: Substitute 12 ounces firm tofu, diced into 1-inch cubes, for the chicken. In addition, add 1

cored and diced green bell pepper to wok when stir-frying the green onion and garlic.

Western-Style Kung Pao: Add ½ cup each diced carrots and diced celery to the wok at the same time as the green onions and garlic.

Flavor the Oil

- Heat a wok over high heat. Add all the vegetable oil. When the oil is hot, add peanuts and cook until browned, about 40 seconds.

- With a slotted spoon, remove peanuts and reserve.

- Add whole garlic cloves, ginger slices, whole dried peppers, and peppercorns to the oil. Cook until brown; remove ingredients with a slotted spoon and discard.

Stir-Fry Chicken

- When stir-frying meat dishes, it's best to cook the meat first over high heat, before the vegetables and before adding extra sauce.

- Place half the chicken mixture in the wok and spread evenly.

- Cook without stirring until edges turn brown. Turn mixture over once, then stir-fry rapidly for a few seconds.

- Spoon browned chicken into a bowl. Repeat with remaining chicken.

DRY-WOK CHICKEN

This home-style dish is easy to prepare, light on sauce, and heavy on flavor

Dry-wok stir-frying is a bit of a misnomer. The wok isn't completely dry, and the final dish does have a hint of sauce. Dry-wok dishes generally involve stir-frying with a small amount of oil in a wok placed over very high heat. The heat sears and slightly dries the ingredients. At that point a small amount of sauce can be added, and the slightly dehydrated ingredients quickly absorb the flavors.

Dry-cooked meats and vegetables can't hide under heavy sauces, and the quick cooking won't tenderize tough meats. That means you must start with very fresh, high-quality ingredients at the peak of flavor.

Yield: Serves 4–6

Ingredients

1 pound boneless, skinless chicken breast

3 tablespoons vegetable oil, divided

$1/2$ teaspoon five-spice powder

1 tablespoon cornstarch

2 stalks celery, sliced diagonally

1 small red bell pepper, cut in strips

2 cups sliced mushrooms

2 cups green beans or snow peas

$2/3$ cup sliced water chestnuts

1 tablespoon soy sauce

1 tablespoon rice wine

$1/2$ teaspoon rice wine vinegar

Pinch sugar

Salt and white pepper to taste

Dry-Wok Chicken

- Cut chicken crosswise into ½-inch slices. Coat with 1 tablespoon oil. Sprinkle with five-spice powder and cornstarch. Cover; let stand 15 minutes.

- Combine celery, bell pepper, mushrooms, green beans or snow peas, and water chestnuts in a bowl.

- Prepare wok; stir-fry chicken and then vegetables over high heat.

- Combine soy sauce, rice wine, vinegar, and sugar. Add to the wok. Stir to coat ingredients with sauce. Season with salt and pepper.

• • • • RECIPE VARIATIONS • • • •

Dry-Wok Pork: Substitute 1 pound boneless pork chops, trimmed of fat and sliced, for the chicken.

Dry-Wok Duck: Substitute 1 pound boneless duck breast, sliced, for the chicken. Add ½ cup diagonally sliced carrots to the vegetable mixture.

Prepare the Wok

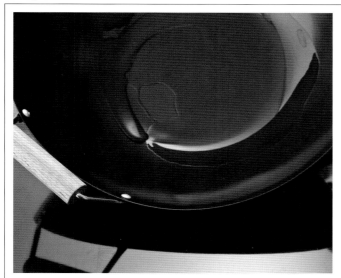

Stir-Fry Vegetables

- Place an empty wok over high heat. When wok is hot, add remaining 2 tablespoons oil. Lift wok (using potholders) and swirl to coat the sides with oil.

- Return wok to high heat. When oil is hot, add chicken. Cook without stirring 1 minute.

- Stir-fry chicken an additional minute, scraping up any bits that have stuck to the bottom.

- Remove chicken to a bowl.

- Add the vegetables to the hot wok, giving the wok a quick shake to coat the vegetables with oil.

- Stir-fry the vegetables 2 to 3 minutes, keeping the ingredients moving at all times.

- When vegetables are crisp-tender, return chicken to wok.

- Stir-fry chicken and vegetables over high heat an additional minute or until chicken is cooked through.

GLAZED CHICKEN WINGS
Chinese flavors meet popular party fare in this tasty finger food

At restaurants in China you won't find a full menu of chicken wings as you might at a Western bistro. However, Chinese cooks do use every part of the chicken (including the feet) in preparing soups and dim sum dishes, so this recipe isn't too much of a stretch.

Marinating the wings in a soy sauce infused with aromatic vegetables allows the chicken skin to soak up these classic Chinese flavors. The wings are fried, then—in a nod to world-

beloved hot wings—glazed with a mixture of sweet honey and hot chile oil. For extra heat, add more chile oil to the glaze, or serve the wings with a side of chile paste along with hoisin sauce.

Yield: Serves 6

Ingredients

24 chicken wings

1 cup soy sauce, divided

³/₄ rice wine

¹/₄ cup rice wine vinegar

1 tablespoon sugar

1 onion or 2 green onions, chopped

1 tablespoon chopped ginger root

3 cloves garlic, chopped

Vegetable oil for frying

2 tablespoons honey

1 teaspoon hot chile oil

2 tablespoons sesame seeds

Glazed Chicken Wings

- Separate chicken wings into three pieces at the joints; discard the tips. In a bowl, whisk together ¾ cup soy sauce, wine, vinegar, and sugar.

- Place chopped onion, ginger root, and garlic in a large resealable plastic bag. Pour sauce mixture in the

bag and add chicken wings; refrigerate.

- Fry wings in hot oil. In a small bowl, whisk together remaining soy sauce, honey, and hot chile oil.

- Brush honey-soy sauce over cooked chicken wings. Sprinkle with sesame seeds.

•••• RECIPE VARIATIONS ••••

Glazed Quail: Cut 6 whole quail in half and use in place of the chicken wings. Follow the recipe, but increase cooking time for the quail halves by 1 minute.

Glazed Chicken Breasts: Cut 1½ pounds chicken breast halves into 24 pieces. Follow the recipe as directed, but reduce cooking time for chicken pieces to 2 minutes.

Glazed Turkey Legs: Turkey doesn't often appear in Chinese cuisine. Think of this as a variation on a county fair favorite. Substitute 6 turkey legs for the chicken wings. Follow recipe as directed, but increase cooking time to 6 minutes.

Marinate Chicken Wings

- Combine soy sauce, wine, vinegar, and sugar.

- Place aromatics in a resealable bag. Add the wings and pour marinade into the bag.

- Close the bag tightly, being careful to press out as much air as possible. Seal the bag, place on a plate or in a shallow bowl, and refrigerate 8 hours or overnight. Turn bag occasionally.

- Before cooking, remove the wings from the marinade and allow excess liquid to drain. Discard marinade.

Fry Chicken Wings

- Place a wok or Dutch oven over high heat. Add vegetable oil to a depth of 3 inches. Use oil with a high smoking point, such as peanut oil.

- Heat oil to 375°F, or to the point when a cube of bread turns brown in a minute or less.

- When oil is hot, cook a few well-drained wings at a time. Use tongs to turn chicken wings during cooking so they brown evenly.

- Fry wings until golden brown, about 4 to 5 minutes. Drain on paper towels.

LEMON CHICKEN

Crispy, boneless fried chicken with lemon sauce makes an elegant luncheon dish

Virtually every cuisine offers some version of lemon chicken. The clean, tart flavor of fresh lemons combines well with a range of herbs and spices to create the perfect accent for rich, succulent chicken. Although this dish appears, with slight variations, throughout China, Chinese cuisine fans throughout the West have enthusiastically embraced it. Crispy fried chicken with sweet-tart lemon sauce . . . what's not to like?

In this version, panko bread crumbs add extra crunch to the fried boneless chicken breasts and the lemon sauce gets an infusion of ginger. If you prefer, the chicken breasts can be replaced with boneless chicken thighs.

Yield: Serves 4

Lemon Chicken

Ingredients

1 cup water

1/2 cup sugar

4 slices ginger root

Juice of 2 lemons

1/2 teaspoon lemon zest

1 tablespoon cornstarch

4 boneless, skinless chicken breast halves

1 cup flour

1/2 teaspoon baking powder

1 teaspoon salt

1/2 teaspoon white pepper

2 eggs

1 tablespoon cold water

1 teaspoon soy sauce

2 cloves garlic, pressed

2 cups panko-style bread crumbs

Vegetable oil for frying

12 romaine lettuce leaves, shredded

Garnish

- In a saucepan, combine water, sugar, and ginger. Bring to a boil, stirring. Reduce heat and simmer 5 minutes.

- Remove ginger slices. Stir in lemon juice and lemon zest; return to a boil.

- Dissolve cornstarch in 2 tablespoons cold water. Stir into lemon mixture. Cook until thickened; remove from heat.

- Flatten, batter, and fry chicken. Place on a bed of shredded lettuce. Drizzle lemon sauce over chicken. Garnish with lemon slices and chopped green onion.

· · · · RECIPE VARIATIONS · · · ·

Cilantro-Lime Chicken: Substitute 3 limes for the lemons. Prepare the recipe as directed, but replace the chive garnish with chopped fresh cilantro.

Peanut-Crusted Chicken: Replace 1 cup of the panko bread crumbs with 1 cup finely chopped (but not ground) peanuts. Prepare recipe as directed. Serve the lemon sauce on the side.

Prepare Chicken

- Place chicken between two sheets of waxed paper.

- Pound chicken with a mallet or roll with a rolling pin until flattened to about ½-inch thick.

- Combine flour, baking powder, salt, and pepper in a shallow bowl. Stir to blend.

- Whisk together egg, water, soy sauce, and garlic in another bowl. Put the panko bread crumbs in a third bowl.

Bread Chicken

- Dredge chicken in the flour mixture, coating each piece completely.

- Dunk each piece in the egg mixture, and finally coat each piece with bread crumbs.

- Place a wok over high heat. Add oil to a depth of 2 inches. When oil is hot, fry chicken 3 to 4 minutes a side or until golden.

- Place fried chicken over a bed of shredded romaine lettuce. Slice each piece horizontally. Drizzle with lemon sauce and garnish.

CASHEW CHICKEN

This Chinese-American restaurant favorite has roots in Chinese country cooking

There's really no dish called "Cashew Chicken" in Chinese cuisine. In China there are chicken dishes that happen to have cashews as an ingredient. One of the most beloved is a creation called gung bo gai ding. A ding is a dish that contains ingredients uniformly cut into small dice. The chicken ding recipe adapted here offers stir-fried diced chicken, crunchy diced vegetables, cashews, and hoisin sauce.

One of the variations reflects a version of the dish seen in Chinese-American restaurants. Commonly called Springfield-style Cashew Chicken, it features deep-fried chicken pieces and oyster sauce in place of the hoisin sauce.

Yield: Serves 4

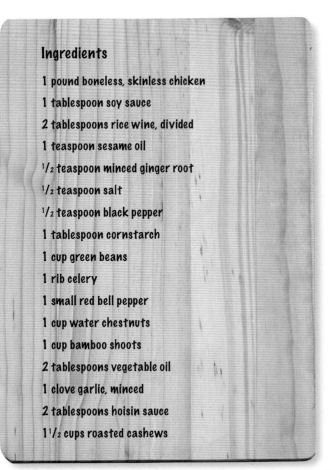

Ingredients

1 pound boneless, skinless chicken

1 tablespoon soy sauce

2 tablespoons rice wine, divided

1 teaspoon sesame oil

1/2 teaspoon minced ginger root

1/2 teaspoon salt

1/2 teaspoon black pepper

1 tablespoon cornstarch

1 cup green beans

1 rib celery

1 small red bell pepper

1 cup water chestnuts

1 cup bamboo shoots

2 tablespoons vegetable oil

1 clove garlic, minced

2 tablespoons hoisin sauce

1 1/2 cups roasted cashews

Cashew Chicken

- Dice chicken into ½-inch cubes; place in a bowl. Mix together soy sauce, half the wine, sesame oil, ginger, salt, and pepper.

- Stir sauce into chicken. Add cornstarch to coat. Cover and refrigerate 30 minutes to marinate.

- Cut and blanch vegetables. Stir-fry chicken, then vegetables. In the wok, combine chicken, vegetables, hoisin sauce, and remaining tablespoon wine.

- Add cashews and stir-fry until hoisin is well distributed and chicken is cooked. Serve with steamed rice.

• • • • RECIPE VARIATIONS • • • •

Springfield (MO) Cashew Chicken: Cut chicken into larger pieces. Marinate as directed, then remove chicken from marinade and dredge in flour. Deep-fry the chicken in 2 inches hot oil. Remove chicken with a slotted spoon. Remove all but 2 tablespoons oil from wok. Stir-fry vegetables and garlic as directed until crisp-tender. Substitute oyster sauce for hoisin sauce. Add sauce to the wok along with the reserved chicken. Stir until blended, add cashews, and serve with rice.

Cashew Shrimp: Prepare recipe as directed, substituting 1 pound peeled, deveined shrimp for the chicken.

Prepare Vegetables

- Trim ends from green beans and discard; cut into ⅓-inch slices. Place beans in a bowl.

- Remove tough fibers from celery and dice into ⅓-inch pieces. Core bell pepper and dice into ⅓-inch pieces. Add celery and pepper to the bowl.

- Dice water chestnuts and bamboo shoots into ⅓-inch pieces. Add to other vegetables.

- Bring a pot of water to a boil. Add vegetables and blanch 1 minute. Drain into a colander and rinse with cold water. Drain.

Stir-Fry Chicken

- Place a wok over high heat. Add oil. Stir-fry garlic in hot oil 30 seconds.

- Add marinated chicken to wok in an even layer. Cook without stirring 1 minute. Then stir-fry briskly, separating chicken pieces. Remove to a bowl.

- Add vegetables to wok and stir-fry 1 minute.

- Return chicken to wok with vegetables and stir-fry 1 minute longer.

FIRECRACKER CHICKEN

Spicy chiles give this chicken with black bean sauce a sinus-clearing kick

The name "Firecracker Chicken" has been applied to fiery chicken dishes of Cajun, Indian, Mexican, and Moroccan origin, just to name a few. In Chinese cuisine the name was popularized by a large Chinese-American restaurant chain.

The concept of cooking chicken—or beef, seafood, or tofu—in spicy black bean sauce is authentic to Guangzhou

and some other regions of China. In this version fermented black beans share the wok with aromatic ginger and garlic, hot chile peppers, and sweet bell peppers. We've added a sweet onion for extra crispness, although an authentic Chinese sauce would use green onions.

Yield: Serves 4–6

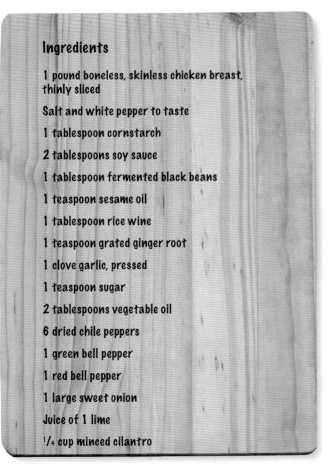

Ingredients

1 pound boneless, skinless chicken breast, thinly sliced

Salt and white pepper to taste

1 tablespoon cornstarch

2 tablespoons soy sauce

1 tablespoon fermented black beans

1 teaspoon sesame oil

1 tablespoon rice wine

1 teaspoon grated ginger root

1 clove garlic, pressed

1 teaspoon sugar

2 tablespoons vegetable oil

6 dried chile peppers

1 green bell pepper

1 red bell pepper

1 large sweet onion

Juice of 1 lime

¹/₄ cup minced cilantro

Firecracker Chicken

- Place chicken in a bowl with salt, pepper, and cornstarch. Stir to coat. Prepare black bean sauce.

- Place a wok over high heat. Add vegetable oil and swirl to coat. Stir-fry chiles until browned; remove.

- Add chicken to wok in an

even layer. Cook without stirring a few seconds, then stir-fry 1 minute; remove to a platter.

- Add bell peppers and onion. Stir-fry 2 minutes. Return chicken and cook 1 minute. Add sauce and stir-fry 1 minute. Stir in lime and cilantro. Serve with noodles.

•••• RECIPE VARIATIONS ••••

Firecracker Duck: Substitute 1 pound boneless duck breast for the chicken breast. Prepare dish as directed.

Touch-of-Thai Chicken: Follow the recipe as directed. Add 1 cup coconut milk and 2 tablespoons sliced lemongrass to the wok. Simmer until heated through and serve with jasmine rice.

Prepare Sauce

- This sauce has sweet, hot, and pungent elements, as well as aromatic touches of ginger, garlic, and sesame oil. It's designed to coat, rather than soak, the ingredients.

- Combine soy sauce, black beans, sesame oil, and wine. Stir to blend.

- Add ginger root, garlic, and sugar. Pressed garlic, unlike minced, will quickly dissipate and flavor the sauce.

- Stir mixture until sugar is completely dissolved. If you prefer a "saucier" sauce, add another teaspoon of wine or water.

Adding Ingredients

- A well-seasoned wok keeps stir-fries from sticking. Heat the wok, then add vegetable oil and swirl to coat.

- Chinese cooks generally work in this order: aromatics, meat, vegetables, meat, sauce, and garnish. Flavoring agents—garlic, ginger, chiles—can be added to hot oil until the aromas blossom.

- Meats should be browned slightly, then stir-fried until almost cooked. Remove meat, stir-fry vegetables, then return meat to pan.

- Add sauce and stir-fry to coat ingredients. Add garnish.

BEEF WITH BROCCOLI

This classic combination gets its rich flavor from stir-fried steak and oyster sauce

Oyster sauce shows the transformative power of long, slow cooking. This sauce, which most cooks buy ready to use in jars, is made by slow cooking oysters with a bit of soy sauce and other ingredients until a thick, uniform, caramelized elixir forms. Surprisingly, oyster sauce doesn't taste like oysters at all. It does add a deep, savory element to a number of Chi-

nese dishes. Oyster sauce gives Beef with Broccoli, a Cantonese classic, a mysterious, rich essence. The sauce stands up to bitter greens and the quick-cooked beef. This dish uses a relatively small amount of sauce. Any leftovers in the jar should be kept tightly covered in the refrigerator.

Yield: Serves 4

Ingredients

4 cups broccoli, cut into bite-size pieces

1 pound lean sirloin or flank steak, thinly sliced

2 tablespoons soy sauce, divided

1 tablespoon rice wine vinegar

1 teaspoon sugar

2 tablespoons vegetable oil

1 clove garlic, minced

2 tablespoons oyster sauce

1 tablespoon rice wine or sherry

2 tablespoons beef broth

1 teaspoon cornstarch dissolved in 1 tablespoon cold water

Salt and pepper to taste

Beef with Broccoli

- Blanch broccoli. Combine beef with 1 tablespoon soy sauce, vinegar, and sugar. Let stand 15 minutes.

- Place wok over high heat. Add vegetable oil. Add beef in an even layer. Cook 30 seconds without stirring, then stir-fry 1 minute.

- Add garlic, oyster sauce, and remaining soy sauce. Add broccoli and stir-fry a few seconds. In a bowl, combine wine and beef broth. Add to wok.

- Stir dissolved cornstarch into wok. Cook until thickened. Add salt and pepper. Serve with steamed rice.

Beef with Rapini: Substitute one bunch rapini, blanched and chopped, for the broccoli.

Chicken with Broccoli: Substitute 1 pound chicken breast, sliced, for the beef.

Lamb with Broccoli: Substitute 1 pound boneless lamb for the beef.

Slice Steak

- Sirloin steak is a great cut for stir-frying. The meat is tender, yet flavorful. Flank steak or round steak can be used, but toughen quickly.

- Beef for stir-fry should be thinly sliced across the grain, briefly marinated, then lightly cooked.

- A Chinese technique called velveting can help seal in moisture. Mix an egg white with a bit of soy sauce or rice wine vinegar and cornstarch.

- Coat cut meat with mixture; refrigerate 30 minutes before cooking.

Chinese Broccoli

- Chinese broccoli is a leafy, thin-stalked plant with a distinctive bittersweet flavor. Supermarkets in large cities and some Asian specialty markets carry this green.

- If you can't find Chinese broccoli, you can substitute rapini or regular broccoli.

- To blanche broccoli for stir-fries, drop trimmed veggies in boiling water and cook 1 to 2 minutes or until color changes to bright green.

- Drain broccoli and plunge into cold water to stop cooking. Drain and let stand in a colander until you're ready to use.

ORANGE-SCENTED BEEF

The heavenly aroma of this dish draws guests to the table with piqued appetites

The innovative, complex balance of flavors in Chinese cooking shines through in this dish. Often called Tangerine Peel Beef, the recipe combines beef—which the Chinese consider to be a "gamy" flavor, with the fresh, sweet essence of citrus. Some versions use candied or preserved citrus peel as an ingredient, which is great if you're willing to make your own. (The stuff in plastic containers in the supermarket won't do the trick.) Instead of preserved peel, this recipe gets extra orange flavor from a little orange juice in the marinade and sauce. We've also used freshly grated orange zest, although slivered tangerine zest can be used as well.

Yield: Serves 4–6

Ingredients

1 pound flank steak, thinly sliced

2 tablespoons soy sauce, divided

2 tablespoons orange juice, divided

1 teaspoon rice wine vinegar

1/4 teaspoon hot chile oil

1 tablespoon cornstarch

3 tablespoons vegetable oil

2 cloves garlic, minced

1 teaspoon minced ginger root

1 teaspoon red pepper flakes

1 red bell pepper, cored and sliced

1 tablespoon rice wine

2 green onions, shredded

1 tablespoon grated orange zest

Salt and pepper to taste

Slivers of orange zest or twisted orange slices for garnish

Orange-Scented Beef

- Combine steak with 1 tablespoon soy sauce, 1 tablespoon orange juice, vinegar, and chile oil. Coat with cornstarch. Cover; refrigerate 30 minutes.

- Sear beef in oil; remove to a plate. Remove all but 1 tablespoon oil from wok.

- Add garlic, ginger, and pepper flakes to wok; stir-fry a few seconds. Add beef and bell pepper slices; stir-fry to combine.

- Add remaining soy sauce, juice, wine, green onion, and orange zest. Stir-fry 1 minute. Add salt and pepper and garnish.

Orange-Scented Chicken: Substitute 1 pound boneless chicken breasts for the flank steak.

Orange-Scented Pork: Substitute 1 pound boneless pork chops for the flank steak.

Fry Beef

- Place a wok over high heat. Add oil. When oil is very hot, add a few slices of beef. Do not crowd the wok.

- Cook beef 30 seconds or until slices are crispy at the edges, but not completely cooked at the center.

- Remove beef slices to a plate lined with paper towels.

- Repeat procedure until all beef has been seared. Beef slices will cook completely when returned to the wok.

Remove Orange Zest

- Citrus zest is the exterior of the peel, the part that carries the color. Zest is filled with citrus oil and essential flavors.

- The white pith underneath the zest is bitter tasting and can add unpleasant flavors to your dish.

- To get fresh orange zest, use a sharp paring knife or vegetable peeler to strip the colored skin off the pith.

- When grating the zest by hand, use a fine-gauge grater. Be careful to grate only the colored skin.

SLICED BEEF WITH LEEKS

Tender leeks add a mellow flavor to this slightly spicy dish from Northern China

Cooks in Beijing and other parts of China value the leek for its ability to impart crispness and a mild onion flavor to dishes. Lamb dishes—such as one variation of this recipe—almost always include leeks because they stand up to strong flavors. Cultivated leeks have been around for 3,000-plus years and before that, wild leeks (which are smaller and more potent)

turned up in cooking pots. Leeks have two parts: tender, white cylindrical bulbs that grow below ground and leathery leaf stalks that grow above ground. Gardeners mound soil around emerging leeks to extend the amount of root produced by each plant. Tough stalks can be used to flavor broths.

Yield: Serves 4–6

Ingredients

1 pound sirloin or flank steak

2 tablespoons soy sauce, divided

2 tablespoons rice wine, divided

1 teaspoon Szechwan peppercorns, lightly toasted in a dry wok and ground

1 tablespoon cornstarch

2-3 tablespoons vegetable oil

3 large leeks, julienned

6 cloves garlic, minced

1/2 teaspoon sugar

2 tablespoons fermented black beans

2 teaspoons sesame oil

1 teaspoon chile paste

Salt to taste

Sliced Beef with Leeks

- Thinly slice beef across the grain. Marinate 30 minutes with 1 tablespoon soy sauce, 1 tablespoon wine, toasted ground peppercorns, and cornstarch.

- Stir-fry beef over high heat in vegetable oil; remove when cooked through.

- Add julienned leeks and garlic to wok; stir-fry 1 minute. Remove a few leeks for garnish. Return beef to wok.

- Combine remaining ingredients. Pour over beef and leeks. Stir-fry 1 minute. Add salt and garnish with reserved leeks.

Sliced Lamb with Leeks: Substitute 1 pound boneless leg of lamb for the beef. Increase sugar to 1 teaspoon and add ⅓ cup soaked, slivered wood ear mushrooms with the leeks. Follow the recipe as directed.

Sliced Wild Boar with Leeks: Substitute 1 pound farm-raised wild boar for the beef. Increase sesame oil to 1 tablespoon.

Prepare Leeks

Return Beef to Wok

- Although related to onions and green onions, leeks are sweeter than bulbous onions and more substantial than green onions. In many stir-fries leeks take the role of starring vegetable, rather than aromatic flavoring.

- Trim roots from leeks and cut off tough green shoots.

- Cut leek in half lengthwise and wash white parts carefully. Gently pull back layers to rinse away any trapped sand.

- Slice leeks lengthwise into thin shreds and place on a paper towel to drain. Blot any excess water.

- Although Chinese cooks almost never serve rare beef, it's important not to overcook beef to the point of toughening it.

- When preparing this dish, the beef should be added to the hot wok in a single layer, then cooked undisturbed 1 minute.

- Briskly stir-fry beef 1 minute, scraping browned bits from the bottom of the pan. Remove beef to a plate.

- Add additional oil to wok if needed. Stir-fry leeks and garlic 1 minute, then return beef to wok to finish cooking.

BEEF WITH BLACK BEAN SAUCE

Few Chinese dishes are as simple, or as well-loved, as this salty-sweet beef

You've probably ordered this Cantonese classic dozens of times. At Chinese restaurants it usually goes by the name Pepper Beef, a reference not to any piquant qualities, but to the abundance of sweet bell peppers in the mix. The multicolored peppers and beef get a savory kick from fermented black bean paste or sauce, which can be found in most supermarkets. The "black beans" are actually black soybeans that have been fermented and salted. Although the fermented beans can be found in some markets, the bean sauce or paste—mashed beans with seasonings and soy sauce—is more readily available. Beef with Black Bean Sauce is Chinese comfort food.

Yield: Serves 4–6

Ingredients

1 pound sirloin or top round, cut into thin, 2-inch square slices

1 tablespoon soy sauce

1 tablespoon rice wine

$1/2$ teaspoon sugar

$1/2$ teaspoon grated ginger root

1 onion, cut vertically into wedges

1 green bell pepper, cut into 1-inch strips

1 red or yellow bell pepper, cut into 1-inch strips

2 cloves garlic, minced

2–3 tablespoons vegetable oil

2 tablespoons fermented black bean paste

$1/2$ cup beef or chicken broth

2 teaspoons cornstarch dissolved in 1 tablespoon cold water

Salt and pepper to taste

Beef with Black Bean Sauce

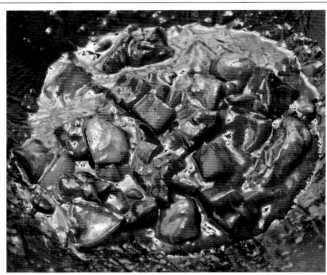

- Combine beef with soy sauce, wine, sugar, and ginger. Pull onion layers apart and mix with pepper strips.

- Add oil to wok over high heat. Add beef in an even layer. Cook without stirring 1 minute. Flip and cook 10 seconds. Stir-fry 1 minute; remove to a plate.

- Add more oil, if needed. Stir-fry onion, peppers, and garlic 2 minutes; add beef.

- Prepare sauce. Add to wok and stir-fry 30 seconds. Add cornstarch; cook until thick. Season with salt and pepper and serve.

Chicken with Black Bean Sauce: Substitute 1 pound boneless chicken breast halves. Butterfly each piece, making the breast halves half as thick, but twice as wide. Then cut each butterflied piece into 4 pieces. Proceed with recipe as directed.

Beef with Summer Squash and Black Bean Sauce: Use this recipe when the backyard garden is overflowing with zucchini. Substitute 2 zucchini and 2 yellow summer squash for the bell pepper. Cut the squash into diagonal slices, then prepare recipe as directed.

Slice Beef

Prepare Sauce

- Buy a fresh, 2-inch-thick sirloin or top round steak or small roast. Place in freezer 30 minutes.

- Place beef on a work surface. With a sharp cleaver, trim large areas of fat or connective tissue.

- For this dish, the meat should be very thinly sliced. Cut across the grain in even slices, no more than ¼-inch thick.

- Cut each slice vertically in half or in thirds to create 2-inch-square pieces. Vegetables can be cut to mimic the beef squares or into longer strips.

- Combing thick pastes with a little broth or water before adding to the wok ensures a uniform, smooth sauce.

- In a small bowl, add the black bean paste to the broth and stir until well blended.

- Add sauce mixture to wok over high heat. Stir-fry 30 seconds. When mixture begins to bubble, prepare thickener.

- Dissolve cornstarch in 1 tablespoon cold water. Add to the wok and cook until sauce is thick and bubbly. Add salt and pepper to taste.

SZECHWAN SHREDDED BEEF
Hold onto your rice bowl; this dish is spicy, crunchy, and very satisfying

In Chinese cuisine, shredding, which suggests meat being pulled apart, is a bit of a misnomer. Instead, Chinese cooks painstakingly slice beef and pork into long, thin strips (or shreds) that meld with similarly cut crunchy vegetables like bamboo shoots, celery, and peppers. The combination offers a balance of ingredients in each and every bite.

This recipe gets most of its heat from fresh hot peppers and dried pepper flakes. However, if you want to add a bit of numbing Szechwan peppercorn flavor, by all means do so. Just throw a few peppercorns into the hot oil and stir-fry 20 to 30 seconds. Remove the peppercorns and proceed with the recipe.
Yield: Serves 4–6

Ingredients

1 pound top round or flank steak

3 tablespoons soy sauce, divided

2 tablespoons rice wine

$1/2$ teaspoon sugar

$1/2$ teaspoon sesame oil

1 tablespoon cornstarch

1 rib celery

$2/3$ cup bamboo shoots

2-4 fresh hot peppers

1 green bell pepper

2 green onions

2-3 tablespoons vegetable oil

2 cloves garlic, minced

$1/2$ teaspoon minced ginger root

$1/2$-1 teaspoon red pepper flakes

Salt to taste

Szechwan Shredded Beef

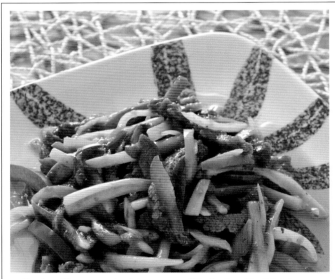

- Cut beef into matchstick-size shreds. Briefly marinate with 2 tablespoons soy sauce, wine, sugar, and sesame oil. Sprinkle cornstarch over mixture and stir to coat.

- Cut vegetables into uniform pieces.

- Stir-fry beef in 2 tablespoons oil over high heat 30 seconds. Remove.

- Add vegetables to wok. Stir-fry 1 minute. Add garlic, ginger, and pepper flakes.

- Return beef to wok. Add remaining soy sauce. Salt to taste. Stir-fry 30 seconds.

Szechwan Shredded Chicken: Substitute 1 pound boneless chicken breasts or thighs for the beef. Proceed with recipe as directed.

Szechwan Shredded Bison: Although not a native Chinese ingredient, North American bison meat works very well in this dish. Substitute 1 pound bison tenderloin or sirloin for the beef.

BEEF

Shred Beef and Vegetables

- Cutting beef into matchsticks is easier if the meat is very cold. Wrap fresh beef and place in freezer 30 minutes to an hour.

- Slice semifrozen beef across the grain into ¼-inch slices. Cut slices lengthwise into ¼-inch-thick matchstick pieces.

- Remove outer fibers from celery; cut into 2-inch pieces. Cut each piece into ¼-inch-thick matchsticks.

- Slice bamboo shoots into ¼-inch matchstick pieces. Core bell pepper and cut into thin strips. Trim green onions and cut into shreds.

Cutting Peppers

- Hot peppers get their heat from capsaicin and related compounds. Capsaicin exists throughout the pepper, but the highest concentration is in the inner membranes and around the seeds.

- A natural tissue irritant, capsaicin can cause burns when peppers are handled barehanded.

- To avoid this, wear thin latex gloves when cutting peppers.

- Cut the hot peppers in half lengthwise. Remove seeds and slice peppers lengthwise into thin strips.

HUNAN CHILI BEEF

This earthy, fiery dish from China's heartland is perfect for adventurous dinner guests

Hunan occupies a vast fertile region, with crops growing on gently sloping hills and fish-filled rivers and lakes. Though land-locked, the area offers an incredible diversity of foodstuffs, in-cluding much of the rice grown in China. The cuisine, which is both creative and complex, relies on fresh local ingredients.

Most dishes from Hunan have layers of flavor, including salty, sweet, sour, and spicy.

Hunan Chili Beef combines hearty flank steak with searing fresh hot peppers and pungent black beans, all tempered with bits of fresh ginger, garlic, wine vinegar, sugar, and salt. It is Hu-nan home cooking that's good enough for company.

Yield: Serves 4–6

Ingredients

1 pound flank steak, thinly sliced

3 tablespoons soy sauce, divided

2 tablespoons rice wine

1 teaspoon rice wine vinegar

1 teaspoon sugar

1 tablespoon cornstarch

5 fresh hot chiles, two or more colors

2–3 tablespoons vegetable oil

3 cloves garlic, minced

1 teaspoon grated ginger root

2 tablespoons fermented black beans, rinsed

1 teaspoon sesame oil

2 tablespoons cilantro, minced

Salt to taste

Hunan Chili Beef

- Combine steak with 2 table-spoons soy sauce, wine, vinegar, and sugar. Add cornstarch and stir. Refriger-ate 30 minutes.

- Cut chiles into thin strips. Add 2 tablespoons oil to a hot wok. Add beef and cook without stirring 1 minute. Stir-fry beef 30 seconds and remove to a bowl.

- Add more oil to wok. Stir-fry garlic, ginger, and chiles 1 minute. Add remaining soy sauce, black beans, and sesame oil.

- Return beef to wok. Stir-fry 30 seconds. Add cilantro and salt. Serve immediately.

···· RECIPE VARIATIONS ····

Hunan Chili Lamb: Substitute 1 pound boneless lamb shoulder for the flank steak. Follow recipe as directed.

Hunan Chili Duck: Substitute 1 pound boneless duck breast for the beef. Add 1 tablespoon orange zest to the sauce.

Slice Flank Steak

- Flank steak is cut from the well-exercised abdominal muscle of the cow. It is both chewy and extremely flavorful.

- To combat toughness, flank steak should either be braised for long periods or carefully cut and lightly cooked.

- Slicing flank steak for this dish starts with cutting the steak lengthwise—with the grain—into several 1½-inch strips.

- The strips should then be cut across the grain into very thin slices, marinated, and stir-fried.

Add Fermented Black Beans

- Unlike black bean paste, which is essentially a ready-to-use sauce, fermented black beans are a stand-alone ingredient.

- These salted, preserved black soybeans have a strong, pungent flavor. A little goes a long way.

- Fermented black beans are used as a seasoning ingredient in several Chinese provinces.

- For a less salty flavor, rinse beans and soak in cold water 30 minutes before using. Mash some of the black beans while stir-frying to disperse flavor.

TWICE-COOKED PORK

Boiling then stir-frying makes this dish melt in your mouth

Hunan specialties often involve multi-stage cooking processes. Meats might be boiled or smoked before turning up in a stew or stir-fry. The extra effort results in complex flavors and often renders tough cuts of meat fork-tender.

Twice-Cooked Pork is among the most famous of such dishes. In this recipe pork shoulder is boiled to break down muscle fibers, then chilled to make the meat easier to slice. The slices then get lightly crisped and sauced in a hot wok. To make this dish for a weeknight supper, boil the pork shoulder the day before, then refrigerate overnight. When you're ready to make dinner, just slice and sear.

Yield: Serves 4–6

Ingredients

1 pound boneless pork shoulder

2 tablespoons rice wine

2 slices ginger root

1 small onion, halved

1 tablespoon soy sauce

1 tablespoon hoisin sauce

2 teaspoons fermented black beans, rinsed

$1/2$ teaspoon chile paste

2 cloves garlic, minced

2–3 tablespoons vegetable oil

2 spring onions or 2 leeks, trimmed and cut in shreds

1 green bell pepper, cored and diced

Salt and pepper to taste

Twice-Cooked Pork

- Boil pork with wine, ginger, and onion; chill and slice. Combine pork with soy sauce, hoisin sauce, black beans, chile paste, and garlic.

- Add 2 tablespoons oil to hot wok. Add pork slices. Cook 1 minute without stirring; flip. Sear 30 seconds, then stir-fry 1 minute.

- Remove pork. Add more oil if needed. Stir-fry spring onions and peppers 2 minutes.

- Add sauce; when bubbly, return pork to wok and stir-fry 30 seconds. Add salt and pepper.

Twice-Cooked Pork with Cabbage: Cut a small head of cabbage into 1-inch squares to yield 2 cups. Follow recipe as directed, but increase soy sauce to 2 tablespoons. Add cabbage to wok with leeks and peppers.

Twice-Cooked Beef: Substitute 1 pound boneless bottom round roast for the pork shoulder. Follow recipe as directed.

Boil Pork

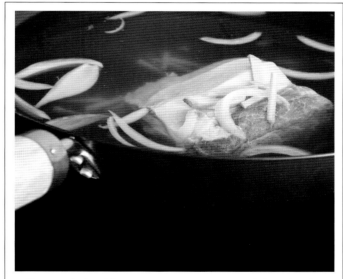

Slice Pork

- Place pork shoulder in a deep saucepan or wok. Add enough water to cover. Add wine, ginger slices, and onion.

- Bring mixture to a boil over high heat. Reduce heat to medium. Simmer, uncovered, until pork is tender, about 40 to 50 minutes.

- Remove pork from broth and set aside 15 minutes to cool. Discard broth.

- Wrap pork or place in a covered bowl. Refrigerate until chilled, about 1 hour.

- Chilling congeals meat juices and stiffens fibers, making the meat easier to slice and less likely to pull apart.

- Place chilled pork on a work surface. Using a sharp cleaver, cut pork into thin slices.

- Cut each slice into pieces about 1-inch wide.

- Place the slices on a platter and cover with foil or a damp paper towel until ready to stir-fry.

SHREDDED PORK IN GARLIC SAUCE

This Szechwan favorite will show off your good taste—and your knife skills

Yes, it's a labor-intensive dish. Shredded Pork in Garlic Sauce gets much of its enticing texture and appearance from a range of savory and crisp ingredients, all cut into the same long, thin matchstick shape. The good news is: All that knife work will be amply rewarded. Grabbed together with chopsticks, the pork and vegetables become a delicious conduit

for the slightly sweet sauce of garlic and hot peppers. Any single element of this dish might be tasty on its own, but stir-fried together, the ingredients create a whole much greater than the sum of its parts. Serve Shredded Pork in Garlic Sauce with plenty of fluffy white rice to cool the palate.

Yield: Serves 4–6

Ingredients

4 dried wood ear mushrooms

1 pound boneless pork butt or loin

3 tablespoons soy sauce, divided

1 teaspoon sesame oil

1 egg white

4 teaspoons cornstarch

2 tablespoon rice wine vinegar

2 tablespoons sugar

1 tablespoon rice wine

2 teaspoons chile paste

6 tablespoons vegetable oil

4 cloves garlic, minced

1 cup matchstick-cut bamboo shoots

²/₃ cup slivered water chestnuts

2 green onions, cut into shreds

Salt to taste

Shredded Pork in Garlic Sauce

- Soak wood ears in hot water 30 minutes. Drain and cut into matchsticks. Prepare pork.

- Combine soy sauce not used for pork with vinegar, sugar, wine, and chile paste. Fry the pork in hot oil; remove along with all but 2 tablespoons oil.

- Stir-fry garlic, wood ears, bamboo shoots, water chestnuts, and green onions 1 minute. Add sauce and cook until bubbly. Return pork; stir-fry 1 minute. Dissolve remaining cornstarch in 2 tablespoons cold water. Add to wok and stir-fry until mixture thickens. Add salt.

Shredded Chicken in Garlic Sauce: Substitute 1 pound boneless chicken breasts for the pork. Prepare dish as directed.

Shredded Beef in Garlic Sauce: Substitute 1 pound sirloin or flank steak for the pork. Prepare dish as directed.

Shrimp in Garlic Sauce: Substitute 1 pound peeled, deveined shrimp for the pork. Instead of cutting shrimp into matchsticks, slice them in half lengthwise. This dish can't quite approximate the texture of the pork version, but the sauce does complement shrimp very well.

Prepare Pork

- Start with well-chilled or partially frozen pork. Place pork on a work surface and cut across the grain into ¼-inch-thick slices.

- Lay slices flat and cut into long ¼-inch-thick matchstick-style strips; place in a bowl.

- Whisk together 1 teaspoon soy sauce, sesame oil, and egg white. Pour over pork and stir to blend completely.

- Sprinkle 1 teaspoon cornstarch over pork and toss to coat. Cover and refrigerate 30 minutes.

Fry Pork

- Place a wok over high heat. When hot, add all 6 tablespoons of vegetable oil.

- Heat until a drop of water sizzles on the surface of the oil.

- Working in batches, keeping the pork in a single layer, fry pork strips in oil 30 to 40 seconds, or until strips are browned.

- Remove pork from oil with a wire mesh strainer. Place on a plate lined with paper towels.

PORK

MU SHU PORK

Wrap a pancake full of this sophisticated mélange from Beijing

Mu shu pork only seems complicated. The mix of shredded pork, vegetables, and eggs in a dark sauce has an earthy, mysterious appearance. But it's actually an easy, forgiving dish. The hardest part is the superthin Mandarin pancakes—the traditional mu shu wrapper. In a pinch you can buy those ready-made or substitute crepes or flour tortillas. Exact recipes for mu shu pork vary greatly from one part of the globe to another. In China wood ear mushrooms, lily buds, bean sprouts, and bamboo shoots give the dish crunch, while Chinese restaurants outside of China rely on shredded cabbage. The recipe below combines all the usual suspects. To eat, dab a little hoisin sauce on a pancake, add a spoonful of mu shu, and roll like a soft taco.

Yield: Serves 4–6

Ingredients

For Mandarin Pancakes:

2¼ cups flour

1 cup boiling water

3 tablespoons sesame oil

For Mu Shu:

4 dried wood ear mushrooms

2 tablespoons dried lily buds

12 ounces boneless pork butt

2 tablespoons soy sauce, divided

2 tablespoons rice wine, divided

½ teaspoon sugar

2 teaspoons cornstarch

3 tablespoons vegetable oil

4 eggs, beaten with 1 tablespoon water

2 cups finely shredded napa cabbage

6 green onions, shredded

2 cloves garlic, minced

⅔ cup matchstick-cut bamboo shoots

Salt and white pepper to taste

Hoisin sauce

Mu Shu Pork

- Make pancakes. Soak wood ears and lily buds in hot water 30 minutes. Drain. Cut wood ears into strips.

- Cut pork into matchsticks; combine with 1 tablespoon soy sauce, 1 tablespoon wine, and sugar. Add cornstarch to coat.

- Make egg strips. Add a tablespoon oil to wok and stir-fry pork 2 minutes; remove. Add remaining oil. Stir-fry vegetables, wood ears, and lily buds 2 minutes. Stir in egg strips, pork, remaining soy sauce, and wine. Stir-fry 1 minute. Add salt and pepper. Serve with pancakes and hoisin sauce.

Mu Shu Chicken: Substitute 1 pound boneless chicken breast or thighs for the pork. Prepare dish as directed.

Mu Shu Vegetables: Cut 2 zucchini and 2 yellow squash into 2-inch strips. Cut 8 ounces portobello mushrooms into slivers. Substitute cut vegetables for the pork. Follow recipe as directed, but reduce pork cooking time by half.

Chicken and Broccoli Mu Shu: Substitute 1 pound boneless chicken breast for the pork and 2 cups packaged broccoli slaw for the cabbage. Follow recipe as directed.

Make Pancakes

Prepare Egg Strips

PORK

- Pour flour in a bowl and whisk to remove lumps. Add boiling water and stir until dough pulls together.

- Knead dough well on a floured surface. Cover; let stand 30 minutes. Roll dough into a tube; cut into 16 slices. Roll slices into paper-thin 6-inch circles.

- Brush circle tops with sesame oil. Place two circles together, oiled sides touching; repeat to make 8 pairs.

- Cook pancakes in a medium-hot nonstick skillet 45 seconds each side. Let stand 1 minute, then separate. Stack and cover.

- Heat wok over high heat. Add 2 teaspoons vegetable oil and swirl to coat.

- Pour in half the beaten eggs and cook undisturbed until set. With a spatula, remove eggs in one piece to a platter.

- Add another teaspoon of oil to wok and cook remaining eggs until set; remove to platter.

- Using a sharp knife or pizza cutter, slice eggs into thin strips. Use as directed in recipe.

SWEET-AND-SOUR PORK

Introduce your children to Chinese cuisine with this fruited pork dish

Pineapple. Ketchup. Fried pork. It may not sound like exotic fare, but what's not to like?

Sweet-and-sour pork is both an authentic Chinese dish and a Chinese restaurant menu favorite. The sweet and tangy sauce gives an extra kick to the crispy pork cubes. (In fact the sauce portion of the recipe can be made separately and used as a dip for other goodies.) Less-than-stellar versions of this dish turn up from time to time, and the failing is usually attributable to one thing: too much cornstarch in the sauce. Ideally sauce should be thick and glossy. If your sauce seems too thick, stir in a small amount of water or broth.

Yield: Serves 4–6

Ingredients

1 pound pork tenderloin, cut into bite-size cubes

2 eggs

2 tablespoons soy sauce, divided

1/2 teaspoon white pepper

2/3 cup flour mixed with 1/3 cup cornstarch

Vegetable oil for frying

1/4 cup sugar

1/4 cup ketchup

1/4 cup rice wine vinegar

1 clove garlic, minced

1/2 cup pineapple juice

1 tablespoon cornstarch dissolved in 2 tablespoons cold water

1 cup fresh or canned pineapple chunks, drained

1 green bell pepper, cored and cut into chunks

Salt to taste

Sweet-and-Sour Pork

- Batter and fry the pork cubes in a wok over high heat. Drain on a plate lined with paper towels.

- In a deep saucepan or clean wok, make the sweet-and-sour sauce. Add pineapple, green peppers, and salt.

- Simmer just until peppers are crisp-tender, about 3 minutes. Ladle a small amount of sauce on a serving platter.

- Arrange fried pork cubes over the sauce. Ladle remaining sauce, pineapple, and peppers over the pork. Serve immediately with rice.

Sweet-and-Sour Chicken: Substitute 1 pound bone-less chicken thighs, cut into bite-size cubes, for the pork tenderloin. Prepare recipe as directed.

Sweet-and-Sour Catfish: Substitute 1 pound raw catfish nuggets for the pork. Prepare recipe as directed.

PORK

Fry Pork

- Place pork in a bowl. In another bowl, whisk together eggs, 1 tablespoon soy sauce, and pepper. Pour over pork and stir to coat.

- In a shallow bowl, combine flour and cornstarch. Remove pork from egg batter and dredge in flour mixture.

- Place a wok over high heat. Add enough oil to reach a depth of 2 inches.

- Fry pork cubes in hot oil 2 to 3 minutes or until golden brown. Remove to a plate lined with paper towels.

Make Sweet-and-Sour Sauce

- In a large saucepan or wok, combine remaining 1 table-spoon soy sauce, sugar, ketchup, vinegar, garlic, and pineapple juice.

- Bring mixture to a boil over high heat, stirring constantly until sugar dissolves and ingredients are well blended.

- Add dissolved cornstarch to sauce.

- Stir and cook until mixture is thick and bubbly.

- Add pineapple and green pepper chunks and salt.

STIR-FRIED PORK TENDERLOIN
Serve this beautiful-yet-simple dish at your next dinner party

Chinese dishes emphasize fresh, flavorful ingredients. But mostly those ingredients are either economical or used in modest quantities. However, sometimes you have to splurge a little. The centerpiece of this recipe is pork tenderloin, juicy and fork tender. The meat needs very little enhancement— just a bit of seasoning and a light dusting of cornstarch to seal in the juices. The fresh vegetables, each with a distinctive texture and shape, have been selected with an eye for color.

Feel free to experiment with your own favorite combinations of leafy and starchy vegetables. The only caveat is to avoid overcooking any element of the dish.
Yield: Serves 4

Ingredients

1 pound pork tenderloin, thinly sliced

3 tablespoons soy sauce, divided

1 tablespoon rice wine

1 teaspoon sugar

2 teaspoons cornstarch

1/2 pound shiitake mushrooms

2 cups baby bok choy

1 cup baby corn

1 red bell pepper

2/3 cup water chestnuts

2 tablespoons vegetable oil, divided

1 tablespoon water

4 cloves garlic, minced, divided

Salt and pepper to taste

Stir-Fried Pork Tenderloin

- Place pork in a large bowl. In another bowl, whisk together 1 tablespoon soy sauce, wine, and sugar. Add to pork. Sprinkle with cornstarch; toss to coat. Refrigerate 30 minutes.

- Cut, steam, and fry vegetables; remove to a platter.

- Add 1 tablespoon oil to wok. Add garlic cloves and pork slices; stir-fry just until pork is no longer pink.

- Stir in remaining soy sauce. Return vegetables to wok; stir-fry until heated through. Add salt and pepper; serve immediately.

Stir-Fried Pork Tenderloin II: This version of the recipe uses veggies you might have on hand. Substitute 1 cup each broccoli florets, cauliflower florets, and halved baby carrots for the bok choy and baby corn. In place of the water chestnuts, use peanuts or cashews.

Stir-Fried Shrimp and Scallops: Substitute ½ pound each large shrimp, peeled and deveined, and sea scallops for the pork. Continue recipe as directed.

Prepare Vegetables

- For this dish the vegetables don't all have to be uniform, but they do have to be easy to grab and lift with chopsticks.

- Cut mushrooms in half; cut halves into slices. Trim bok choy; cut into 1-inch pieces.

- Baby corn ears can be left whole or halved. Combine mushrooms, bok choy, and corn in a bowl.

- Core bell pepper and cut into 1-inch pieces. Halve water chestnuts; add to bowl of vegetables.

Steam and Fry Vegetables

- This cooking technique combines steaming and stir-frying, which results in tender, but crisp vegetables.

- Place wok over high heat; add 1 tablespoon oil and 1 tablespoon water.

- Add cut vegetables to wok; cover and steam 1 minute.

- Remove cover from wok, allowing water to completely evaporate. Stir-fry vegetables 2 minutes. Remove to a platter.

PORK

STEAMED HAM WITH PEARS

This luscious, salty-sweet treat pays homage to a Yunnan delicacy

Most Chinese provinces have their own pork-based specialties. But the fragrant, satin-textured ham of Yunnan is widely praised and sought after throughout China. Unfortunately, Yunnan ham can be tough to find outside Asia. However, dry-cured, salty Smithfield ham—a variety of country-style ham—produced in the southeastern United States can substitute. This dish pairs Smithfield ham with Asian pears. Asian pears come in a variety of shapes and shades, but most Asian

pears in supermarkets are round, pale gold, and firm. When ripe they're juicy and crisp. Don't try to use ripe Bartlett or Comice pears, which are too soft for steaming.

Yield: Serves 6–8

Ingredients

2 pounds Smithfield ham

$^1/_3$ cup brown sugar

6 Asian pears, peeled and cored

$^1/_3$ cup soy sauce

$^1/_4$ cup honey

2 tablespoons apple juice

1 teaspoon rice wine vinegar

1 tablespoon cornstarch dissolved in 2 tablespoons water

$^1/_4$ cup cold water

$^1/_4$ cup minced cilantro or chives

Steamed Ham with Pears

- Cut ham into thin slices, about 2 inches wide. Layer slices in a steamer basket. Add brown sugar and steam 20 minutes.

- Cut each pear into 6 wedges. In a saucepan, combine soy sauce, honey, apple juice, and vinegar.

- Bring mixture to a boil over medium-high heat. Dissolve cornstarch in water. Add to sauce; stir until thickened.

- Add pears to steamer. Brush with sauce; steam 10 minutes. Remove ham and pears to a platter, drizzle with remaining sauce, and garnish with herbs.

Steamed Ham with Pears II: For softer pears and captured juices, layer ham and pears in a bowl that can fit inside a wok steamer rack. Sprinkle layers with brown sugar, add water, and cover wok. Steam 20 minutes, then let stand off heat for 10. Prepare sauce as directed and serve on the side.

Steamed Ham with Gala or Granny Smith Apples: Substitute 6 large Gala or Granny Smith apples for the Asian pears.

Steam the Ham

- Layer the slices of ham in a steamer basket. Sprinkle brown sugar over each slice of ham.

- Cover the steamer basket; place in a wok or pot. Add water to a depth just below the ham.

- Bring water to a boil. Steam ham 20 minutes.

- Check water often and add more as needed.

Add Pears

- Remove wok from heat. Using potholders and tongs, carefully add pear wedges to ham slices in steamer basket.

- Brush pears and ham slices with some of the thickened sauce.

- Close steamer and return wok to a burner. Steam pears with ham 10 minutes.

- Remove pears and ham from basket and arrange on a platter. Drizzle with remaining sauce.

PORK

95

FRAGRANT STEAMED SNAPPER

No Chinese celebration is complete without a whole fish, a symbol of happiness and prosperity

Delicate red snapper steams into a firm, sweetly flavored entree. However, other small whole fish such as bass, trout, or carp can be substituted. Order the freshest fish available from your market and have it cleaned and scaled. Resist the urge to lop off its head. Keeping the fish whole helps retain both flavor and moisture. To the Chinese it is also more aesthetically pleasing.

Seasonings can be adjusted to reflect different Chinese regional signatures. The most important thing to remember is that fish keeps cooking after it is removed from a hot wok. Steam the fish for 10 minutes per pound, then let stand a minute or two before serving.

Yield: Serves 2–3

Ingredients

1½ pounds whole snapper, cleaned and scaled

1 teaspoon coarse salt

½ teaspoon coarsely ground black pepper

4 thin slices ginger root

1 whole green onion, trimmed

2 whole sprigs cilantro

2 tablespoons peanut oil

1 tablespoon dark sesame oil

2 tablespoons soy sauce

1 tablespoon dry sherry

1 teaspoon grated fresh ginger

2 green onions, trimmed and cut into strips

Fragrant Steamed Snapper

- Pat fish dry. Place on a nonporous cutting board. Make three shallow cuts on each side of the fish.

- Sprinkle salt and pepper over the fish and inside the belly cavity.

- Place ginger slices, evenly spaced, inside the fish cavity. Top ginger with green onion and cilantro.

- Add oil mixture and steam 10 minutes per pound (15 minutes for a 1½-pound fish). Let stand 2 minutes, garnish, and serve.

Cantonese Fish with Black Beans: Soak 2 tablespoons fermented black beans in warm water for 10 minutes. Drain and mince the beans. Combine the beans with 1 clove garlic, minced, and ½ teaspoon grated fresh ginger. Press bean mixture into shallow slits in the fish before steaming as directed.

Spicy Whole Fish: Prepare recipe as directed, but sprinkle ⅓ cup sliced fresh chile peppers over the fish before steaming for 10 minutes per pound (15 minutes for a 1½-pound whole fish).

Baste Snapper, Prepare Wok

- Whisk together peanut oil, sesame oil, soy sauce, sherry, and ginger.

- Place fish on a heat-safe plate. Drizzle a small amount of oil mixture into the cuts on one side of the fish.

- Turn the fish over and pour remaining oil mixture into the slits and over the top of the fish.

- Place a metal rack inside the wok. Add water to a level just below the rack. Bring the water to a boil over high heat.

Steam Snapper

- Reduce heat to medium. When water is simmering, place plate with snapper on the steaming rack.

- Cover the wok. Steam snapper over simmering water 15 minutes, or 10 minutes per pound.

- Remove wok cover to vent steam. Carefully remove the plate from the steaming rack and place on a trivet or serving tray.

- Baste fish with juices from the plate; let stand briefly. Garnish with green onions.

FISH

ORANGE SESAME SEA BASS

Fragrant citrus and sesame complement each other and the delicate sea bass in this elegant entree

Cooking mildly flavored fish in a moist environment results in tender, sweet flesh—the perfect foil for a light, clean sauce. However, make sure you don't overcook the steaks or fillets, which could result in a steamer basket full of mushy fish.

Sea bass is a favorite fish for roasting or steaming, but be aware the term sea bass covers a variety of saltwater fish.

Popular Chilean sea bass is actually Pantagonian Toothfish, a threatened species that should only be purchased when labeled "certified sustainable." Otherwise, widely available black sea bass—a member of the grouper family—is a perfect choice for this recipe.

Yield: Serves 6

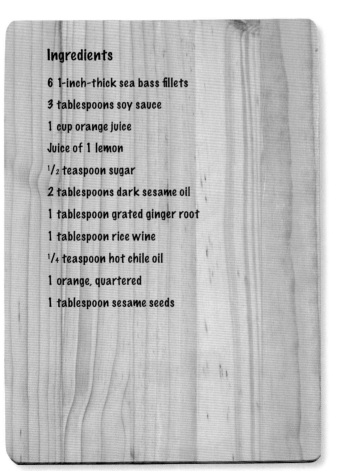

Ingredients

6 1-inch-thick sea bass fillets

3 tablespoons soy sauce

1 cup orange juice

Juice of 1 lemon

$1/2$ teaspoon sugar

2 tablespoons dark sesame oil

1 tablespoon grated ginger root

1 tablespoon rice wine

$1/4$ teaspoon hot chile oil

1 orange, quartered

1 tablespoon sesame seeds

Orange Sesame Sea Bass

- Rinse bass fillets and pat dry; place in a baking dish.

- Whisk together soy sauce, orange juice, lemon juice, sugar, sesame oil, ginger root, wine, and chile oil.

- Pour marinade over fillets, cover, and refrigerate 1 hour.

- Steam fillets 8 to 10 minutes. Boil marinade until reduced by half. Drizzle over fillets, garnish with sesame seeds, and serve.

Baked Orange Sesame Salmon: Substitute 6 1-inch-thick salmon steaks for the sea bass. Brush the tops of the salmon with oil and bake at 350°F 10 minutes. While salmon is baking, combine soy sauce, orange juice, lemon juice, sugar, ginger, and rice wine in a saucepan. Boil until reduced by half. Stir in chile and sesame oils. Drizzle over salmon, garnish with orange slices and sesame seeds.

Steamed Bass with Ginger-Soy Sauce: Marinate sea bass fillets in 1 cup orange juice mixed with 2 table-spoons rice wine and 1 teaspoon sugar. Steam as directed. Combine ⅓ cup soy sauce; 1 tablespoon rice wine vinegar; 1 tablespoon rice wine; 1 teaspoon honey; 1 clove garlic, pressed; 2 teaspoons grated ginger; and 1 minced green onion. Drizzle over steamed bass fillets.

Steam Fish Fillets

Reduce Marinade

- Remove fillets from the marinade; place in a steamer basket.

- Place quartered orange in wok and add water to a level just below the fish. Cover the steamer.

- Bring the water to a boil; reduce heat to medium. Steam fish 8 to 10 minutes, until fillets are opaque.

- Place fillets on a serving platter.

- Pour marinade into a saucepan.

- Bring to a boil over medium-high heat.

- Cook until marinade is thick and reduced by half, about 8 minutes.

- Spoon marinade over the sea bass fillets. Garnish with sesame seeds.

FISH

SWEET-AND-SOUR FISH

Serve this palate-rousing dish to friends who think they don't like fish

Chinese cuisine is full of subtle, light fish dishes. This isn't one of them. Seasoned, crisp-fried fish fillets get a tart-and-fruity kick from the classic sweet-and-sour sauce. Shredded, raw napa cabbage adds a fresh, crunchy contrast to the rich flavors in the sauce.

Select firm, not-too-thick fillets of fish such as tilapia, floun-

der, snapper or even farm-raised catfish. Fish strips offer plenty of crunch, but for a more impressive presentation, fillets can be left whole and served with a crisscross of sweet-and-sour sauce, with peppers and pineapple on the side. Steamed white rice should accompany this dish.

Yield: Serves 6

Ingredients

1 1/2 pounds firm white fish fillets

2 eggs

3 tablespoons soy sauce, divided

1/2 teaspoon dark sesame oil

1/2 teaspoon five-spice powder

2/3 cup flour combined with 1/3 cup cornstarch

Vegetable oil for frying

2 tablespoons rice wine

3 tablespoons sugar

3 tablespoons rice wine vinegar

2 tablespoons ketchup

1/2 cup pineapple juice

1/2 cup water or fish broth

1 tablespoon cornstarch dissolved in 2 tablespoons cold water

2 bell peppers, one red and one green, cored and sliced

1 cup mandarin orange slices

3 cups shredded napa cabbage

2 green onions, shredded

Sweet-and-Sour Fish

- Rinse fish and pat dry. Cut fillets crosswise into 1-inch strips.

- Whisk together eggs, 2 tablespoons soy sauce, sesame oil, and five-spice powder. In a shallow bowl, combine flour and cornstarch.

- Dip fish in egg mixture, dredge in flour mixture, and deep-fry until golden.

- Prepare sauce. Place shredded cabbage on a serving platter. Arrange fried fish on the cabbage. Ladle sauce over the fish and garnish with green onions.

100

Extra-Crispy Sweet-and-Sour Fish: Replace half the flour with panko-style bread crumbs. Cut fish fillets in half vertically before dipping in eggs and breading.

Mixed Seafood Sweet-and-Sour: Substitute ½ pound each large, peeled, deveined shrimp; sea scallops; and grouper strips for the fish fillets.

Fry the Fish

- Batter each piece of fish by dipping in eggs, then flour.

- Place a wok over high heat and add enough oil to reach a depth of 3 inches.

- Working in batches, fry fish strips until golden brown, about 2 to 3 minutes.

- Remove from oil with a wire basket strainer. Drain on paper towels.

Prepare Sauce

- Whisk together remaining soy sauce, wine, sugar, vinegar, ketchup, pineapple juice, and water or fish broth.

- Place mixture in a saucepan and bring to a boil. Dissolve 1 tablespoon cornstarch in 2 tablespoons cold water. Stir into saucepan.

- When sauce is thickened, add peppers; cook 1 minute. Stir in orange sections and remove from heat.

FISH

STIR-FRIED FISH WITH VEGETABLES

Give your catch of the day a quick stir-fry with plenty of crisp-tender veggies

Stir-frying is the most basic Chinese cooking technique, and it works perfectly with firm, meaty fish. It also offers an alternative to the baked-or-fried cycle many fish lovers fall into.

A quick sear in a hot wok seals in juices and gives fish slices a crisp edge. Plus, the relatively small quantity of sauce enhances, rather than drowns, the flavors of the ingredients.

Don't be afraid to mix different varieties of fish in this dish. Salmon, tuna, and halibut together would not only offer a subtle, delicious mix of flavors, but also add to the visual appeal of the stir-fry. Vegetables can be varied as well, depending on your preferences.

Yield: Serves 6

Ingredients

1 pound skinless tuna or salmon fillets

1 teaspoon sesame oil

3 teaspoons cornstarch, divided

4 tablespoons vegetable oil

1 clove garlic, minced

1/2 teaspoon minced ginger root

4 ounces sliced mushrooms

1 red bell pepper, cored and diced

1 cup snow peas

1 cup bamboo shoots

1 cup small broccoli pieces

2 green onions, shredded

2 tablespoons oyster sauce

2 tablespoons soy sauce

1 tablespoon rice wine

1 tablespoon cold water

Salt and pepper to taste

Stir-Fried Fish with Vegetables

- Rinse fish and pat dry. Cut into 1-inch-wide slices. Toss with sesame oil, then with 2 teaspoons cornstarch to coat.

- Place a wok over high heat; add vegetable oil. Gently stir-fry fish 1 minute; remove from wok.

- Remove 2 tablespoons oil from wok and discard. Prepare vegetables. Stir-fry 3 minutes. Add sauce mixture.

- Return fish to wok and stir-fry gently to coat with sauce. Add salt and pepper. Serve immediately.

• • • • RECIPE VARIATIONS • • • •

Swordfish and Mushroom Stir-Fry: Replace tuna or salmon with 1 pound swordfish. Substitute 3 cups mixed wild mushrooms for the broccoli, bamboo shoots, and snow peas.

Grouper and Bok Choy Stir-Fry: Cut 1 pound grouper fillets crosswise into thick strips. Sear in oil, then prepare wok for stir-frying vegetables. Stir-fry garlic, ginger, and mushrooms. Substitute 9 baby bok choy, cut in half vertically, for the peppers, snow peas, bamboo shoots, and broccoli. Return grouper to the wok and stir in sauce and green onions.

Prepare Fish

- Delicate fish won't withstand the heat and tossing of a stir-fry. Use salmon, tuna, or even swordfish.

- Start with thick fillets or steaks and cut into thick, 1-inch-wide slices. Coat with a little sesame oil and cornstarch for flavor and browning.

- Stir-fry fish in a hot wok, using a little more oil than usual. Remove the browned fish pieces to a plate after about 1 minute.

- Remove excess oil before stir-frying vegetables.

Prepare Vegetables

- Add garlic, ginger, mushrooms, and peppers to the wok. Stir-fry 20 seconds.

- Add snow peas, bamboo shoots, broccoli, and green onions. Stir-fry 2 minutes longer.

- Combine oyster sauce, soy sauce, and wine. Add to the wok. Dissolve remaining 1 teaspoon cornstarch in 1 tablespoon cold water. Stir into hot sauce.

- When sauce is thickened and bubbly, return fish to the wok and cook just until heated through. Add salt and pepper.

CRISPY CARP WITH CHILES

Serve this Szechwan "good luck" favorite when you need strong flavors and a dramatic presentation

Carp originated in China, where they still rank as one of the most prized food fish. A member of the cyprinid family, carp come in hundreds of varieties, including common goldfish and ornamental koi fish. Connoisseurs prefer smallish carp—under 5 pounds—for eating, while anglers seek the 30-plus-pound fighting carp that grow in large lakes around the world. Carp were introduced to North America and some parts of Europe to control pond vegetation, but they adapted well and grew prolifically. Carp generally offer mild, sweet-tasting meat. However, they are quite bony, making them much easier to serve whole, with napkins, than to attempt filleting.

Yield: Serves 4

Ingredients

1 2-pound whole carp or other whole fish, cleaned and scaled

Salt and pepper

4 tablespoons cornstarch

Vegetable oil for frying

4 cloves garlic, minced

2 tablespoons grated ginger root

6 fresh chile peppers, cored and sliced

2 green onions, sliced

2 tablespoons fermented black beans, rinsed

2 tablespoons soy sauce

1 tablespoon rice wine

1 teaspoon sesame oil

1 teaspoon sugar

2 tablespoons chopped cilantro

Crispy Carp with Chiles

- Rinse fish well, then pat dry. Make two or three shallow cuts in each side of the fish.

- Sprinkle with salt and pepper, then dust with cornstarch until well coated.

- Heat a wok over high heat. Add vegetable oil to a depth of 3 inches. When oil is hot, add fish and fry 6 to 8 minutes a side.

- Place the fish on a platter. Prepare chile sauce and pour over the fish. Garnish and serve.

Crispy Carp with Shrimp: Add 1 pound peeled, de-veined shrimp to the hot oil after cooking the carp. Just as shrimp turn opaque, remove from the oil with a slotted spoon. Prepare sauce as directed. Dice cooked shrimp and add to sauce before pouring over the carp.

Crispy Tilapia or Catfish Fillets: Although the Chinese vastly prefer a whole fish, both for flavor and presentation, you can substitute fillets from the market for a mid-week supper. Lightly dust 1 pound fish fillets with salt, pepper, and cornstarch, then fry in hot oil until browned. Remove to a platter and prepare sauce as directed.

Frying a Whole Fish

- Cutting slits in a whole fish helps it cook faster and allows flavors to seep into the fish.

- The rule of thumb for cooking fish is 10 minutes an inch or per pound for whole fish. However, frying in hot oil cooks the fish a little faster.

- It's important to add the cornstarch-dusted fish to very hot oil. Hot oil sears the outside of the fish and keeps it from getting soggy or oily.

- When fish is brown and crispy, place on a serving platter and keep warm.

Prepare Chiles

- After fish has fried, remove all but 1 tablespoon oil from wok.

- Return wok to high heat. Add garlic, ginger, peppers, and green onions. Stir-fry 2 minutes.

- Combine black beans, soy sauce, wine, sesame oil, and sugar. Add to wok and stir-fry another minute.

- Pour sauce and peppers over the fish and garnish with chopped cilantro.

FISH

STEAMED FISH CAKES

Serve these versatile fish cakes over spinach or dressed salad greens for your next luncheon

Steamed fish cakes are a mainstay of Korean and Japanese cuisines, where they are often prepared in long rolls and sliced after steaming. Chinese adaptations appear in some regions of China, but especially among Chinese cooks in Hawaii and other Pacific Rim cities. Mild, white saltwater fish combine with the distinctive flavors of leeks, radishes, and ginger to make this dish memorable without the masking of a heavy sauce. Feel free to experiment with different types of fish and vegetables in the cakes. Although tomatoes don't find their way into many Chinese dishes, these taste wonderful when topped with thick slices of heirloom tomatoes.

Yield: Serves 8

Ingredients

1 pound grouper, cod, or mahi-mahi fillets, cut in ¼-inch cubes

4 ounces baby portobello or shiitake mushrooms

1 leek or spring onion

½ daikon radish

⅓ cup minced cilantro

2 teaspoons grated ginger root

1 clove garlic, pressed

2 tablespoons soy sauce

1 tablespoon lemon juice

1 teaspoon sugar

½ teaspoon sesame oil

½ teaspoon hot chile oil

1 egg, beaten

2-3 tablespoons cornstarch

6 cups fresh baby spinach

1 cucumber, sliced

2 fresh hot peppers, seeded and diced

Steamed Fish Cakes

- Place fish in a large bowl. Finely chop mushrooms. Shred leek or onion and radish. Add vegetables to fish, along with cilantro, ginger, and garlic.

- Whisk together soy sauce, lemon juice, sugar, sesame oil, and chile oil. Add to fish and gently stir. Add egg and mix with hands, being careful not to crush the fish.

- Add enough cornstarch so mixture can be shaped into cakes.

- Steam cakes and serve over fresh spinach garnished with cucumber and peppers. Serve immediately.

Steamed Clam Cakes: Substitute 2 cups well-drained, minced clams for the fish. If mixture seems too moist, sprinkle a small amount of bread crumbs onto the clams.

Mixed Seafood Cakes: Combine ⅓ pound each diced scallops and diced shrimp with ⅓ pound lump crab-meat or sliced crab legs. Mix gently and use in place of diced fish.

Prepare Leeks and Radish

- These fish cakes boast a mix of flavors and textures: soft and crunchy, tart and sweet.

- The best way to showcase these combinations is by finely dicing or shredding solid ingredients, but never crushing or pureeing them.

- A crisp leek and daikon rad-ish cut into very thin shreds should lace through the diced fish and mushrooms in the finished cakes.

- For more color, shredded carrots can be substituted for the radish.

Shape Fish Cakes

- Using hands, shape fish mixture into 8 fish cakes. If mixture is too soft, add a little more cornstarch.

- Place cakes, 4 at a time, on a heat-safe plate. Place a steaming rack into a wok or saucepan and add water to reach just below the rack.

- Bring water to a boil and carefully add plate to rack.

- Reduce heat to medium. Cover wok or pan and steam cakes 8 minutes. Remove plate from rack and repeat with remaining cakes.

FISH

SHRIMP IN CHILI SAUCE

This hot, tart, and sweet dish looks beautiful and makes taste buds dance

This restaurant favorite has roots in Szechwan cooking, where chiles and crisp celery enhance a classic sweet-and-sour sauce. In other Asian cuisines this recipe might take a splash of coconut milk, a tablespoon of hot curry paste, or a selection of blanched vegetables. Ideally the sweet, sour, and hot aspects of the sauce balance one another. Individual cooks may want to experiment by adding more or less vinegar, sugar, and pepper to the dish. Ketchup, a sweet-tart condiment that gives this dish color, also can be added with a heavier or lighter hand. The technique of quickly frying shrimp in hot oil seals in juices.

Yield: Serves 6

Ingredients

1 1/2 pounds large shrimp, peeled and deveined

4 tablespoons vegetable oil

2 cloves garlic, minced

2 teaspoons grated ginger root

4 dried chile peppers, minced

1 rib celery, thinly sliced

2 green onions, trimmed and sliced

1/3 cup ketchup

2 tablespoons rice wine

1 teaspoon hot chile paste

1 teaspoon dark sesame oil

1 teaspoon sugar

1/4 cup water or shrimp stock

1 tablespoon cornstarch, dissolved in 2 tablespoons water

Salt to taste

Shrimp in Chili Sauce

- Rinse shrimp and drain well. Place a wok over high heat. Add vegetable oil.

- Fry a few shrimp at a time in very hot oil 1 minute. Remove with a basket strainer to a platter.

- Remove all but 1 tablespoon oil from wok. Add garlic, ginger, peppers, celery, and green onions. Stir-fry 1 minute.

- Add ketchup mixture to wok; add dissolved cornstarch. When sauce is thick, return shrimp and cook 1 minute. Add salt and serve.

Lobster in Chili Sauce: Substitute 2 pounds diced spiny lobster tail meat for the shrimp.

Chicken in Chili Sauce: Substitute 1½ pounds diced boneless, skinless chicken thighs for the shrimp.

Tofu in Chili Sauce: Substitute 1 pound diced, firm tofu for the shrimp. Double the celery and add 1 small, diced green bell pepper to the vegetable mixture.

Prepare Shrimp

- Shrimp are largely made up of water. Cooked properly, they're juicy and succulent.

- To keep shrimp from becoming dry or tough, it's important to cook them quickly at high temperatures.

- Before adding shrimp to the wok, add a drop of water to the hot oil. The water should immediately pop and evaporate.

- Cook only a few shrimp at a time to keep the wok temperature high. When shrimp begin to turn opaque, remove from oil.

Prepare Sauce

- Drain all but 1 tablespoon oil from wok after frying shrimp. Stir-fry garlic, ginger, peppers, celery, and green onions.

- Whisk together the ketchup, wine, chile paste, sesame oil, sugar, and water or stock. Add to wok and bring to a boil.

- Add dissolved cornstarch to the mix. When sauce is thick and bubbly, return shrimp to wok.

- Cook just until shrimp is well coated with sauce and opaque all the way through.

SHELLFISH

SCALLOPS WITH SNOW PEAS

Golden-seared sea scallops and bright green snow pea pods capture the essence of spring

Some combinations—like sweet, juicy scallops and crisp snow peas—require only gentle handling and the slightest hint of seasoning to be transformed into a regal entree. Medium-size, tender sea scallops work best for this dish. If your market only offers very large scallops, use a "velveting" technique to make the scallops tender. Cut the scallops in half and mix with a marinade of 1 tablespoon rice wine, 1 egg white, salt and pepper, and 1 tablespoon cornstarch. Cover and refrigerate for 30 minutes, then blanch the scallops very briefly in boiling water; drain. Sear scallops in hot oil and proceed with recipe.

Yield: Serves 4

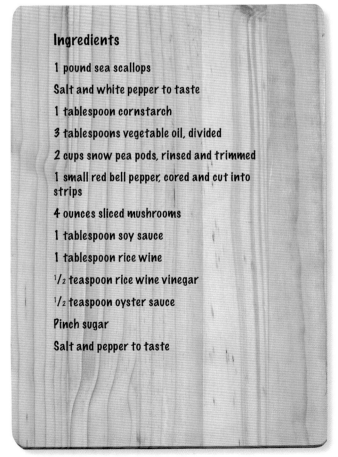

Ingredients

1 pound sea scallops

Salt and white pepper to taste

1 tablespoon cornstarch

3 tablespoons vegetable oil, divided

2 cups snow pea pods, rinsed and trimmed

1 small red bell pepper, cored and cut into strips

4 ounces sliced mushrooms

1 tablespoon soy sauce

1 tablespoon rice wine

$1/2$ teaspoon rice wine vinegar

$1/2$ teaspoon oyster sauce

Pinch sugar

Salt and pepper to taste

Scallops with Snow Peas

- Rinse the scallops and pat dry; sprinkle with salt and pepper, then dust with cornstarch.

- Place a wok over high heat. Add 2 tablespoons vegetable oil. Sear a few scallops at a time in hot oil.

- Remove browned scallops.

Add remaining oil. Add snow peas, pepper, and mushrooms to the hot wok and stir-fry 1 minute.

- Whisk together sauce. Add to wok and cook until bubbly. Return scallops to wok; stir-fry 1 to 2 minutes. Serve immediately.

Bay Scallops with Snow Peas: Substitute 1 pound bay scallops for the sea scallops and cut the snow pea pods in half crosswise. Cook bay scallops in batches, using a spoon or long chopstick to keep the small scallops from sticking together. Continue recipe as directed.

Turkey with Snow Peas: Substitute 1 pound thinly sliced boneless turkey breast for the scallops. Cook as directed.

Prepare Snow Peas

Prepare Sauce

- Depending on the age and size of the snow peas, the tips can be tender or woody.

- Also, larger pea pods may have a tough fiber running along one side.

- After rinsing the snow pea pods, slice off the ends. On large pods, break the stem end and pull downward to remove the fiber.

- Snow peas are at their best when cooked until just bright green and crisp-tender. Don't let them get soggy.

- This dish has a very minimal sauce, allowing the fresh flavors to shine through.

- Whisk together the soy sauce, wine, vinegar, oyster sauce, and sugar.

- Once scallops are seared and veggies stir-fried, add sauce to the wok. Cook sauce until it begins to bubble.

- Return scallops to wok to finish cooking in the sauce. Depending on the thickness of the scallops, this should take 1 to 2 minutes.

SHELLFISH

CRAB WITH GINGER-SOY

Indulge your guests with soft-shell crabs, gently fried and scented with garlic and ginger

Crabs can't expand beyond the size of their hard shells, so in order to grow, they molt. For a few days a year, usually during warm weather, this results in the crab being covered in a papery, completely edible skin. Soft-shell crabs should be alive when purchased and cleaned and cooked promptly. Ask your seafood purveyor to clean your soft shells, or do it yourself just before cooking. Cleaning is just a matter of pulling the feathery gills from the underskirt of the crab and snipping off the crab's face with a sharp knife. Most soft shells are molting blue crabs from the Atlantic Ocean or Gulf of Mexico, although in Asia some cooks prepare soft-shell mangrove crabs.

Yield: Serves 6

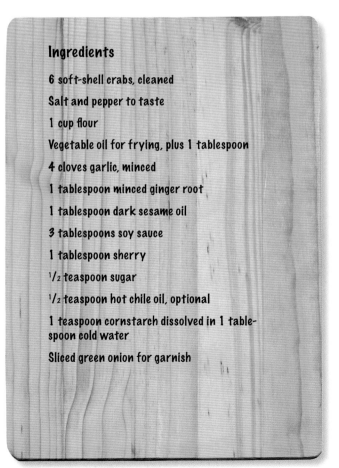

Ingredients

6 soft-shell crabs, cleaned

Salt and pepper to taste

1 cup flour

Vegetable oil for frying, plus 1 tablespoon

4 cloves garlic, minced

1 tablespoon minced ginger root

1 tablespoon dark sesame oil

3 tablespoons soy sauce

1 tablespoon sherry

$1/2$ teaspoon sugar

$1/2$ teaspoon hot chile oil, optional

1 teaspoon cornstarch dissolved in 1 tablespoon cold water

Sliced green onion for garnish

Crab with Ginger-Soy

- Rinse crabs and pat dry. Sprinkle each with salt and pepper, then dredge in the flour.

- Heat a wok or deep skillet over high heat. Add oil to a depth of 2 inches and fry crabs, being careful not to overcrowd them.

- Fry the crabs twice, then drain on paper towels.

- In a hot wok, prepare the sauce. Drizzle sauce over the fried crabs and garnish with green onion. Serve immediately.

Cocktail Crab Cakes with Ginger-Soy: Substitute 12 to 18 miniature crab cakes, either commercially prepared or your own recipe, for the soft-shell crabs. Fry the crab cakes until golden and drain on paper towels. Prepare sauce. Place each crab cake on a small, pressed circle of rice or on a toasted bruschetta. Drizzle with sauce and serve as an appetizer.

Flounder with Ginger-Soy: Substitute 1½ pounds flounder fillets for the soft-shell crabs. Season fillets and coat in flour. Fry in oil until browned on each side, about 2 to 3 minutes altogether. Do not fry a second time. Cook remaining ingredients as directed.

Prepare the Soft Shells

- Soft-shell crabs are a seasonal delicacy. Buy fresh, cleaned crabs shortly before you cook them. Everything is edible on a cleaned soft shell.

- Season crabs, then dredge in flour. Fry in hot oil, 2 or 3 at a time, 1 minute. Turn once.

- Drain crabs on paper towels. After crabs have been fried once, return them to the oil and fry again 2 minutes each.

- Crabs should be golden and very crisp. Drain on paper towels and place on a serving platter.

Prepare Sauce

- Heat a clean wok over high heat. Add 1 tablespoon vegetable oil. Add minced garlic and ginger. Stir-fry just until fragrant, 20 to 30 seconds.

- Add sesame oil, soy sauce, sherry, sugar, and chile oil, if using. Cook just until bubbly.

- Add dissolved cornstarch to sauce and cook until thickened and translucent.

- Either drizzle sauce over crabs or place crabs on a sauce-covered platter and turn fried crabs in sauce to coat. Garnish with green onions.

SHELLFISH

113

LOBSTER CANTONESE

Serve this metropolitan restaurant classic at your next Mid-Century Modern—theme party

Culinary historians debate whether a dish resembling Lobster Cantonese actually originated in Canton, now Guangzhou. Everyone agrees the dish has been prepared with flourish by the chefs at high-end Chinese restaurants since the 1940s. Lobster Cantonese, with its mysterious, pork-laced white sauce and shell-on lobster pieces, was an exotic favorite. Later the

dish became more egalitarian by substituting shrimp for lobster. This was the genesis of Shrimp in Lobster Sauce. Lobster Cantonese lovers fall into two camps—people who like thick, eggy sauce and those who prefer a lighter sauce with black beans. Here we offer the original and a black bean variation. _Yield: Serves 4_

Lobster Cantonese

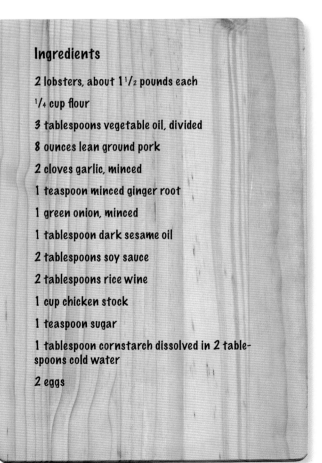

Ingredients

2 lobsters, about 1 1/2 pounds each

1/4 cup flour

3 tablespoons vegetable oil, divided

8 ounces lean ground pork

2 cloves garlic, minced

1 teaspoon minced ginger root

1 green onion, minced

1 tablespoon dark sesame oil

2 tablespoons soy sauce

2 tablespoons rice wine

1 cup chicken stock

1 teaspoon sugar

1 tablespoon cornstarch dissolved in 2 tablespoons cold water

2 eggs

- Bring a large kettle of water to a boil. Drop lobsters in the water headfirst. Cover and cook 2 minutes.

- Remove lobsters from boiling water; rinse with cold water. Cut lobster into pieces and dredge in flour.

- Place a wok over high heat.

- Add 2 tablespoons oil. When oil is hot, add lobster pieces in the shell and stir-fry 1 minute.

- Remove lobster pieces with a slotted spoon and prepare sauce. Return lobster to the sauce and simmer until opaque. Serve immediately.

Lobster Cantonese with Black Beans: Prepare lobster as directed. Add 2 tablespoons rinsed fermented black beans to the pork mixture. Mash the beans against the side of the wok as you stir-fry. Reduce chicken stock to ⅓ cup and omit eggs.

Shrimp in Lobster Sauce: Substitute 1 pound large shrimp, peeled and deveined, for the lobster. Skip the boiling water bath. Stir-fry the raw shrimp in hot oil for 1 minute. Remove from the wok and prepare sauce, reducing stock to ⅔ cup. Return shrimp to the wok and simmer until shrimp is opaque.

Prepare Lobsters

- When blanched lobsters are cool enough to handle, remove the tails and twist off the claws.

- With a cleaver, cut the tails in half lengthwise, then crosswise into 2-inch pieces.

- Cut the claws at the joints, then use a mallet or the side of a cleaver to crack each piece.

- Dredge the pieces in flour and stir-fry in hot oil for 1 minute. Remove from wok.

Prepare Sauce

- Add remaining tablespoon of oil to the wok. When hot, add pork, garlic, ginger, and green onion to wok.

- Stir-fry until pork is no longer pink. Combine sesame oil, soy sauce, wine, stock, and sugar. Stir well; cook until liquid is hot.

- Add dissolved cornstarch to wok. Cook on high until sauce is thick. Return lobster to wok.

- Beat eggs and drizzle over contents of wok. Cover wok; let ingredients cook undisturbed 2 minutes. Gently stir egg into mixture.

SHELLFISH

CILANTRO-GARLIC STEAMED CLAMS

Chinese flavors enhance a coastal summer classic in this easy-to-prepare feast

Clams exist in every corner of the world and have helped sustain numerous civilizations. These bivalves range in size from less than an ounce to hundreds of pounds. Although thousands of different varieties of clams exist, many are location-specific. That means, your purchasing options depend on where you live. In general, small clams tend to be more tender and manageable for steaming. In Atlantic coastal areas, that might mean some variety of quahog clam, such as littlenecks or cherrystones, while Pacific Rim shoppers are more likely to find Manila and longneck clams. Cooking times will vary, depending on the size of the mollusks.

Yield: Serves 4

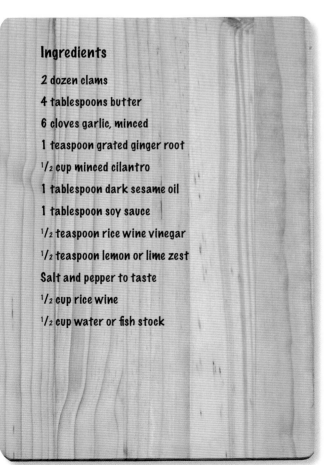

Ingredients

2 dozen clams

4 tablespoons butter

6 cloves garlic, minced

1 teaspoon grated ginger root

$1/2$ cup minced cilantro

1 tablespoon dark sesame oil

1 tablespoon soy sauce

$1/2$ teaspoon rice wine vinegar

$1/2$ teaspoon lemon or lime zest

Salt and pepper to taste

$1/2$ cup rice wine

$1/2$ cup water or fish stock

Cilantro-Garlic Steamed Clams

- Carefully scrub clam shells to remove any dirt. Rinse with cold water.

- In a saucepan combine butter, garlic, ginger, cilantro, sesame oil, soy sauce, vinegar, and zest. Season sauce with salt and pepper.

- Heat sauce over medium-high heat, stirring often. Simmer 2 minutes, then remove from heat.

- Steam clams and remove to a bowl. Reduce steaming liquid by half; whisk into sauce. Serve clams with sauce.

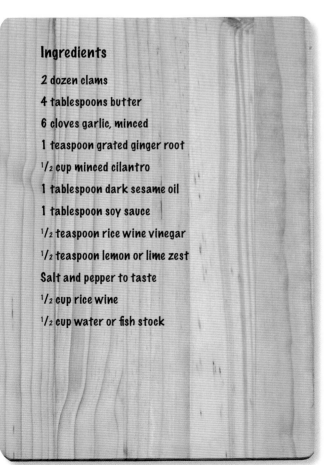

Steamed Clams with Beer: Substitute Chinese beer for rice wine and stock in the steaming liquid.

Cilantro-Garlic Steamed Mussels: Substitute 2 dozen mussels for the clams.

Roasted Oysters with Cilantro-Garlic Sauce: Roast 2 dozen scrubbed oysters in a closed barbecue pit for 10 minutes, or until shells pop open. Prepare butter sauce. Combine ¼ cup each wine and seafood stock. Boil until reduced by half, then whisk into the butter sauce. Serve oysters on the half shell with sauce for dipping.

Place Clams in Steamer

- Place clams, hinge side down, in a steamer basket. Discard any open clams that don't close when tapped.

- Pour wine and water or stock into a wok or large saucepan that can accommodate the steamer basket.

- Cover pot and place over high heat. Steam clams 6 to 8 minutes, or until clams open.

- Remove clams to a serving bowl. Discard any that did not open.

Prepare Sauce

- Remove steamer basket from wok or saucepan. Place pot with cooking liquid from clams over high heat.

- Cook clam liquid until reduced by half.

- Whisk cooking liquid into sauce until well blended.

- Drizzle sauce over steamed clams or serve in a separate bowl for dipping.

SHELLFISH

SALT & PEPPER SQUID

This is fried calamari with a difference—coarse sea salt and toasted Szechwan peppercorns

Some cooks insist the exquisite flavor of this dish comes from the hot and numbing quality of the Szechwan peppercorns. Others argue the dish was meant to be prepared with ordinary black peppercorns, which actually are somewhat exotic in China, where white pepper is usually used for seasoning. Either way, the common ground is freshness: fresh squid,

freshly ground spices, and freshly decanted vegetable oil. Because Salt and Pepper Squid has so few ingredients, each must shine. This recipe uses readily available young squid. However, if you have access to fingertip-size baby squid, by all means, use them. Just season, flour, and fry them whole.
Yield: Serves 4

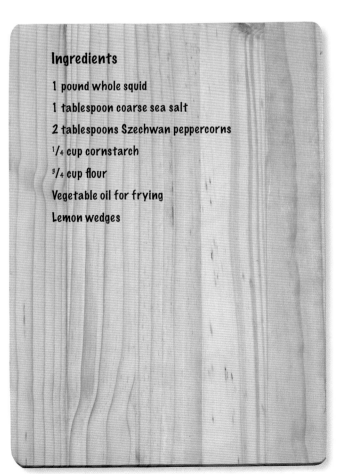

Ingredients

1 pound whole squid

1 tablespoon coarse sea salt

2 tablespoons Szechwan peppercorns

1/4 cup cornstarch

3/4 cup flour

Vegetable oil for frying

Lemon wedges

Salt and Pepper Squid

- Rinse and clean the squid. Score and cut into pieces; sprinkle with sea salt.

- Place peppercorns in a dry skillet over high heat. Toast the peppercorns. Grind peppercorns in a spice grinder or mortar and pestle.

- Combine cornstarch and flour in a bowl. Stir in pepper. Place a wok over high heat. Add oil to a depth of 2 inches.

- Dredge squid pieces in flour-pepper mixture and fry until golden, about 1 to 2 minutes. Serve hot with lemon wedges.

Salt and Pepper Squid with Black Peppercorns: Substitute black peppercorns for the Szechwan peppercorns. Do not toast the peppercorns, just grind them in a pepper mill or spice grinder.

Salt and Pepper Shrimp: Substitute 1 pound large shrimp, peeled, deveined, and butterflied, for the squid.

Clean Squid

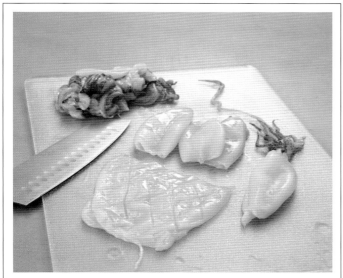

- Holding squid body firmly and gently, pull head away from body. Discard head and attached organs.

- Cut tentacles off just below eyes and reserve. Remove cartilage from body and rinse out the tube.

- Remove any membrane on the outside of tube. Slice tube open and lay flat. Score squid with shallow diagonal cuts.

- Slice squid in half vertically, then crosswise into 3 or 4 pieces. Pinch the hard beak from the base of the tentacles and discard.

Toast Peppercorns

- Place a small, heavy skillet over high heat.

- Add peppercorns, stirring constantly to keep them from scorching. Toast peppercorns 1 to 2 minutes, until fragrant.

- Pour peppercorns in a bowl to cool. Then pulverize in a spice grinder or with a mortar and pestle.

- Stir ground peppercorns into flour and cornstarch mixture.

SHELLFISH

STEAMED STUFFED TOFU

These layered packages make a striking first course or a light vegetarian entree

Tofu comes with many different labels. Basically there are two varieties of tofu—silken and regular or firm tofu. Silken tofu has a custardlike texture, while regular tofu has the texture of semisoft cheese. However, within the two general categories, there are products that offer various levels of firmness. These range from very moist tofu to very dry, crumbly tofu. In general silken tofu should be used in recipes that require the least handling, while regular or firm tofu can withstand frying, stir-frying, and marinating. This recipe calls for a dry, firm tofu that can withstand frying. The steaming-only variation can be prepared with a silken tofu.

Yield: Serves 4

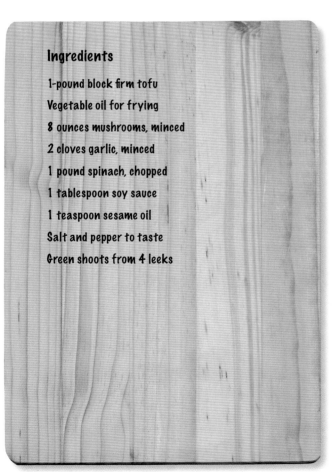

Ingredients

1-pound block firm tofu

Vegetable oil for frying

8 ounces mushrooms, minced

2 cloves garlic, minced

1 pound spinach, chopped

1 tablespoon soy sauce

1 teaspoon sesame oil

Salt and pepper to taste

Green shoots from 4 leeks

Steamed Stuffed Tofu

- Rinse, drain, and cut tofu into 8 pieces. Place a wok over high heat and add 2 inches oil. Deep-fry the tofu 1 to 2 minutes in hot oil. Remove with a basket strainer.

- Remove all but 1 tablespoon oil from the wok. Stir-fry mushrooms, garlic, and spinach 2 minutes. Add soy sauce, sesame oil, and salt and pepper.

- Remove mushrooms. Press out as much liquid as possible.

- Layer mushroom mixture between two slices of tofu, wrap with blanched leek shoots and steam.

• • • • RECIPE VARIATIONS • • • •

Steamed Stuffed Tofu with Ham: Layer a thin slice of Smithfield ham, cut to fit, on the bottom cube of fried tofu before layering spinach and mushrooms on top. Prepare tofu bundles and steam as directed.

Steamed Silken Tofu: Skip the frying step. Cut tofu into cubes as directed, layer vegetables between the cubes, tie with leeks, and steam just until warmed through.

Slice Tofu

Steam Tofu

- Although it's a good source of protein, tofu is bland and takes on the flavor of other ingredients.

- Use a wet, sharp knife to cut tofu block into four quarters. Cut each quarter in half horizontally.

- Deep-fry tofu to give the exterior a crisp texture. When tofu is cool enough to handle, make four "sandwiches" with mushroom filling at the center.

- Blanch leek shoots until limp. Use them to gently tie each tofu quarter together, using 2 shoots per quarter.

- Place a steaming rack in a wok and add enough water to reach just below the rack.

- Place tied tofu packets on a plate and fit the plate into the wok. Cover wok tightly and bring water to a boil over high heat.

- Steam tofu 4 minutes or until heated through.

- Drain any excess liquid from the plate. Serve stuffed tofu immediately.

SPICY TOFU WITH PORK

Entice even those who are suspicious of tofu with this spicy, savory pork sauce

This hearty dish from Szechwan province offers a wonderful juxtaposition of textures and flavors. The ground pork and mushrooms feel rough to the palate, while the tofu cubes have a smooth, soothing texture. The tofu adds high-quality protein and substance to the mix, but little flavor. The predominant tastes are from the pork, soy sauce, and chile paste,

all of which coat and flavor the tofu.

If you don't have chile paste on hand, this dish also can be made by adding fresh hot peppers, or by grinding dried hot chiles in a food processor with a tiny bit of oil. The perfect foil for Spicy Tofu with Pork is a big bowl of fluffy steamed rice. *Yield: Serves 6*

Ingredients

4 dried wood ear mushrooms

8 ounces lean ground pork

1/4 cup soy sauce, divided

1 tablespoon rice wine

2 teaspoons dark sesame oil

1 pound firm tofu

2 tablespoons vegetable oil

3 cloves garlic, minced

2-3 teaspoons chile paste

1/2 teaspoon five-spice powder

2 green onions, minced

1 teaspoon sugar

1 tablespoon cornstarch dissolved in 2 tablespoons cold water

Salt to taste

Spicy Tofu with Pork

- Soak wood ears in hot water 30 minutes. Drain and finely chop.

- Combine pork, 1 tablespoon soy sauce, wine, and sesame oil. Cut tofu into ½-inch cubes. Place wok over high heat; add vegetable oil.

- Stir-fry pork in hot oil until no longer pink, about 2 minutes. Add wood ears, garlic, chile paste, five-spice powder, green onions, and sugar.

- Stir-fry 1 minute, then add tofu and remaining soy sauce. Add cornstarch. Stir-fry 1 minute.

···· RECIPE VARIATIONS ····

Spicy Tofu with Chicken or Beef: Substitute 8 ounces ground chicken or beef for the ground pork.

Spicy Tofu with Mushrooms: Substitute 8 ounces minced fresh mushrooms for the pork.

Soak Wood Ears

Chop Pork

- Wood ears are known by many names: tree ears, silver ears, and jelly ears among them.

- Wood ears are almost exclusively cultivated in China. They're hard to find fresh, so they must be reconstituted before use.

- Pour very hot water over wood ears and let steep 30 minutes. Remove from soaking liquid and chop or cut into slivers to add color and texture to dishes.

- The soaking liquid is flavorful. Strain it through a coffee filter and use instead of water in cooking.

- Many Chinese dishes benefit from the rich flavors of pork, sausage, and ham. For maximum impact the fat is rarely drained from these meats as dishes are prepared.

- Some cooks may prefer to add precooked and drained ground pork to recipes to

reduce overall fat content.

- Another alternative is to use cubes of lean pork to make ground or minced raw meat.

- Place partly frozen (not hard) pork cubes in a food processor and pulse until finely chopped.

123

DEEP-FRIED TOFU

The crunchy coating yields to a smooth, creamy center in this simple dish

Deep-fried tofu can never be confused with health food. But it is both tasty and addictive—like any good snack should be. Offered with a variety of dipping sauces, fried tofu triangles make a great cocktail party treat or a nosh for the book club meeting. Select sweet hoisin sauce, spicy hot chile paste, and aromatic ginger-soy sauce for a variety of dipping sensations.

Fried tofu also can substitute for pork in a sweet-and-sour preparation. Remember to drop battered tofu into hot oil a few pieces at a time, without crowding the wok, to ensure a crisp coating. *Yield: Serves 4*

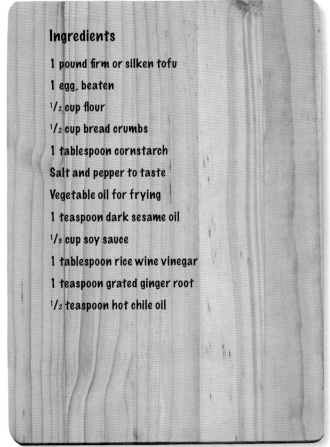

Ingredients

1 pound firm or silken tofu

1 egg, beaten

$^1/_2$ cup flour

$^1/_2$ cup bread crumbs

1 tablespoon cornstarch

Salt and pepper to taste

Vegetable oil for frying

1 teaspoon dark sesame oil

$^1/_3$ cup soy sauce

1 tablespoon rice wine vinegar

1 teaspoon grated ginger root

$^1/_2$ teaspoon hot chile oil

Deep-Fried Tofu

- Drain tofu. Using a wet knife, cut diagonally, forming 1-inch triangles.

- Coat tofu in beaten egg. Combine flour, bread crumbs, and cornstarch; dredge tofu in mixture.

- Place wok over high heat. Add vegetable oil to a depth of 2 to 3 inches. When oil is very hot, fry tofu until golden, about 2 minutes.

- Drain tofu on paper towels. Sprinkle with salt and pepper. Whisk together sesame oil, soy sauce, vinegar, ginger, and chile oil. Serve immediately.

• • • • RECIPE VARIATIONS • • • •

Deep-Fried Tofu Salad: Prepare fried tofu as directed. Toss together 4 cups mixed salad greens, 1 cup shredded napa cabbage, ½ cup shredded daikon radish, and ½ cup red bell pepper strips. Whisk together 1 tablespoon soy sauce, 1 tablespoon dark sesame oil, 2 tablespoons vegetable oil, 1 teaspoon honey, and 3 tablespoons rice wine vinegar. Toss with salad greens and serve with fried tofu on top.

Salt and Pepper Fried Tofu: Combine 1 tablespoon sea salt with 1 tablespoon cracked black peppercorns. Stir into the bread crumbs. Prepare fried tofu as directed.

Fry Tofu

- Chinese cooks use deep-frying to add crispness and flavor to dishes.

- Heat oil to a temperature of 350°F to 375°F before adding food. High temperatures sear the food, resulting in a crunchy exterior and tender, moist center.

- If you don't have a food thermometer, drop a cube of bread in the fat. If the oil bubbles around the bread immediately, the oil is hot.

- Always use fresh oil for deep-frying. Peanut oil maintains its quality at higher temperatures better than other vegetable oils.

Prepare Dipping Sauce

- Authentic Chinese dishes are rarely laden with heavy sauces.

- Instead, a small amount of sauce serves as seasoning or offers an interesting flavor counterpoint to other ingredients.

- Dipping sauces are a favorite way to introduce hot, sweet, salty, sour, and savory flavors to hors d'oeuvres and fried foods.

- Experiment by blending soy sauce with sugar, garlic, ginger, vinegar, or chiles. Or start with a thick hoisin or tart-sweet duck sauce and layer in other ingredients.

SILKEN TOFU WITH MUSHROOMS

An assortment of mushrooms gives this dish a range of textures and flavors

Imagine a savory custard, richly sauced with a cascade of stir-fried mushrooms in a deep brown sauce. Now drop a spoon into this silken tofu feast. The soft, satin-textured tofu instantly brings to mind that rich custard, and the mushrooms bestow a meaty essence to the sauce. The best mix of mushrooms might include shiitakes, chanterelles, and morels, but in a

pinch, portobello and white mushrooms will do.

Oyster sauce gives the sauce depth, but also makes the dish nonvegetarian. A vegetarian version of oyster sauce—actually made from mushrooms—exists, but you may have to shop diligently to find it.

Yield: Serves 4

Ingredients

1 pound silken tofu

1 pound assorted mushrooms

2 tablespoons vegetable oil

2 cloves garlic, minced

2 green onions, minced

2 tablespoons soy sauce

1 tablespoon oyster sauce

1 tablespoon rice wine

1/2 teaspoon sugar

Salt and pepper to taste

2 teaspoons cornstarch dissolved in 1 tablespoon cold water

Silken Tofu with Mushrooms

- Place tofu on a heat-safe plate. Set a steamer rack into a wok and add water to just below rack. Bring water to a boil, place plate on rack, and cover wok.

- Steam tofu 5 minutes. Remove; drain liquid from plate.

- Slice mushrooms. Heat oil in wok over high heat. Stir-fry garlic, green onions, and mushrooms 2 to 3 minutes. Stir in soy sauce, oyster sauce, wine, sugar, salt, and pepper.

- Stir in dissolved cornstarch. When sauce is thickened, pour over tofu. Serve.

···· RECIPE VARIATIONS ····

Silken Tofu with Spinach: Substitute 1 pound washed, drained spinach leaves for all or part of the mushrooms. Add the spinach after stir-frying the garlic and green onions for 2 minutes. Continue stir-frying according to the recipe.

Silken Tofu with Mushrooms and Shrimp: Stir-fry 8 ounces of peeled, deveined, and diced shrimp in 2 tablespoons of hot oil for 1 minute. Remove the shrimp, then stir-fry the garlic, green onions, and mushrooms for 2 minutes. Return shrimp to the wok and continue stir-frying for 1 minute longer. Complete recipe as directed.

Prepare Mushrooms

Drain Tofu

- Select at least three different varieties of fresh mushrooms. Different shapes and textures make the dish interesting to the eye and palate.

- Meaty, firm shiitakes are a favorite in many Asian cuisines. Mix them with delicate chanterelles and white buttons, full-flavored morels or creminis.

- Shop for firm, dry, blemish-free mushrooms that have a clean or slightly earthy scent.

- Remove dirt with a soft brush, rinse quickly, then slice.

- No surprise here: Water dilutes flavor. Reducing the amount of unneeded water in a dish can mean the difference between an exciting taste experience and a bland dish.

- Both tofu and mushrooms have high water content, so it's important to be vigilant.

- Drain tofu well both before and after steaming.

- Blot mushrooms dry before adding to the wok and make sure the oil is hot. Thicken sauce with cornstarch diluted in a small amount of water.

TOFU WITH ALMONDS

Tofu absorbs soy, ginger, and garlic flavors in this vegetarian entree with sweet almonds

Substitute tofu for virtually any mild-tasting animal protein and you've got an instant vegetarian entree. However, this dish was designed with tofu in mind. The crunchy almonds offset the soft tofu, and the savory sauce both coats and infuses the porous bean curd. Tofu with Almonds is a gently spiced recipe. Chile lovers can add minced hot peppers or a bit of hot chile oil to the mix. Sweet, mild almonds complement the other ingredients perfectly, but in a pinch, blanched peanuts or cashews can be used instead. Steamed white rice is a perfect accompaniment for this dish.

Yield: Serves 4

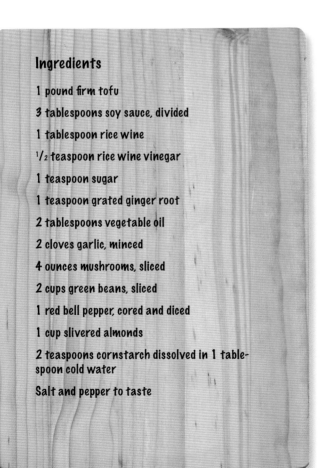

Ingredients

1 pound firm tofu

3 tablespoons soy sauce, divided

1 tablespoon rice wine

1/2 teaspoon rice wine vinegar

1 teaspoon sugar

1 teaspoon grated ginger root

2 tablespoons vegetable oil

2 cloves garlic, minced

4 ounces mushrooms, sliced

2 cups green beans, sliced

1 red bell pepper, cored and diced

1 cup slivered almonds

2 teaspoons cornstarch dissolved in 1 tablespoon cold water

Salt and pepper to taste

Tofu with Almonds

- Drain tofu and cut into 1-inch cubes. Toss tofu with 1 tablespoon soy sauce. In a bowl, combine remaining soy sauce, wine, vinegar, sugar, and ginger root.

- Place a wok over high heat. Add oil. Stir-fry garlic, mushrooms, green beans, and red bell pepper in hot oil 2 minutes.

- Add almonds and tofu. Stir-fry for 1 minute. Add sauce mixture and stir to coat ingredients.

- Add dissolved cornstarch. Cook until sauce is thick and bubbly. Serve immediately.

···· RECIPE VARIATIONS ····

Tofu with Black Bean Sauce: Add 2 tablespoons minced fermented black beans and 1 tablespoon water to the ginger and soy sauce mixture. Prepare recipe as directed, but double the amount of mushrooms and omit the almonds.

Tofu with Mixed Vegetables: In place of green beans, add 1 cup sugar snap peas, ½ cup sliced carrots, and 1 cup broccoli florets.

Select Almonds

- Nuts and seeds play a vital role in Chinese cuisine, adding texture, protein, and flavor.

- In this dish, crunchy almonds offer a counterpoint to the tender tofu. The nuts brown in the stir-fry process and get a nice coating of sauce.

- For extra flavor, toast nuts before adding them to recipe. Dry-toast them on a baking sheet in a 350°F oven, turning often, until browned.

- Or, toast nuts in a small amount of butter in wok or skillet. Keep nuts moving to prevent scorching.

Tofu as an Ingredient

- Asian cooks use tofu simply as another well-loved ingredient in their vast repertoire.

- Often it is flavored with meats or included in recipes that feature animal-based products.

- However, vegetarian and vegan cooks value tofu for the ready, easily digested protein it provides.

- Soy-based products like tofu offer a complete spectrum of amino acids as well as calcium, fat, and other essential nutrients. A ½-cup serving of tofu has 10 grams of protein.

TOFU WITH EGGS

Love a weeknight supper of eggs and hash browns? For variety, try this protein-packed egg dish

Purists prefer this dish almost plain, just the creamy white tofu and the yellow eggs cooked until set, with a sprinkle of salt and white pepper. Others go for a little oomph—green onions, peppers, and a dash of soy sauce. Either way, Tofu with Eggs makes a great brunch offering or casual supper. Unlike omelets, Tofu with Eggs isn't cooked until browned,

so either watch the wok carefully or cook the mixture over low heat. Stir-fry a wok full of greens or mushrooms to serve beside the eggs and tofu for a well-rounded, colorful platter. *Yield: Serves 4*

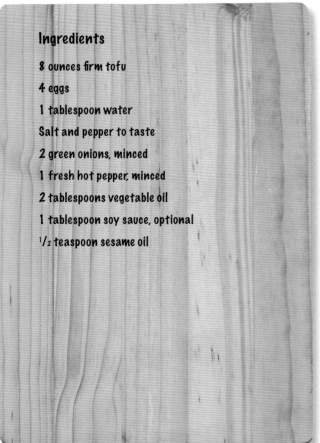

Ingredients

8 ounces firm tofu

4 eggs

1 tablespoon water

Salt and pepper to taste

2 green onions, minced

1 fresh hot pepper, minced

2 tablespoons vegetable oil

1 tablespoon soy sauce, optional

1/2 teaspoon sesame oil

Tofu with Eggs

- Slice tofu into ½-inch cubes. In a bowl, whisk eggs with water until eggs are light and fluffy.

- Stir in salt, pepper, green onions, and hot pepper. Place wok over high heat. Add oil.

- Gently stir-fry tofu in hot oil 1 minute. Reduce heat to medium. Pour eggs over tofu and cook without stirring until eggs begin to set.

- Combine soy sauce, if using, and sesame oil and sprinkle over the eggs. Cook until eggs are done.

• • • • RECIPE VARIATIONS • • • •

Cholesterol-Free Tofu with Eggs: Replace eggs with a cholesterol-free egg substitute equivalent to 4 eggs.

Tofu with Eggs in a Nest: Boil 4 vermicelli noodle nests in water until just tender. Remove carefully with a slotted spoon. Pour oil to a depth of 2 inches in a deep skillet or wok. When the oil is hot, slip the noodle nests into the oil. Fry just until the nest bottoms are browned and crisp. Drain well. Prepare recipe as directed and slip a portion of the cooked tofu-egg mixture into each nest.

Cook the Eggs

- Cooking eggs in a wok requires a gentle touch. Always use a well-seasoned or nonstick wok and swirl oil around the sides.

- Pour eggs into the hot wok and allow bottom of eggs to set. Do not disturb for at least 30 seconds.

- Once eggs begin to set, gently push them toward the middle of the wok, allowing uncooked eggs to slide to the wok surface.

- When outer edges of eggs begin to set, gently break them up and stir-fry the pieces.

Pancake-Style Tofu with Eggs

- Tofu with Eggs is a favorite no-fuss vegetarian (but not vegan) dish.

- This recipe can be served as is for lunch or an evening meal. The eggs can also be flipped, pancake style, instead of stir-fried. Cut the tofu-egg cake into wedges and serve.

- Another favorite way to serve eggs in China is soft-boiled. Warm, soft eggs star with stir-fried vegetables, tofu, chiles, and sweet-and-sour sauces.

- Runny eggs carry a risk of salmonella contamination, so cook until firm.

STIR-FRIED LONG BEANS

You'll be tempted to put this veggie side dish at the center of your table

Long beans have an honored tradition in many Asian cuisines. When lightly cooked, the beans take on a meaty, chewy texture and sweet flavor. Add long beans to stir-fries, soups, and curries. Green-colored long beans are the most readily available, but if you live near a large farmers' market, you may be able to find dark purple or very pale varieties.

During Chinese New Year feasts, long beans are often served uncut, as a symbol of long life. They can be steamed and tossed with a bit of sesame oil. Some chefs add blanched long beans to main-dish salads. This recipe can be made into an entree with the addition of chicken or tofu.

Yield: Serves 6

Ingredients

1 pound Chinese long beans

Vegetable oil for frying

2 tablespoons soy sauce

1 teaspoon sugar

$1/2$ teaspoon rice wine vinegar

1 tablespoon dark sesame oil

4 cloves garlic, minced

2 hot peppers, sliced

2 leeks or 4 green onions, trimmed and sliced

Salt and pepper to taste

Stir-Fried Long Beans

- Clean long beans. Trim ends; discard. Slice beans into 2-inch lengths.

- Place wok over high heat. Add enough vegetable oil to reach a level of 2 inches. Fry beans in hot oil 2 minutes; remove with a strainer.

- Combine soy sauce, sugar,

vinegar, and sesame oil. Remove all but 2 tablespoons oil from wok. Over high heat, stir-fry garlic, peppers, and leeks or green onions 30 seconds.

- Add beans. Continue stir-frying 1 minute. Add soy sauce mixture and stir-fry 1 minute longer. Serve hot.

Long Beans with Pork: Add 8 ounces of cooked, drained ground pork to the garlic, leeks, and peppers.

Long Beans with Chicken and Wood Ears: Soak 4 wood ear mushrooms in hot water for 30 minutes. Drain and slice. Cut 3 boneless chicken breast halves crosswise into thin slices. Combine 1 egg white with 1 tablespoon rice wine and 1 teaspoon soy sauce. Toss the chicken in this mixture, then sprinkle with 1 tablespoon cornstarch. Refrigerate 30 minutes. Fry the beans in 2 inches of oil according to the recipe. Remove all but 3 tablespoons of the oil, then stir-fry the chicken and remove. Add the garlic, leeks, and peppers; stir-fry. Add the beans, wood ears, and chicken and continue recipe as directed.

Buy Long Beans

- Chinese long beans, also known as yard-long beans and asparagus beans, grow to a length of almost 3 feet, but they are best when 1 to 1½ feet long.

- They're the seedpods of an annual vine and grow throughout the warmest areas of Asia.

- Fresh long beans can be found in specialty stores and some supermarkets in the West. However, fresh green beans make a fine substitute.

- Shop for light to dark green beans that are firm and blemish free.

Flavor Long Beans

- Stir-fried long beans are often augmented with ingredients from the onion family, such as garlic, leeks, green onions, and chives.

- For a dramatic dish, add chile paste, dried hot chiles, and minced Szechwan-style preserved vegetables to the seasoning blend.

- Peanuts and sesame seeds are favorite additions as well.

- Deep-frying long beans or green beans results in a slightly dehydrated bean that soaks up sauces and flavorings when stir-fried.

BABY BOK CHOY WITH OYSTER SAUCE
Oyster sauce gives this mild green a rich salty-sweet flavor

Greens, prepared simply and lightly sauced, are common side dishes on the Chinese table. Bok choy and sweeter, smaller baby bok choy rank as favorites. Although native to Asia, bok choy can be grown in any temperate climate. The most important rule in handling these antioxidant and fiber-rich vegetables is to cook them only until crisp-tender. Overcooked bok choy becomes mushy and loses flavor.

In a pinch, bok choy can be steamed until just tender, then tossed with sesame oil or drizzled with warm oyster sauce diluted with a little wine and soy sauce.

Yield: Serves 6

Ingredients

6 baby bok choy, trimmed and halved lengthwise

2 tablespoons vegetable oil

2 slices ginger root

2 cloves garlic

2 tablespoons oyster sauce

1 tablespoon soy sauce

$1/2$ teaspoon sugar

$1/4$ cup water or broth

1 teaspoon cornstarch dissolved in 1 tablespoon water

1 tablespoon dark sesame oil

Salt and pepper to taste

Baby Bok Choy with Oyster Sauce

- Rinse and drain bok choy. Place wok over high heat. Add vegetable oil. Stir-fry ginger and garlic 30 seconds; remove.

- Stir-fry bok choy 40 seconds; remove. Stir oyster sauce, soy sauce, sugar, and water or broth in wok. Bring to a boil.

- Reduce heat and return bok choy to wok. Cover and simmer 1 minute; remove to serving platter.

- Bring sauce mixture to a boil. Add dissolved cornstarch. When sauce is thick, stir in sesame oil, salt, and pepper. Ladle sauce over bok choy; serve.

···· RECIPE VARIATIONS ····

Asparagus with Oyster Sauce: Substitute 1 pound of asparagus, well trimmed and cut into 1-inch pieces, for the baby bok choy.

Broccoli with Oyster Sauce: Trim 1 head of broccoli and cut into florets. Blanch in boiling water for 2 minutes and

drain. Prepare recipe as directed, using broccoli in place of bok choy.

Baby Bok Choy with Peanuts: Prepare recipe as directed. Sprinkle ½ cup chopped peanuts over the top of the bok choy before serving.

Baby vs Regular

- Bok choy is a versatile leafy green and cabbage family cousin. It can grow in virtually any temperate climate, but is primarily seen in Chinese dishes.

- Baby bok choy—a miniature variety of bok choy—is slightly sweeter and more tender than the larger head.

- Regular bok choy can be substituted, although thick stems should be discarded and cooking time lengthened.

- Buy firm, blemish-free bok choy. Keep refrigerated and use within 2 to 3 days. Wash well before using.

Adding Veggies to Sauce

- Simmering vegetables in sauces allows for a valuable exchange of flavors.

- As long as stir-fried vegetables aren't allowed to "stew"—or overcook—in the sauce, the result should be both flavorful and aesthetically pleasing.

- If a beautiful presentation is essential, consider preparing the sauce separately.

- For Baby Bok Choy in Oyster Sauce, whole bok choy can be blanched in boiling water, drained, then arranged on a serving platter. Prepare the sauce, then drizzle a little over the vegetables.

WARM SLIVERED RADISHES

Discover the versatility and varieties of radish in this surprising dish

If your experience with radishes has been limited to red globe radishes sliced into salads, you're in for a mind-expanding treat. Chinese cooks employ a variety of types of radishes to add crunch, color, and flavor to dishes. A root vegetable related to turnips, radishes can be eaten raw or cooked. In this dish three different radishes, blanched, offer layers of peppery flavor. The sauce resembles a warm dressing, with sweet and tart elements, as well as aromatics. Designed to be served as a vegetable side dish, this recipe also can be served cold. After a few hours in the refrigerator, the blanched radish slivers absorb the sauce and take on the character of soft pickles.

Yield: Serves 6

Ingredients

1 cup slivered daikon radishes

1 cup slivered red radishes

1 cup slivered watermelon heart radishes

$\frac{1}{2}$ cup water

2 slices ginger root

1 tablespoon rice wine

1 tablespoons soy sauce, optional

1 tablespoon rice wine vinegar

2 teaspoons sugar

$\frac{1}{3}$ cup minced fresh cilantro

Warm Slivered Radishes

- Combine three varieties of radishes in a bowl.

- Place a wok over high heat and add water, ginger, and wine. When liquid begins to boil, add the radishes.

- Cook just until radishes are heated through, about 1 minute. Drain radishes and place in a bowl.

- Whisk together soy sauce (if using), vinegar, and sugar. Pour over the slivered radishes and mix well. Garnish with cilantro. Serve immediately.

Warm Radish Salad: Cut the radishes into thin slices. Add 1 cup of thinly sliced celery and ½ cup of thinly sliced carrots to the radishes and blanch all together. Double the amount of dressing and pour over the radish mixture. Substitute 1 minced green onion for the cilantro.

Quick-Fix Root Veggie Stir-Fry: Cut three varieties of radishes in 1-inch chunks to yield 2 cups total. Combine with ½ cup each diced turnips, diced rutabaga, and diced beets. Stir-fry in 2 tablespoons hot vegetable oil for 1 minute. Add rice wine, rice wine vinegar, sugar, and 1 tablespoon dark sesame oil and stir-fry just to blend. Remove from heat and add 1 tablespoon grated orange zest.

A World of Radishes

Slice Radishes

- As in the rest of the world, radishes are valued in Asia for their crisp, peppery bite. Common globe radishes are available in China, along with many other types.

- Daikon radishes, a long, white, mild-tasting Japanese variety, turn up in cold dishes, pickles, and stir-fries.

- Sweet watermelon radishes have a white and green exterior and bright red flesh, making them popular for eye-appeal.

- Shop for watermelon hearts in stores and farmers' markets that sell heirloom produce.

- In Chinese cooking, preparation often trumps cooking. That means the amount of time devoted to slicing, dicing, and mixing exceeds the cooking effort.

- The appearance and mouth feel of many dishes depend on how ingredients are cut. When a recipe specifies

"slivers," it means short, thin, oblong pieces.

- To make radish slivers, cut round radishes horizontally into thick disks. Then cut disks into 3 or 4 strips.

- For long radishes, slice on the diagonal to get more surface area, then cut strips.

EGGPLANT WITH GARLIC SAUCE

This vegetarian entree won't make any of your guests feel deprived

Eggplant is a great chameleon in Italian, French, Cajun, and Chinese cuisines. It takes on the flavors of the ingredients around it, and it can be slurpy or crispy, meaty or saucy. This dish, adapted from a Szechwan staple, can be served as is or with a portion of ground pork in the sauce. Either way, it's considered a main dish, with a robust sauce that should be paired with steamed white rice. If you can't find long, thin Asian eggplants at the market, small Italian-style eggplants

will work as well. To use large globe-type eggplant, sprinkle the cut pieces with salt and drain on a rack or paper towels for 1 hour. Rinse before using.

Yield: Serves 4

Eggplant with Garlic Sauce

KNACK CHINESE COOKING

Ingredients

4 small Asian eggplants

Vegetable oil for frying

3 tablespoons soy sauce

3 tablespoons rice wine vinegar

3 tablespoons sugar

1 tablespoon rice wine

1 green onion, minced

1 tablespoon minced ginger root

6 cloves garlic, minced

1 tablespoon minced fermented black beans

1 teaspoon hot chile paste

1 tablespoon dark sesame oil

1 tablespoon cornstarch dissolved in 2 tablespoons cold water

- Trim top and bottom tips from eggplants; discard. Cut eggplants into 1½-inch pieces.

- Pour oil in wok to a depth of 2 inches; heat until hot. Fry eggplant. Drain all but 2 tablespoons oil.

- In a bowl, whisk together soy sauce, vinegar, sugar, and wine.

- Stir-fry green onion, ginger, garlic, black beans, and chile paste over high heat 20 seconds. Add eggplant and sauce to wok. Stir-fry 30 seconds. Add dissolved cornstarch to wok and cook until sauce is thick. Serve.

Meaty Eggplant with Garlic Sauce: Add 8 ounces cooked ground pork or ground beef to the wok with the sauce ingredients.

Shrimp and Eggplant with Garlic Sauce: After removing all but 2 tablespoons of the oil from the wok, stir-fry 8 ounces peeled, deveined and diced shrimp for 45 seconds. Remove the shrimp and continue the recipe as directed. Return the shrimp to the wok with the eggplant and stir-fry until cooked through.

Cut Eggplant

- Asian eggplants are longer and thinner than the Mediterranean variety.

- They also have less of a problem with bitterness, so no advance salting and draining are required.

- Buy firm, unblemished eggplants that feel heavy for their size. Cut right before cooking, using a sharp knife to lop off the ends.

- Create even pieces by cutting the trimmed eggplant in half lengthwise, then splitting the two halves lengthwise to form four spears. Slice spears crosswise into 1½-inch pieces.

Fry Eggplant

- Eggplants have a spongy texture and a tendency to soak up liquids.

- To avoid a grease-laden mess, fry eggplant in very hot oil, a few pieces at a time, no more than 30 seconds.

- Remove pieces with a wire mesh strainer and drain in a colander or on paper towels. The hot oil will sear the outside of the eggplant.

- If you prefer a lighter dish, blanch the eggplant in boiling water, then add to wok; stir-fry until cooked through.

BUDDHA'S DELIGHT

This dish has many different faces, all vegetarian and all delicious

This dish complies with the general Buddhist aversion to violence by including only vegetarian ingredients. However, the name should not imply a strict interpretation of any particular Buddhist tradition. While some Buddhists follow a general vegetarian diet, others eschew root vegetables (which do violence against animals that make their home in the earth) or strongly flavored foods that excite the senses. Still others eat meat or seafood under certain circumstances. Feel free to adjust the roster of vegetables to your own beliefs, to your own tastes, or to whatever vegetables and herbs look good at the market. If you can find fresh lotus root, a few lacy slices would be a good addition.

Yield: Serves 4–6

Ingredients

4 dried wood ear mushrooms

2 tablespoons dried tiger lily buds

2 tablespoons vegetable oil

2 cloves garlic, minced

1 tablespoon minced ginger root

1 cup green beans

1 red bell pepper, cored and diced

1 cup bamboo shoots

1/2 cup sliced water chestnuts

1 cup canned straw mushrooms

1 cup cabbage, cut into 1-inch squares

1 cup snow pea pods, trimmed

1 cup canned gingko nuts

2 tablespoons soy sauce

1 tablespoon rice wine

1 teaspoon sugar

2 teaspoons cornstarch dissolved in 1 tablespoon cold water

1 teaspoon dark sesame oil

Buddha's Delight

- Soak wood ears and lily buds in hot water 30 minutes. Drain, reserving ¼ cup wood ear liquid. Slice wood ears.

- Add oil to wok. Briefly stir-fry garlic and ginger over high heat. Add green beans and bell pepper. Stir-fry 1 minute. Add remaining vegetables and gingko nuts. Stir-fry 2 minutes. Add wood ears and lily buds.

- Whisk together reserved liquid, soy sauce, wine, and sugar. Add to wok.

- Add cornstarch; cook until sauce thickens. Stir in sesame oil and serve.

Buddha's Delight Noodle Bowl: Follow the recipe as directed. At the end of cooking, add 1 cup water or vegetable broth to the wok. Cook 12 ounces Chinese noodles in boiling water, drain, and add to the wok. Serve Buddha's Delight with broth and noodles.

Buddha's Delight Also: Substitute 1 cup zucchini, quartered and cut in 1-inch pieces, for the green beans in the recipe. Substitute yellow squash, quartered and cut in 1-inch pieces, for the cabbage. Continue the recipe as directed, but add ½ cup cashews at the end of cooking.

Working with Canned Ingredients

- Traditional Chinese dishes include some ingredients that are very difficult, if not impossible, to find fresh outside of China.

- Fortunately, things like straw mushrooms, bamboo shoots, water chestnuts, and gingko nuts can be found readily in supermarkets.

- Experiment with different brands of canned Chinese fruits and vegetables to find your favorites.

- Help these ingredients shed their "tinny" taste by draining them well and rinsing in cold water. In the case of bamboo shoots, a brief soak in ice water can help.

Vegetable Alternatives

- Buddha's Delight is a time-honored Chinese vegetarian dish. However, there are many variations.

- Traditional Chinese vegetables, such as straw mushrooms, bamboo shoots, and water chestnuts, almost always make an appearance in this dish.

- Some versions add sliced lotus root and dried tofu sticks, while other cooks insist the vegetables must be served over cellophane noodles.

- Don't be afraid to experiment.

SESAME SPINACH

Serve this aromatic dish alongside meaty stir-fries or as a bed for steamed fish

Cooked properly—that is, very lightly—spinach has a bright color and silky texture that pair well with almost any simply prepared meat or fish dish. Buy superfresh greens, then use the bunch promptly. Spinach originated in Central Asia and has been part of Chinese cuisine for many centuries. Crinkly, flat-leaf, and hybrid varieties exist, as well as a number of greens related to spinach that can be used interchangeably. Unlike diners in the West, where raw spinach accounts for most of the spinach consumed, the Chinese vastly prefer cooked greens. In this recipe the spinach is only lightly gilded with a little garlic, sesame oil, and sesame seeds.

Yield: Serves 4

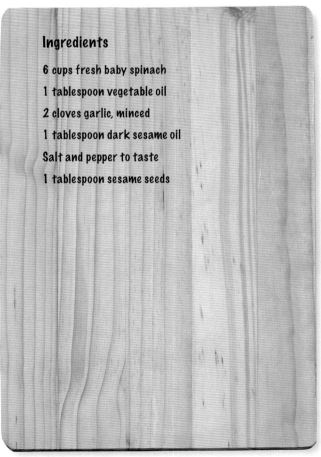

Ingredients

6 cups fresh baby spinach

1 tablespoon vegetable oil

2 cloves garlic, minced

1 tablespoon dark sesame oil

Salt and pepper to taste

1 tablespoon sesame seeds

Sesame Spinach

- Rinse spinach leaves under running water in a colander. Remove any tough stems or blemished leaves.

- Place a wok over high heat. Add vegetable oil and swirl to coat.

- Add garlic to the wok and stir-fry 30 seconds. Add the spinach all at once and cover the wok. Allow spinach to steam 30 seconds.

- Remove cover and stir-fry quickly, just until spinach is limp. Add sesame oil and salt and pepper to taste. Sprinkle with sesame seeds and serve.

Sesame Chard: Substitute 6 cups fresh, chopped Swiss chard for the spinach.

Sesame Endive: Blanch 12 small endive in boiling water for 2 minutes. Drain and cut in half lengthwise. Substitute for the spinach.

Prepare Spinach

- Popeye had it right. Spinach is a nutritional powerhouse, filled with iron, vitamin A, vitamin C, folic acid, and a range of antioxidants.

- The best way to cook spinach, and preserve the nutrients, is to quickly steam or stir-fry it.

- Wash spinach well. Cook it in a hot pan with only the rinse water clinging to the leaves.

- Cover pan to steam spinach quickly. Or, you can open-lid stir-fry the spinach with or without oil. Flat-leaf or baby spinach is best for stir-frying.

About Sesame Seeds

- The Chinese were using sesame seeds for edible oils as well as lamp oil some five thousand years ago.

- Sesame seeds come from the seedpods of an annual flowering plant. They come in ivory, black, red, and brown varieties.

- Toasting brings out the flavor and aroma of the seeds. Toast them on a baking sheet at 350°F, or in a dry skillet, stirring often to avoid scorching.

- Refrigerated seeds will keep for 2 to 3 months.

PORK LO MEIN

Soft egg noodles absorb savory flavors in this Chinese lunchtime favorite

Chinese, Italians, and Middle Easterners have long staked competing claims on the invention of noodles. However, recent archaeological evidence suggests residents of Northern China have been eating wheat flour noodles since 1,000 B.C.E. Northern China still boasts a plethora of noodle-based dishes. But satisfying noodles in all forms turn up on the menus of Chinese noodle shops around the world. Lo mein, which means "stirred or tossed noodles," is a Cantonese dish that pairs cooked egg noodles with oyster sauce, vegetables and meats or seafood. Chinese-style egg noodles tend to be a bit more dense and chewy than Italian-style pasta.

Yield: Serves 4–6

Ingredients

3 dried wood ear mushrooms

1 pound Chinese egg noodles

1 tablespoon dark sesame oil

8 ounces lean pork

2 cloves garlic

1 rib celery

1 carrot

1 green onion

2 to 3 tablespoons vegetable oil

2 tablespoons oyster sauce

2 tablespoons soy sauce

1 teaspoon sugar

Salt and pepper to taste

Pork Lo Mein

- Soak wood ears 30 minutes in hot water; drain. Slice and set aside.

- Prepare noodles and toss with sesame oil. Cut pork into matchsticks. Mince garlic; cut celery, carrot, and green onion into matchsticks.

- Add oil to wok. Working in batches, stir-fry the pork until no longer pink; remove. Add additional oil if needed; stir-fry vegetables 2 minutes.

- Add noodles and pork; stir-fry 1 minute. Combine oyster sauce, soy sauce, and sugar. Stir into wok; add salt and pepper.

Shrimp Lo Mein: Substitute 8 ounces medium shrimp, peeled and deveined, for the pork.

Chicken Lo Mein: Substitute 8 ounces boneless chicken for the pork. Add ½ teaspoon grated ginger to the sauce.

Prepare Noodles

- Depending on whether you're using fresh or dried noodles, cooking times will vary.

- Bring a kettle or large wok full of water to a rolling boil. Drop noodles in the water and stir to separate.

- If using fresh noodles, boil 2 to 3 minutes. For dried noodles, boil 4 to 5 minutes.

- Drain noodles in a colander and rinse with cold water. Drain well; transfer to a bowl. Toss with sesame oil.

Stir-Frying Starchy Ingredients

- Food science studies have detailed the molecular underpinnings, but it all comes down to this: Starchy foods are more likely to stick when subjected to moisture and heat.

- To avoid a sticky mess, make sure cooked lo mein noodles are well coated with sesame oil before adding to wok.

- The wok should be well seasoned and all ingredients hot when noodles are added.

- Stir-fry rapidly, using the wok handle to give the entire vessel a few shakes while stirring.

BEEF CHOW FUN

Wide rice noodles give this Cantonese specialty a silky texture

Chow fun, and its cousin Mei fun, offers southern China's staple rice in noodle form. Chow fun combines meat—usually beef—with crispy mung bean sprouts, fragrant green onions, and translucent rice noodles in a light coating of soy and oyster sauce. The dish is usually "dry fried" with the noodles lightly browned or kissed by the wok before the sauce is added. Mei fun dishes feature thin rice noodles, sometimes called rice vermicelli. Rice noodles are less elastic than wheat noodles and must be handled gingerly to avoid creating a pile of broken or sticky strands. The noodles are soaked to soften, then lightly stir-fried in a well-seasoned, hot wok. Rice noodles appear in dishes throughout Southeast Asia.

Yield: Serves 4–6

Ingredients

1 pound medium rice noodles

8 ounces beef round, flank, or sirloin, sliced crosswise into thin strips

3 tablespoons soy sauce, divided

1 tablespoon rice wine

1 teaspoon rice wine vinegar

1 teaspoon cornstarch

3 tablespoons vegetable oil, divided

4 ounces mushrooms, sliced

2 green onions, sliced

2 cups bean sprouts

²/₃ cup bamboo shoots, sliced

2 tablespoons oyster sauce

Salt and pepper to taste

Beef Chow Fun

- Prepare rice noodles. Place beef in a bowl with 1 tablespoon soy sauce, wine, and vinegar. Sprinkle on cornstarch to coat.

- Place wok over high heat. Add 2 tablespoons oil. Stir-fry beef in 2 batches. Remove beef when no longer pink.

- Add additional oil to the wok. Stir-fry mushrooms, green onions, bean sprouts, and bamboo shoots 2 minutes.

- Add drained noodles and toss. Return beef to wok and stir in oyster sauce. Season with salt and pepper and serve.

146

Beef Mei Fun: Substitute 1 pound rice vermicelli for the medium rice noodles. Reduce the noodle soaking time to 3 to 4 minutes.

Singapore Chow Fun: Substitute 4 ounces each peeled and deveined shrimp and matchstick-sliced pork for the beef. Follow recipe as directed. Add 1 teaspoon Madras curry powder or Singapore curry oil to the wok before adding softened rice noodles.

Softening Rice Noodles

About Bean Sprouts

- Rice noodles must be softened before adding to recipes. Since they break more easily than wheat noodles, they are usually steeped rather than boiled.

- Place dried rice noodles in a large bowl. Add boiling water to cover.

- Allow noodles to steep in water 5 to 7 minutes, stirring occasionally to separate. Drain and use as directed.

- Noodles can steep longer for a more tender texture. Rice noodles should be soft, but not mushy.

- Alfalfa, radish, and wheat berry sprouts are great additions to salads and sandwiches, but they cannot substitute for mung bean sprouts in cooking.

- Crisp, sturdy mung bean sprouts can be eaten raw, but most Chinese cooks add them to stir-fries or blanch, and toss them with a dressing.

- Crisp sprouts with silvery white stalks will keep in the refrigerator up to a week.

- Briefly soak sprouts in cold water, drain well, and store in a resealable plastic bag in the refrigerator.

SHREDDED LAMB & CRISP NOODLES

Fried noodle pancakes give this Hunan-inspired lamb dish a unique presentation

Shredded lamb ranks among Hunan province's most renowned dishes, pairing savory lamb with spicy chiles and slivered wood ears. The accompanying crispy noodles in this recipe—pan-fried into browned cakes—are more common to the dishes of Guangdong province. Together this intra-country fusion creates a dish perfect for a meat course or small plate in a multicourse dinner party. Cantonese food aficionados might miss the traditional gravy over the noodles. For those cooks and diners, we have a saucy variation.

Yield: Serves 4, or makes 6 small plates

Ingredients

3 dried wood ear mushrooms

12 ounces boneless lamb

3 tablespoons soy sauce, divided

1 tablespoon rice wine

1 teaspoon hot chile paste

1/2 teaspoon sugar

1 teaspoon cornstarch

1 pound thin Chinese egg noodles

1 tablespoon dark sesame oil

4 tablespoons vegetable oil, divided

2 cloves garlic, minced

1/2 teaspoon minced ginger root

2 green onions, minced

Shredded Lamb and Crisp Noodles

- Soak wood ears in hot water 30 minutes; drain and chop.

- Cut lamb into matchsticks. Combine with 1 tablespoon soy sauce, wine, chile paste, and sugar. Toss with cornstarch to coat. Prepare noodle pancakes.

- Add 2 tablespoons vegeta-ble oil to wok. Stir-fry garlic, ginger, and green onions 30 seconds. Add wood ears and half the lamb.

- Cook lamb 1 minute without stirring; stir-fry quickly until no longer pink. Repeat. Return lamb to wok, add remaining soy sauce; stir-fry 20 seconds.

Saucy Shredded Beef and Crisp Noodles: Substitute 12 ounces flank steak for the lamb. Prepare recipe as directed, but omit chile paste. Before adding final 2 tablespoons of soy sauce, combine it with 1 tablespoon each oyster sauce and rice wine or broth. Add the sauce to the wok and bring to a boil. Dissolve 1 teaspoon cornstarch in 1 tablespoon cold water. Add to the wok and cook until thick and bubbly.

Shredded Duck and Crisp Noodles: Substitute 12 ounces boneless duck breast for the lamb.

Make Crisp Noodles

- Fill a soup pot or wok with water and bring to a boil.

- Add noodles and stir to separate. Boil 3 to 5 minutes or until tender. Drain and rinse with cold water. Toss with sesame oil.

- Heat 2 tablespoons oil in a wok or large skillet. Working in batches, drop noodles into pan in pancake-size circles.

- Fry noodles over high heat until crisp and lightly browned on the bottom, about 1 to 2 minutes. Flip noodle cakes over and cook until browned. Remove to a platter.

Prepare Lamb

- Many cultures embrace lamb as a staple. Sheep are an economical source of meat, with the advantage of also providing milk and wool.

- For those who didn't grow up eating lamb, it can be an acquired taste.

- For the mildest flavor, buy young, farm-raised lamb and trim off all visible fat. Lean leg or loin steaks work well for stir-fries.

- Slice lamb steaks across the grain into thin slices, then cut the slices into thin matchsticks.

VEGGIE CELLOPHANE NOODLES

Translucent mung bean noodles make this a pasta dish with a difference

Cellophane noodles, also called glass noodles or bean threads, are made from mung bean starch. They're brittle and slightly opaque when dried and plump and resilient when softened. Dishes made with cellophane noodles can be served hot or cold, dry or saucy. Since cellophane noodles absorb the flavor and color of sauces, all you have to do is cook the noodles

in sauce a bit longer to get a drier dish.

Dry cellophane noodles can be added directly to soups, but must be softened before they are added to any other recipes.

Yield: Serves 4–6

Ingredients

1 pound cellophane noodles

1 tablespoon vegetable oil

4 ounces mushrooms, sliced

1 carrot, cut into matchsticks

1 rib celery, cut into matchsticks

1/2 cup bamboo shoots, cut into matchsticks

1 cup snow pea pods

1 red bell pepper, cored and cut into strips

2 green onions, cut into shreds

2 cloves garlic, pressed

2 tablespoons soy sauce

1 tablespoon dark sesame oil

1 teaspoon sugar

1/2 teaspoon hot chile paste

Salt to taste

Veggie Cellophane Noodles

- Prepare cellophane noodles and set aside. Place a wok over high heat. Add vegetable oil and swirl to coat the wok.

- Add mushrooms, carrots, celery, bamboo shoots, snow peas, red bell pepper and green onions to the hot oil. Stir-fry 3 minutes.

- In a bowl, mix together garlic, soy sauce, sesame oil, sugar, and chile paste. Add cellophane noodles to the wok. Toss to mix. Stir in the sauce.

- Stir-fry until noodles are well coated and heated through; add salt and serve.

Cellophane Noodles with Minced Pork: Follow recipe as directed. Add 8 ounces cooked ground pork to the wok with the sauce ingredients.

Cold Cellophane Noodles with Shrimp: Follow recipe as directed. Add 8 ounces peeled, deveined, cooked shrimp to the wok with the sauce mixture. Toss in noodles and remove from heat. Let stand 10 minutes. Spoon noodles into a shallow bowl or platter, cover, and refrigerate for 2 hours. Garnish with chopped cilantro or sesame seeds before serving.

Prepare Cellophane Noodles

- Cellophane noodles are extremely brittle until softened.

- Place coiled cellophane noodles in a large bowl. Fill bowl with hot water to cover.

- If the noodles float to the surface initially, weigh them down with a heavy saucer until they become softer.

- Let the noodles stand 20 to 30 minutes or until softened; drain.

Select Vegetables

- This lightly sauced dish uses traditional Chinese vegetables for color and crispness.

- If you happen to have a different mix of vegetables in your refrigerator, or growing in your garden, feel free to vary the recipe.

- Zucchini, yellow squash, green beans, wax beans, edamame beans, sugar snap peas, broccoli rabe, and asparagus are all acceptable additions.

- Simply cut veggies uniformly into long, thin pieces to complement the noodles.

NOODLES & RICE

PERFECT STEAMED RICE

The cornerstone of most Chinese meals is a beautiful bowl of white rice

China produces more rice than any other country in the world. Hybrid strains of long-grain rice, which is polished to produce the white rice that sustains families and culinary traditions, have made it possible for most regions of the country to produce rice. Rice is so connected to the notion of well-being in China that an ancient greeting citizens offered one another translates to, "Have you had your rice today?"

Although flavored rice dishes certainly exist, the vast majority of rice in China is eaten plain, balancing other boldly flavored dishes. Steaming, which results in full, tender, but never mushy grains, is the preferred cooking method.

Yield: Serves 3–4

Ingredients

1 cup long-grain white rice

1 1/2 cups cold water

Steamed Rice

- Place rice in a bowl. Add several cups water and swirl the rice to rinse. Drain the water.

- Pour the rice in a saucepan with a tight-fitting lid. Add the water.

- Bring the rice and water to a boil over medium-high heat. Reduce heat to medium-low. Cover the pot. Steam 20 minutes, without opening the lid.

- After 20 minutes, remove the rice from the heat. Let stand 2 minutes, then open lid and fluff the rice.

Steamed Brown Rice: To prepare brown rice, which is rice that still has its bran layer intact, simply count on using more water and a longer cooking time. In a saucepan, bring 3 cups water and 1 cup brown rice to a boil. Reduce heat to medium-low, cover the pot, and steam for 40 minutes or until all the water is absorbed.

Steamed Jasmine Rice: Jasmine rice is wonderfully aromatic and very commonly served in Thailand and other parts of Asia. The recipe for jasmine rice is the same as white rice—just substitute 1 cup of jasmine rice for the white rice.

Varieties of Rice

- In China most families enjoy white rice for meals and short, fat-grained glutinous rice (also called sticky rice) for desserts and snack dishes.

- The Chinese also produce heirloom strains of rice, often available at Asian markets and gourmet shops.

- Varieties include red rice and black rice, or so-called forbidden rice, which is a short-grain dark rice that turns a wonderful purple when cooked.

- Black rice is a whole grain rice and should be cooked in the same way as brown rice.

Serve the Rice

- One very important thing to remember: Rice continues to cook after it's removed from the heat.

- In order to interrupt the process, and prevent gooey rice at the center of the pot, you must "mess up" the rice.

- Let the rice stand, covered, for a few minutes after steaming, then remove the cover.

- Take a heat-safe plastic paddle or wooden spoon and gently fluff the rice, allowing air to reach deep into the center of the rice pot.

SHRIMP FRIED RICE

This home and restaurant favorite can be as simple or elaborate as you like

Jambalaya, pilaf, risotto, and paella all owe a debt to the original stirred-rice entree, fried rice. In China, fried rice heavily laced with shrimp and pork sometimes turns up at banquets, while simple dishes of rice flavored with oil, eggs, and vegetables can be purchased from street vendors.

Outside of China, Shrimp Fried Rice is a restaurant favorite, while home cooks think of it mostly as a way to stretch leftovers. Either way, the secret to great fried rice is to start with day-old rice that has been refrigerated. The slightly dehydrated rice will be less sticky and more likely to absorb added flavors.

Yield: Serves 4–6

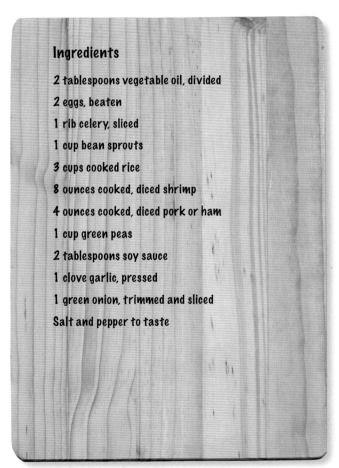

Ingredients

2 tablespoons vegetable oil, divided

2 eggs, beaten

1 rib celery, sliced

1 cup bean sprouts

3 cups cooked rice

8 ounces cooked, diced shrimp

4 ounces cooked, diced pork or ham

1 cup green peas

2 tablespoons soy sauce

1 clove garlic, pressed

1 green onion, trimmed and sliced

Salt and pepper to taste

Shrimp Fried Rice

- Place wok over high heat. Add ½ tablespoon oil. Add beaten eggs to hot oil and cook, without stirring, until eggs are set. Remove eggs and cut in strips.

- Add remaining oil to wok. Stir-fry celery and bean sprouts 1 minute. Add cooked rice and stir-fry rapidly 2 minutes.

- Add shrimp, pork, and peas. Stir-fry 1 minute. Add soy sauce and garlic to the rice and stir-fry until sauce is evenly distributed.

- Add cooked eggs, green onion, salt, and pepper. Serve immediately.

Pork Fried Rice: Substitute 8 ounces chopped or shredded cooked pork for the shrimp, and use 4 ounces of diced ham, rather than pork.

Vegetarian Fried Rice: Substitute 4 ounces diced firm tofu and 8 ounces sliced mushrooms for the pork and shrimp.

Add Day-Old Rice

- Refrigerated, day-old rice is best for preparing fried rice.

- To avoid lumps in the dish, transfer day-old rice to a large bowl.

- Using your fingers, break up the rice until the grains are separate.

- When adding the rice to the wok, do it all at once and stir-fry quickly to coat the grains evenly with sauce.

Alternative Egg Method

- Some cooks prefer to have eggs coat the rice, rather than egg ribbons tossed with the rice.

- For this method, stir-fry the rice with the vegetables, shrimp, and pork. Add the soy sauce and garlic.

- Before adding the green onion, pour beaten eggs over the rice. Stir-fry quickly, distributing the eggs evenly through the dish.

- When the eggs are cooked through, add the green onion, salt, and pepper.

CLAY POT CHICKEN

Slow cooking in a ceramic pot makes this chicken juicy and fork-tender

Chinese clay pots, also known as sand pots, have ancient origins, with specimens emerging from archaeological sites dating to 5,000 B.C.E. and historical references going back even further. Typically the pots are glazed inside, to protect both the food and the pot, and unglazed outside, to absorb heat and moisture.

This recipe can be prepared in an ordinary Dutch oven on the stove or in a stove top–safe ceramic casserole. If you aren't sure your ceramic dish can take direct heat, simply prepare the recipe ingredients in a wok, transfer it all to a covered casserole, and cook in a 325°F oven for an hour.

Yield: Serves 4–6

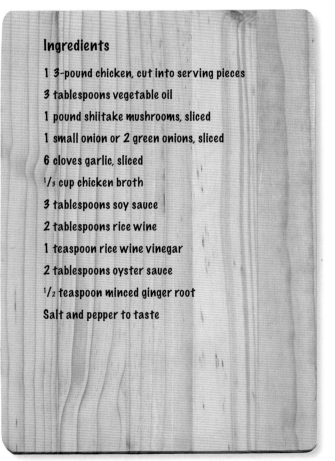

Ingredients

1 3-pound chicken, cut into serving pieces

3 tablespoons vegetable oil

1 pound shiitake mushrooms, sliced

1 small onion or 2 green onions, sliced

6 cloves garlic, sliced

1/3 cup chicken broth

3 tablespoons soy sauce

2 tablespoons rice wine

1 teaspoon rice wine vinegar

2 tablespoons oyster sauce

1/2 teaspoon minced ginger root

Salt and pepper to taste

Clay Pot Chicken

- Rinse chicken pieces and pat dry. Prepare clay pot as directed. In a wok or skillet, brown chicken in hot oil.

- Remove browned chicken. Add mushrooms, onion, and garlic to the hot oil. Stir-fry 2 minutes.

- Combine broth, soy sauce, wine, vinegar, oyster sauce, and ginger. Pour sauce mixture in the clay pot and slowly heat until bubbly. Add chicken pieces, mushrooms, onion, and garlic.

- Cover; simmer on medium-low until chicken is cooked through, about 45 minutes. Season. Serve with rice.

Clay Pot Cornish Hen: Substitute 3 Cornish hens, halved, for the chicken.

Clay Pot Whole Chicken: Substitute one 3-pound fryer for the cut-up chicken. Brown the chicken breast side down, then place in the clay pot breast side up. Follow recipe as directed, but increase cooking time to 1 hour.

Prepare Chicken and Pot

The Oven Alternative

- Before using, be sure to rinse the chicken and pat dry. Cut with chef's knife into small, bite-size pieces.

- Before using a new sand pot or Chinese clay cooker, the pot should be soaked in cold water overnight, then drained and allowed to air dry. Also, before cooking

with a clay pot, it should be soaked in cold water 20 minutes.

- Sand pots shouldn't be subjected to rapid changes in temperature. Allow the pot filled with ingredients (never empty) to heat slowly. Never put a hot sand pot directly on a cold or wet surface.

- Chinese sand pots or ceramic pots, unlike most terra-cotta pots, can take direct heat from a stove top.

- However, sometimes it's just easier to throw a dish in a slow oven for an hour or so.

- To cook this recipe in a

conventional oven, simply prepare the dish on the stove to the point where all ingredients have been added.

- Carefully place the covered pot in a 325°F oven and bake 1 hour. Remove and let stand, covered, 15 minutes before serving.

ROASTS & STEWS

ROAST PORK
Cilantro and kumquats give this dish a unique herbal signature

This isn't a traditional Chinese dish. However, it does combine traditional Chinese ingredients, such as pork in a soy marinade, plus hoisin sauce and garlic, with a citrus coating. The sweet-tart kumquats give off a heavenly aroma while cooking, making this a great dinner-party entree, with or without a full Chinese menu. If you prefer to cook a large pork loin roast, rather than quick-cooking tenderloins, just double the sauce quantities and increase the cooking time according to the weight of the roast. White rice and Sesame Spinach (see Vegetables) would make wonderful accompaniments.
Yield: Serves 6

Ingredients

2 pounds pork tenderloin

²/₃ cup soy sauce, divided

2 tablespoons sugar

2 tablespoons lemon juice

2 tablespoons rice wine

2 tablespoons hoisin sauce

1 tablespoon ketchup

1 clove garlic, pressed

4 kumquats

¹/₄ cup cilantro leaves

Roast Pork

- Rinse pork and pat dry. Combine ⅓ cup soy sauce, sugar, lemon juice, and wine. Pour marinade over pork, refrigerate 2 hours.

- Preheat oven to 375°F. Place pork in roasting pan and discard marinade. Combine remaining soy sauce, hoisin sauce, ketchup, and garlic.

- Baste pork with hoisin mixture and roast 20 minutes. Finely chop kumquats and cilantro in a food processor.

- Baste pork with more hoisin mixture, sprinkle with kumquat-cilantro mixture, and roast 10 minutes longer. Let stand 10 minutes before serving.

Roast Venison with Kumquats and Cilantro: Substitute 2 pounds of farm-raised venison for the pork. Add 2 slices of ginger root to the kumquat-cilantro mixture in the food processor before pulsing. Prepare recipe as directed, but adjust cooking time and temperature to 325°F for 3 hours. Baste with sauce in the last half hour of cooking.

Roast Duck with Kumquats and Cilantro: Substitute a whole, cleaned duck for the pork. Roast at 350°F for 3 hours, basting with hoisin and cilantro-kumquat mixture during the last half hour of cooking.

Roasting Pork

- Pork should never be served rare, but that doesn't mean it has to be cooked to the point of dryness.

- Cook pork to an internal temperature of 140°F, then let stand before carving. The meat will continue to cook a little while resting.

- Thin tenderloins, in particular, have almost no fat for self-basting, which makes this cut perfect for glazes and herb coatings.

- If you want pork to have a crusty exterior, quickly sear on the stove before roasting.

Prepare Kumquats

- Oval, grape-size kumquats are tiny citrus-like fruits that originated in China.

- The fruits come in several varieties, but all are designed to be eaten whole. The yellow-to-orange zest carries the sweetness of the fruit, while the inner flesh is extremely tart.

- This sweet-tart dichotomy makes the kumquat perfect for marmalades, jams, and glazes.

- Some varieties do have seeds, so you may want to split kumquats in half to remove them before pulsing in a food processor.

ROASTS & STEWS

BEER-BASTED PORK
Bold Chinese beer pumps up the flavor in this red-cooked dish

Rice wine or sherry mingles with soy sauce in the classic Chinese-style braising liquid. In this recipe we take the liberty of replacing the wine with Chinese beer, which has a highly malted, crisp quality that complements the sweet pork nicely. (In fact, the broth would make a nice simmering bath for sausages or even bratwurst.)

Long simmering distinguishes this dish from a stir-fry. The boneless pork butt can be cooked as a roast, rather than in cubes, if you prefer. Just add 30 minutes or so to the simmering time. For traditional red-cooked flavor, just omit the beer. In its place add ½ cup of rice wine and ½ cup of water.
Yield: Serves 6–8

Ingredients

2 pounds boneless pork butt, cut into 2-inch cubes

1 teaspoon five-spice powder

¹/₂ teaspoon salt

1 star anise

1 rib celery, sliced

3 cloves garlic, minced

2 dried hot chile peppers

2 green onions, sliced

¹/₃ cup soy sauce

2 tablespoons sugar

1 cup Chinese beer

2 cups chicken broth

1 tablespoon cornstarch, dissolved in 2 tablespoons cold water

Beer-Basted Pork

- Sprinkle pork with five-spice powder and salt. Place a wok over high heat. Add the anise, celery, garlic, hot peppers, green onions, soy sauce, sugar, beer, and broth. Bring to a boil.

- Add pork to the wok. Reduce heat to medium. Cover the wok and simmer 15 minutes; remove the cover.

- Simmer 1 hour longer, adding more broth or water if needed.

- Bring pork mixture to a boil; add dissolved cornstarch. Cook until sauce is thick and bubbly.

Beer-Basted Chicken: Cut a 3-pound fryer into serving pieces. Rinse and pat dry. Use chicken pieces in place of pork.

Beer-Basted Beef: Substitute a whole 2-pound bottom round roast for the pork. Substitute beef broth for the chicken broth and add 30 minutes to the cooking time. Add extra broth or water as needed during cooking.

Chinese Braising

- Western braising techniques involve browning meats in oil before adding liquid.

- In China, braising or "red cooking" means simmering meats or vegetables in a broth of soy sauce, broth, seasonings, and wine. (In this recipe we substitute beer for wine.)

- The result is fork-tender meat and a rich, red brown sauce. The style of cooking takes its name from the sauce's color.

- Some cooks save sauce from one braised dish to add richness to the next red-cooked dish.

Chinese Beer

- The Chinese have been brewing beer for 9,000 years, using a variety of grains, fruits, and herbs in the process.

- However, the most well-known Chinese beer, Tsingtao, pays homage to German brewmasters who established breweries in China around 1900.

- Most modern widely distributed Chinese beers resemble European pilsners, with a clear, pale gold color and crisp flavor.

- More limited-distribution beers include dark brews made from rice.

SLOW-COOKED BEEF STEW
Enjoy Chinese flavors without having to focus on a hot wok

Chinese braising or stewing doesn't usually involve browning meat in fat before adding liquid. Instead the beef or pork is simply simmered in a broth seasoned with soy sauce and other ingredients. However, this version of Chinese beef stew uses a slow cooker to achieve rich flavor and tenderness, with minimal hassle. In general, beef that's going in the slow cooker tastes better when it has been seared first. Since the wok has already been heated up, we also give the sauce a

bubbly head start before adding it all to a Crock-Pot or slow cooker. Put this dish to simmering just after noon and you'll enjoy a hearty supper that evening.

Yield: Serves 6

Ingredients

2 pounds beef brisket, trimmed and cut into 1¹/₂-inch cubes

1 teaspoon five-spice powder

¹/₂ teaspoon coarse salt

1 tablespoon cornstarch

2 tablespoons vegetable oil

2 leeks, trimmed and sliced

¹/₄ cup beef broth

3 tablespoons soy sauce

2 tablespoons hoisin sauce

2 tablespoons fermented black bean paste

3 tablespoons rice wine

1 teaspoon sugar

1 teaspoon hot chile paste

2 cloves garlic, minced

1 star anise

1 large carrot, sliced

1 large daikon radish, sliced

1 teaspoon dark sesame oil

Slow-Cooked Beef Stew

- Sprinkle beef with five-spice powder and salt. Coat with cornstarch.

- Place wok over high heat. Add oil. Working in batches, brown the beef in hot oil and remove to a slow cooker. Add leeks to wok and stir-fry 2 minutes.

- Add beef broth and stir to deglaze pan. Stir in soy sauce, hoisin sauce, black bean paste, wine, sugar, chile paste, and garlic. Bring to a boil.

- Pour sauce over beef. Add star anise, carrot, radish, and sesame oil. Cook on high 5 hours.

Slow-Cooked Eye Round Roast: Substitute a 2-pound eye round roast for the brisket in the recipe. Do not cut into pieces. Coat the whole roast with five-spice powder, salt, and cornstarch and brown in vegetable oil. Cook leeks and sauce ingredients in the wok. Place roast, sauce, and remaining ingredients in a slow cooker and cook on medium for 6 hours.

Slow-Cooked Beef Stew with Spring Vegetables: Prepare stew as directed, but omit daikon radish. Two hours before beef is cooked, add 8 ounces sliced mushrooms, 3 cups quartered pattypan squash, and 1 cup grape tomatoes to the slow cooker. Continue cooking until beef and vegetables are tender.

Prepare Vegetables

- In this stew, treat the daikon radish as you would a parsnip.

- Slice the root into ½-inch-thick pieces and stir to blend with the beef at the bottom of the slow cooker.

- Slice the carrot, or use baby carrots if you prefer, and stir to mix.

- The root vegetables will absorb the flavors of the sauce and beef as they cook, as well as add moisture and aromatic flavors to the stew.

Slow Cooking Meats

- Even on high, a slow cooker cooks foods at a temperature around 300°F.

- Perhaps more important, the cooker surrounds ingredients with an even heat that allows foods to simmer in their own juices.

- This moist cooking method

breaks down tough fibers and renders even tough cuts fork-tender.

- Slow cookers also can turn beef into a cauldron of mush. If you must leave your stew cooking longer than recommended, turn the setting to medium.

ROASTS & STEWS

BRAISED LAMB CHOPS
Lamb lovers will enjoy the Asian-influenced sauce in this easy dish

As discussed, Chinese braised meats don't usually start with a browning phase. Instead the meat is colored and tenderized by the dark soy sauce–infused braising liquid. The meat simmers in a way that resembles poaching.

When applied to lamb, this cooking method brings out the full flavor of boiled lamb, which isn't always pleasing to those who prefer ultramild-tasting chops. To compromise, we browned the chops in this recipe, giving the exterior a

nice caramelized crust. From there we added a braising liquid infused with soy, fennel, anise, ginger, and coriander.

If you would prefer a classic Chinese dish, just skip the pan-frying step. Stir-fry the mushrooms in half the oil, add the braising ingredients, and simmer the lamb for 30 to 40 minutes.

Yield: Serves 4

Ingredients

- **1 pound lamb chops**
- **2 tablespoons vegetable oil**
- **4 ounces sliced mushrooms**
- **2 green onions, coarsely chopped**
- **2 cloves garlic, chopped**
- **2 dried red chiles**
- **1 cup water**
- **3 tablespoons soy sauce**
- **2 tablespoons rice wine**
- **1 teaspoon minced ginger root**
- **1 teaspoon sugar**
- **1 whole star anise**
- **¼ teaspoon fennel seeds**
- **¼ teaspoon coriander**
- **1 teaspoon cornstarch, dissolved in 1 tablespoon cold water**
- **2 tablespoons minced chives**

Braised Lamb Chops

- Prepare lamb chops. Add mushrooms, green onions, garlic, and chiles. Stir-fry 2 minutes.

- Add water to skillet. Stir to deglaze pan. In a bowl, mix together soy sauce, wine, ginger, and sugar. Add to skillet.

- Bring sauce to a boil; reduce heat to medium. Return lamb to skillet in a single layer.

- Add star anise, fennel, and coriander to the sauce; cover. Cook 30 minutes, adding water as needed. Thicken sauce, garnish with chives, and serve.

Braised Veal Chops: Substitute veal loin chops for the lamb chops.

Braised Pork Chops: Substitute pork loin chops for the lamb chops. Omit the ginger, fennel, and coriander. Increase garlic to 3 cloves.

Prepare Lamb Chops

- For this dish you can use pricey eye-appealing rib chops or less expensive sirloin chops. Rinse lamb and pat dry.

- Place a large, deep skillet over high heat and add oil. When oil is hot, add the lamb; brown on each side.

- Remove lamb to a plate while stir-frying vegetables and adding sauce to the skillet.

- Return lamb to skillet, reduce heat to medium, cover, and cook as directed.

Thicken Sauce

- When lamb chops, vegetables, and sauce have cooked 30 minutes, remove skillet cover.

- Simmer lamb chops, uncovered, 10 minutes longer. Remove lamb to a serving platter.

- Bring sauce to a boil. Add dissolved cornstarch mixture to the sauce.

- Cook and stir the sauce until thick and bubbly. Spoon sauce over lamb chops, garnish with chives, and serve.

ROASTS & STEWS

TOFU & VEGETABLE STEW

Even vegetarians crave a nice hearty stew every now and then

This stew contains classic ingredients found in many beefy stews—with one exception: We've replaced the meat with tofu. Serve this stew with rice or noodles as a vegetarian entree, or offer it as a side dish in a meal that includes meat or fish entrees.

Although firm tofu cubes dominate this stew, those who don't happily embrace bean curd can also prepare the recipe with un-fried tofu crumbles, which will take on the appear-

ance and texture of ground beef or pork.

Yield: Serves 4–6

Ingredients

4 dried wood ear mushrooms

1 pound firm tofu, cut into 1-inch cubes

4 tablespoons vegetable oil

8 ounces white mushrooms, sliced

1 red bell pepper, cored and diced

2 cloves garlic, minced

1 rib celery, sliced

1 cup sliced parsnip or daikon radish

1 cup sliced carrots

1 cup bamboo shoots

1 cup straw mushrooms

4 tablespoons soy sauce

2 tablespoons oyster sauce

2 tablespoons rice wine

1/2 teaspoon hot chile paste, optional

1 teaspoon sugar

1 tablespoon dark sesame oil

1/2 cup water

Tofu and Vegetable Stew

- Soak wood ears in hot water 30 minutes. Drain, reserving ½ cup soaking liquid. Slice mushrooms. Drain tofu.

- Add oil to wok. Fry tofu in batches, browning on all sides. Set aside. Remove all but 2 tablespoons oil from wok.

- Stir-fry vegetables 2 minutes. Whisk together soy sauce, oyster sauce, wine, chile paste (if using), sugar, and sesame oil.

- Add sauce to wok, along with soaking liquid and water. Add tofu and simmer on medium 20 minutes, stirring occasionally.

Sweet Potato Stew: Substitute 1 pound of sweet potatoes, peeled and diced, for the tofu. Fry the sweet potato cubes as directed for the tofu. Continue the recipe as written, replacing the oyster sauce with hoisin sauce.

Tofu and Vegetable Stew with Noodles: Prepare the stew as directed, adding an extra cup of water or vegetable broth to the sauce. Cook 12 ounces of cellophane noodles separately, drain, and add to the hot stew.

Simmering Tofu

Adding Carrots

- Buy firm tofu for slow cooking and handle it gently.

- Frying tofu cubes before cooking in simmering broth helps keep them from disintegrating in the wok.

- Simmering allows the sauce to seep into the porous, mostly bland tofu, giving the tofu all the flavors of the liquid.

- All stews require stirring, but be very gentle when working with tofu. A gentle turn with chopsticks or a wooden spoon should be sufficient.

- It's virtually impossible to buy food from a corner Chinese restaurant outside China without finding carrots and celery in the vegetable mix.

- Carrots are an understandable adaptation to available ingredients. However, within China, they aren't routinely added to stews and stir-fries.

- When preparing Chinese dishes, use carrots for color and according to your own tastes.

- Cut carrots in harmony with other ingredients in the dish.

DRUNKEN CHICKEN

An extra dose of rice wine gives this classic chicken dish a jolt of flavor

Serve this wonderfully rich cold dish as an appetizer or summer luncheon entree. Chicken thighs with skin on give a level of flavor that stands up to chilling and can't be overpowered by the wine marinade. However, if you prefer a milder flavor, substitute boneless chicken breasts for the chicken thighs. Drunken Chicken can be the crowning touch on a bed of

mixed greens, lightly coated with a ginger-soy dressing, or a topping on a tangle of cold sesame noodles.
Yield: Serves 6

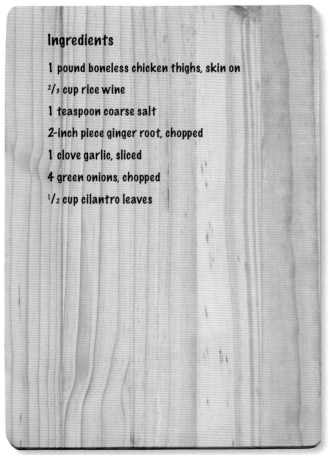

Ingredients

1 pound boneless chicken thighs, skin on

²/₃ cup rice wine

1 teaspoon coarse salt

2-inch piece ginger root, chopped

1 clove garlic, sliced

4 green onions, chopped

¹/₂ cup cilantro leaves

Drunken Chicken

- Rinse chicken thighs and place in a single layer in a shallow bowl. Combine wine, salt, ginger, garlic, and green onion. Pour over chicken; cover and refrigerate 12 hours, turning occasionally.

- Place chicken and marinade in a deep, heat-safe dish.

- Place a steaming rack in a wok and add water to a level just under the rack.

- Cover and steam 45 minutes. Remove chicken from steamer and place in a clean, deep dish.

- Strain marinade over chicken. Refrigerate overnight.

Drunken Turkey: Substitute 1 turkey breast half, skin on, bone removed, for the chicken thighs.

Not-So-Drunken Chicken: Substitute ⅔ cup nonalcoholic white wine for the rice wine.

Marinating Chicken

- Remember how Mom marinated chicken in salad dressing, then used the dressing as a baste?

- Depending on the timing and temperature, that could be dangerous. Raw chicken can contaminate marinades with bacteria.

- The only way to kill bacteria is to bring marinade to a full boil or hold it at a high temperature for an extended period.

- The marinade in this dish cooks with the chicken, killing bacteria. Never reuse marinade that has not been thoroughly cooked.

Preparing Chicken and Aspic

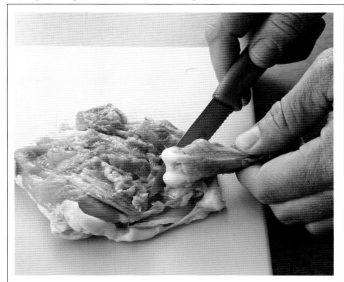

- After refrigerating overnight, the chicken marinade and cooking juices will have gelled into flavorful aspic.

- To serve the Drunken Chicken, first scrape off any fat that has risen to the top of the aspic.

- Pull the chicken from the aspic and cut into thin slices. Place the slices on a serving platter and sprinkle with cilantro.

- Turn the aspic onto a plate and cut into cubes. Arrange aspic around the sliced chicken and serve.

COLD DISHES

HACKED CHICKEN

Ordinary chicken salad won't seem as satisfying after this Chinese favorite

Cold plates rarely appear in Chinese restaurants in the West, so many Chinese food lovers are unaware of the extensive repertoire of Chinese cold dishes. In China, cold plates are served at the start of most banquets, and sometimes they form the basis for an entire meal. Dishes like Hacked Chicken, which may look like simple meat salads, can surprise and de-light taste buds with their complexity. In this case, the slightly sweet, slightly numbing sesame dressing transforms plain poached chicken into a dish you'll crave.

Yield: Serves 4–6

Ingredients

4 chicken breast halves

3 cloves garlic

2 green onions, trimmed

$1/3$ cup cilantro leaves

4 tablespoons sesame paste

3 tablespoons rice wine

3 tablespoons soy sauce

1 tablespoon rice wine vinegar

1 tablespoon dark sesame oil

2 tablespoons sugar

2 teaspoons hot chile oil

$1/2$ teaspoon Szechwan peppercorns, toasted

Salt to taste

6 cups leafy greens

Hacked Chicken

- Place chicken in a wok or saucepan with enough water to cover. Bring to a boil; reduce heat to medium.

- Poach chicken 30 minutes. Let stand in the cooking broth to cool; remove to a work surface and then shred. Place shreds in a bowl.

- Prepare the sauce. Toss chicken with sauce until chicken pieces are well coated.

- Add salt. Layer chicken over a plate of fresh spinach, shredded cabbage, or other greens and serve.

Hacked Duck: Substitute 1 pound cooked duck breast for the chicken.

Hacked Turkey: Turkey isn't a common Chinese ingredient, but this is a great way to use up Thanksgiving leftovers. Substitute 1 pound cooked, shredded turkey meat for the chicken.

Shred the Chicken

- Texture is essential to this dish. Although the name of the dish suggests chopped chicken, the meat is actually pulled.

- The chicken should be cooked just until no longer pink and allowed to cool in the cooking liquid.

- Place warm or room temperature chicken on a hard surface and pull the meat apart, with the grain, into long, thick shreds.

- The strips should be moist and thick enough to absorb the dressing.

Prepare the Sauce

- In a food processor bowl fitted with a metal blade, combine garlic, green onions, and cilantro.

- Pulse until finely chopped; remove to a bowl.

- Add sesame paste, wine, soy sauce, vinegar, sesame oil, sugar, chile oil, and peppercorns to the food processor. Pulse until smooth.

- Combine the sesame paste mixture with the herbs. Pour over the chicken and toss to coat.

COLD DISHES

SPICY GINGER BEEF SALAD

Move over steak Caesar, this salad is ready to take center plate

Hearty main-dish salads are more North American than Asian. However, this dish draws influences from several Chinese favorites, including orange beef, to create a satisfying luncheon entree or light supper.

Marinating overnight ensures the beef slices on this salad will be both tender and infused with flavor. Sear the steak quickly in a hot pan, and remember the residual heat will continue to cook the steak after it has been removed from the stove. Dress the steak while it's still warm, and serve immediately over cold, crisp greens.

Yield: Serves 4–6

Ingredients

1 pound sirloin steak

²/₃ cup plus 1 tablespoon vegetable oil, divided

²/₃ cup soy sauce, divided

¹/₃ cup orange juice

2 slices ginger root

1 onion, sliced

2 teaspoons grated ginger root

¹/₃ cup rice wine vinegar

1 teaspoon sugar

¹/₂ teaspoon hot chile oil

1 clove garlic, pressed

¹/₂ teaspoon hot pepper flakes

1 red bell pepper, cored and sliced

1 tablespoon sesame seeds

8 cups salad greens

1 cup diced cucumbers

1¹/₂ cups grape tomatoes, optional

1 green onion, minced

Spicy Ginger Beef Salad

- Place steak in a resealable plastic bag. Combine ⅓ cup vegetable oil, ⅓ cup soy sauce, orange juice, and ginger slices. Pour over beef; add onion.

- Marinate steak overnight. Sear drained steak in 1 tablespoon oil and slice.

- Whisk together remaining oil and soy sauce, grated ginger, vinegar, sugar, chile oil, garlic, and pepper flakes.

- Combine steak with bell pepper; toss with dressing. Sprinkle with sesame seeds. Layer over salad greens. Top with green onion.

Spicy Seared Tuna Salad: Substitute 1 pound of sushi-grade tuna for the beef. Prepare recipe as directed, but reduce marinating time to 30 minutes.

Spicy Seared Bison Salad: Substitute 1 pound of bison sirloin steak for the beef.

Marinate Steak

- Resealable plastic bags make marinating meats neat and easy.

- Slide the steak into a gallon-size bag. Whisk together marinade ingredients and carefully pour into the bag.

- Add any aromatic veg-

etables, like onion. Seal bag almost completely closed. Press excess air from bag and seal completely.

- Place sealed bag on a plate or in a shallow baking dish in the refrigerator. Every couple of hours, flip the bag over to redistribute the marinade.

Slice the Steak

- Remove steak from marinade, allowing excess marinade to drain from meat.

- Sear steak on both sides as directed. Place on a heat-safe cutting board or platter. Trim any thick strips of fat and discard.

- Working across the grain, slice steak into thin strips. Place strips into a shallow bowl with the red pepper.

- Add sauce to steak and peppers and toss until well coated. Layer over greens and vegetables.

COLD DISHES

COLD SESAME NOODLES
Cucumber cools the spicy sesame sauce in this Szechwan favorite

Many North Americans got their first taste of Szechwan cuisine by ordering a container of slurpy, spicy cold sesame noodles. In spite of the peppery kick, the peanut butter–like flavor of the noodles (in fact, some chefs actually use peanut butter in the recipe) proves irresistible to young and old diners alike. The secret to making really good sesame noodles is creating a smooth emulsion of oil, sesame paste, vinegar, and seasonings.

This version is mildly spicy and mildly tart. If you like more strongly flavored noodles, by all means increase the vinegar and chile paste in the recipe.

Yield: Serves 4–6

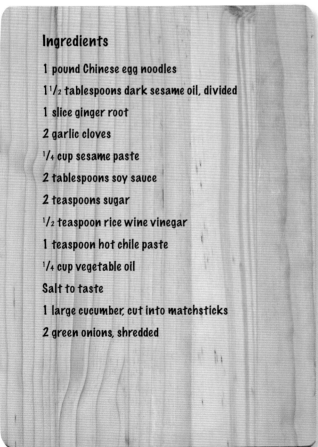

Ingredients

1 pound Chinese egg noodles

1¹/₂ tablespoons dark sesame oil, divided

1 slice ginger root

2 garlic cloves

¹/₄ cup sesame paste

2 tablespoons soy sauce

2 teaspoons sugar

¹/₂ teaspoon rice wine vinegar

1 teaspoon hot chile paste

¹/₄ cup vegetable oil

Salt to taste

1 large cucumber, cut into matchsticks

2 green onions, shredded

Cold Sesame Noodles

- Bring a large pot of water to a boil. Add noodles; cook until tender, about 3 to 5 minutes.

- Drain noodles well and toss with ½ tablespoon sesame oil. Cover and refrigerate until chilled.

- In a food processor, combine remaining sesame oil, ginger root, garlic cloves, sesame paste, soy sauce, sugar, vinegar, chile paste, and vegetable oil. Pulse until smooth.

- Pour sauce over noodles; toss to coat evenly. Add salt. Serve garnished with cucumbers and green onions.

Cold Sesame Noodles with Chicken: Add 2 cups cooked, shredded chicken to the cold noodles. Prepare sauce as directed and toss with chicken and noodles.

Cold Sesame Noodles with Cabbage: You won't find this variation listed among classic dishes, but shredded cabbage and shredded daikon radish transform this recipe into a Chinese-style cold pasta salad. Simply add 2 cups finely shredded cabbage and ½ cup shredded daikon radish to the completed noodle dish. Toss well.

Chinese Sesame Paste

Tossing the Noodles

- Chinese sesame paste is made from toasted sesame seeds, for a rich, distinctive flavor.

- Tahini—which is Middle Eastern–style sesame paste—is made from hulled, raw sesame seeds. It is not a good substitute for the Chinese product.

- If you don't have Chinese sesame paste on hand, or can't find it at the supermarket, grab a jar of natural-style smooth peanut butter.

- Mix a small amount of sesame oil into the peanut butter and use the mixture in the same quantity.

- Start with a big bowl. When tossing ingredients into pasta, you need plenty of room to move.

- Using two large forks, tongs, or chopsticks, reach into the bottom of the bowl and pull the ingredients from the bottom to the top.

- Repeat the motion several times, each time distributing more of the sauce and solids through the pasta.

- Tossing differs from stirring or mixing; the process incorporates air into the noodles, keeping individual strands separate.

COLD DISHES

CUCUMBER SALAD

Welcome summer with this elegant, flavor-infused side dish

Cucumbers originated in India and have been cultivated throughout Asia for more than 2,000 years. The Chinese love cucumbers and use them in cooked dishes as well as salads and pickles. Both seedless and seeded varieties are grown throughout the country.

The cucumbers in this dish readily absorb the sweet-tart dressing and take on the crisp texture of a bread-and-butter pickle. Serve cold Cucumber Salad as a nibble with a crisp white wine or citrusy summer cocktails. It makes a nice accompaniment to a hot pot meal.

While not exactly Chinese, these cucumbers also go very well with smoked salmon or tuna tartare.

Yield: Serves 4–6

Ingredients

2 seedless cucumbers, peeled

2 teaspoons coarse salt

1 tablespoon sugar

3 tablespoons soy sauce

2 tablespoons rice wine vinegar

1 tablespoon vegetable oil

½ teaspoon dark sesame oil

½ teaspoon grated ginger root

2 tablespoons chopped cilantro

Cucumber Salad

- Cut cucumbers in half lengthwise, then slice the halves into ⅓-inch slices. Sprinkle with salt and sugar, and toss to mix. Cover and refrigerate 1 hour.

- Place cucumbers in a colander to drain; press to release more moisture. Return cucumbers to the bowl.

- Whisk together soy sauce, vinegar, vegetable oil, sesame oil, and ginger. Pour over the cucumbers and toss well.

- Let salad stand briefly to absorb dressing. Sprinkle cucumbers with cilantro and serve.

Shrimp and Cucumber Salad: Toss 8 ounces cooked, peeled, and deveined shrimp with the cucumbers and dressing.

Cucumber Salad with Peanuts: Prepare salad as directed. Sprinkle ½ cup chopped peanuts over the salad before serving.

Cucumber Varieties

- Fat, juicy, seedy cucumbers are the most aromatic and flavorful. They're also the preferred cucumber for pickling.

- That said, they don't hold up very well once cut, and some cooks object to the tough seeds.

- English-style hothouse cucumbers solve that problem. These long, thin cucumbers have dense flesh and very small seed pockets.

- Most Asian-grown table cucumbers resemble English cucumbers, though are usually shorter in length.

Pick a Pickle

- Although Cucumber Salad doesn't technically qualify as a pickle—because the dish isn't actually preserved—it does play a similar roll on the table.

- China actually has a long history of preserving vegetables in vinegar or salt brine.

- The vegetables are then used as accompaniments to other dishes or as ingredients in soups and stir-fries.

- Pickled vegetables can include cucumbers, radishes, thick mustard green stems, cabbage, and peppers.

COLD DISHES

TOFU SALAD

Silken tofu blends with crisp vegetables in this surprising salad

Silken tofu only looks cool and creamy in this dish. In fact the bean curd absorbs the tart, sweet, and spicy dressing. One bite will give your palate a kick, which can only be cooled by the surrounding crispy vegetables.

This salad is light but filling. Make no mistake, however. Tofu takes center plate in this dish, which is for tofu lovers only. Those who don't really embrace the texture and chameleon-like flavor of bean curd might want to consider one of the non-tofu variations, such as potato salad or beet salad.
Yield: Serves 4–6

Ingredients

1 pound silken tofu

2 tablespoons soy sauce

2 tablespoons dark sesame oil

1 tablespoon rice wine vinegar

1 tablespoon rice wine

1 teaspoon hot chile paste

1 teaspoon sugar

1 cup shredded daikon radish

6 cups shredded napa cabbage

1 cup peanuts, chopped

2 green onions, minced

Tofu Salad

- Drain cold tofu and cut the block in half lengthwise. Slice each half crosswise into ½-inch-thick slices.

- In a bowl, whisk together soy sauce, sesame oil, vinegar, wine, chile paste, and sugar. Prepare the tofu.

- Toss together the radish and cabbage. Arrange to cover a serving plate.

- Layer the dressed tofu slices over the shredded vegetables. Sprinkle with peanuts and green onions. Serve immediately.

Potato Salad: Substitute 1½ pounds peeled, boiled, and sliced red potatoes for the tofu.

Beet Salad: Substitute 1½ pounds peeled, lightly boiled, and sliced baby beets for the tofu.

Prepare the Tofu

- Place the tofu slices in a baking dish or large, shallow casserole.

- Drizzle dressing evenly over the tofu.

- Gently jostle the tofu to distribute the dressing without breaking up the slices.

- Use a spatula to transfer the slices from the baking dish to the serving platter.

Crush the Peanuts

- Oh sure, you could just put the peanuts in the food processor. But what fun would that be?

- Instead, try this low-tech method of coarsely chopping nuts.

- Pour the peanuts into a resealable plastic bag; press the air out and seal the bag. Place the bag on a work surface.

- Using a meat mallet or rolling pin, quickly and lightly strike the bag, crushing the peanuts. Use the peanuts immediately or refrigerate until later.

COLD DISHES

JIAOZI DUMPLINGS

Make these New Year favorites the easy way, or the authentic way, with this recipe

Many cooks have a horror—born of too many leaden kitchen experiments—of making pasta and bread doughs. We understand. True Jiaozi dumplings are made with hand-rolled warm-water dough. The dough is kneaded until pliable, then rolled, trimmed, shaped, and filled. If that seems like a daunting task, fear not. Our main recipe allows for cheating by us-

ing wonton wrappers. But if you're adventurous, or have a taste for authentic Jiaozi, the instructions are here. Either way you'll have a New Year dish to savor.

Yield: Serves 6

Ingredients

8 ounces lean ground pork

Salt and white pepper to taste

1 teaspoon dark sesame oil

1 green onion, chopped

$1/2$ cup chopped napa cabbage

$1/2$ teaspoon coarse salt

$1/4$ teaspoon five-spice powder

24 small wonton wrappers

1 teaspoon cornstarch

Jiaozi Dumplings

- Combine pork, salt, pepper, and sesame oil. Prepare green onion and cabbage.

- Mix pork with green onion, cabbage, and salt mixture, plus five-spice powder. Freeze 20 minutes.

- Lay a wonton wrapper on a work surface. Place a

teaspoon of filling at the center. Fold and seal with cornstarch.

- Bring a pot of cold water to a boil. Add some of the dumplings, reduce heat to simmer and cover. Cook 5 minutes. Remove dumplings. Repeat with remaining dumplings.

• • • • RECIPE VARIATIONS • • • •

Jiaozi with Shrimp and Scallops: Combine 6 ounces peeled, deveined shrimp and 4 ounces scallops in a food processor; pulse to mince. Drain well and use in place of the pork.

Jiaozi with Beef: Substitute 8 ounces finely ground round for the pork. Stir in 1 teaspoon soy sauce and continue recipe as directed.

Press Liquid from Cabbage

- Place green onion, cabbage, and coarse salt in a food processor. Pulse until finely chopped, but not pureed.

- Place cabbage mixture in a strainer over a sink or bowl. Press with a paper towel to remove excess liquid.

- Add cabbage mixture to the pork mixture and stir well to combine.

Dumpling Technique II

- To make warm-water dough Jiaozi, mix together 1½ cups flour with a generous pinch of salt in a large bowl. Slowly stir in ¾ cup warm water.

- Stir until mixture forms a dough. Knead 20 times on a floured surface. Let dough rest 40 minutes.

- Roll dough into two tubes. Slice each into 12 to 14 pieces. Roll each piece into a circle.

- Add filling and fold dough to form a half-moon shape. Pleat or crimp edges and press to seal.

NEW YEAR SALMON SALAD

Fish represent prosperity and health in this adaptation of a New Year's tradition

In China and the Chinese communities of Southeast Asia, New Year fish salads resemble ceviche. That is, the fish is raw but infused with an acidic dressing. This version is safer, uses readily available wild-caught or farm-raised salmon, and can be served to guests of all ages. That said, we've also included a raw variation of the salad for more adventurous diners.

You don't have to wait until Chinese New Year to serve this dish, which makes an excellent luncheon entree. Feel free to vary the selection of greens and garnishes.

Yield: Serves 4

Ingredients

1 pound salmon fillet, poached

1 tablespoon honey

1 teaspoon hot mustard

1/4 cup plus 1 teaspoon soy sauce, divided

1/4 cup rice wine

2 tablespoons rice wine vinegar

1 tablespoon sugar

1/2 teaspoon grated ginger root

1 tablespoon vegetable oil

1 teaspoon dark sesame oil

1/2 teaspoon pepper

6 cups fresh baby spinach

2 green onions, shredded

1 pomelo

1/3 cup minced cilantro

New Year Salmon Salad

- Prepare salmon. In a small bowl combine 1/4 cup soy sauce, wine, vinegar, sugar, ginger, and oils. Whisk in pepper.

- Mix spinach and green onions on a platter. Drizzle greens with dressing mixture and toss to coat. Place salmon on the greens.

- Peel and section pomelo. Remove membranes and cut sections into pieces.

- Distribute fruit around the salmon on the platter. Sprinkle with cilantro and serve.

• • • • RECIPE VARIATIONS • • • •

Tuna New Year Salad: Thinly slice 1 pound raw sushi-grade tuna. Combine all dressing ingredients from the honey to the pepper. Whisk well, then divide in half. Add 1 tablespoon lemon or lime juice to half the dressing. Toss citrus dressing. Refrigerate 20 minutes. Toss the remaining ingredients with the other half of the dressing. Layer the marinated tuna over the salad and serve.

Seared Salmon or Tuna Salad: Sear 1 pound boneless, skinless salmon or tuna in a hot skillet with 1 tablespoon oil. Fish should be rare at the center. Baste with honey-mustard mixture. Thinly slice. Prepare salad according to recipe, but substitute drained mandarin oranges for the pomelo, and sprinkle peanuts or cashews to garnish.

Prepare Salmon

- Poach salmon, skin side down, in simmering water just until opaque, about 10 minutes.

- Remove salmon to a platter and let stand until cool enough to handle.

- Using a sharp paring knife or fish knife, cut the skin away at the corner. Pull the skin, using the knife in a gentle sawing motion to sever connective fibers.

- Combine honey, mustard, and 1 teaspoon soy sauce. Lightly brush the top of the salmon with the honey mixture. Cover and refrigerate until chilled.

Prepare Pomelo

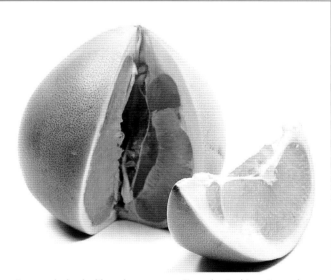

- A pomelo looks like a huge grapefruit and is one of the cultivars that contributed to the modern grapefruit.

- It is native to Southeast Asia and appears in Chinese cold plates and desserts. The flavor is milder and slightly sweeter than grapefruit.

- Pomelo rind is extremely thick, but easy to peel. Slice the pomelo vertically into quarters. With a paring knife, cut through the pith at a corner and remove the peel.

- Pull the inner membranes and cut the slices into chunks.

NEW YEAR CAKE

Bribe the Kitchen God with this relatively easy version of New Year cake

According to Chinese legend, the Kitchen God knows all about a family's behavior during the year. When New Year approaches, it's his job to take final inventory then report back about domestic goings-on. The only acceptable way to sweeten the Kitchen God's perceptions, it is said, is to feed him New Year cake or sticky cake made with glutinous rice flour and dried fruits. New Year cake is steamed and often cut into small slices, which are then fried until crispy outside. Different families have different preferences for fruit fillings, and some New Year cakes get a fancy layer of fondant over the top. This recipe errs on the side of simplicity and sweetness.

Yield: Serves 8

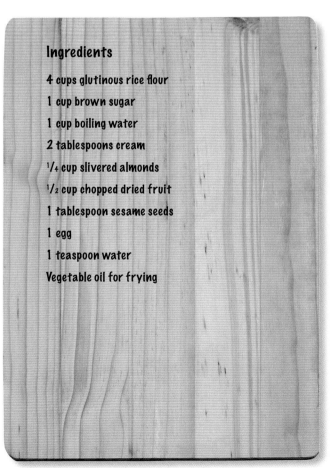

Ingredients

4 cups glutinous rice flour

1 cup brown sugar

1 cup boiling water

2 tablespoons cream

1/4 cup slivered almonds

1/2 cup chopped dried fruit

1 tablespoon sesame seeds

1 egg

1 teaspoon water

Vegetable oil for frying

New Year Cake

- Place flour in a large bowl. Make a well at the center. In another bowl, dissolve brown sugar in boiling water. Pour sugar water into the well and stir to combine.

- Knead dough and add almonds and fruit. Grease an 8-inch, deep, round casserole. Place dough in the dish and sprinkle with sesame seeds.

- Place dish on a steamer rack, cover, and steam over boiling water 1 hour.

- Unmold cake and cool to room temperature. Refrigerate until ready to fry.

···· RECIPE VARIATIONS ····

Cherry Almond New Year Cake: Substitute ½ cup dried cherries and ¼ cup chopped fresh cherries for the dried fruit. Omit sesame seeds and add ½ teaspoon of almond extract.

Kids' Chocolate and Peanut Butter Chip New Year Cake: Substitute ½ cup chocolate chips and ½ cup peanut butter chips for the almonds and dried fruit. Dust the fried cake strips with a generous amount of confectioner's sugar.

Knead the Dough

- Place dough on a work surface and lightly knead.

- Add cream as needed to make the dough more pliable.

- Add almonds and dried fruit, a little at a time, while kneading dough.

- Work the dough to make sure the almonds and fruit are evenly distributed.

Serve the Cake

- Place chilled cake on a hard surface and cut into quarters. Cut quarters horizontally into three layers, then cut each layer into thin strips.

- Whisk together egg and water. Dip strips of cake in the egg wash.

- Add 2 inches vegetable oil to a wok or skillet. Turn heat to high.

- When oil is hot, fry cake strips a few at a time until nicely browned. Serve immediately.

ALMOST DRAGON BOAT DUMPLINGS
Pay homage to China's annual "double five" festival with these wraps

On the fifth day of the fifth month of the lunar calendar, China celebrates the Dragon Boat Festival. This summer solstice fete is known by several names in Asia, but Dragon Boat Festival is best known in the West. The name pays homage to one of the most popular festival events: dragon boat races. Dragon boats are elaborately carved sculls manned by precision row-

ing teams. Dumplings are the snack of the day; they come in both savory and sweet varieties. Authentic dumplings are wrapped in bamboo leaves for steaming. Since bamboo leaves can be hard to come by, we made these with cabbage leaves. Corn husks and banana leaves are other alternatives.
Yield: Serves 8

Almost Dragon Boat Dumplings

Ingredients

4 ounces minced raw chicken breast

2 ounces ground pork

4 ounces shiitake mushrooms, minced

1 tablespoon soy sauce

1 teaspoon sesame oil

1/4 teaspoon grated ginger root

1/4 teaspoon hot chile paste

1 egg, beaten

3 cups cooked glutinous rice, chilled

8 whole napa cabbage leaves

- Combine chicken, pork, mushrooms, soy sauce, sesame oil, ginger root, and chile paste in a bowl. Add egg and mix well. Cover and refrigerate.

- Spread rice on a baking sheet lined with waxed paper. Blanch cabbage leaves.

- Place a rounded teaspoon of chicken mixture on a section of rice. With wet hands, mound the rice, forming a triangle with the chicken mixture at the center.

- Wrap the rice dumpling in a cabbage leaf. Steam the packets over boiling water 20 minutes.

• • • • RECIPE VARIATIONS • • • •

Sweet Bean Dumplings: Replace the filling with 1⅓ cups sweet red bean paste. Prepare the dumplings as directed, using bamboo leaves or corn husks to wrap the dumplings.

Walnut-Date Dumplings: Soak 1 cup dates in cold water for 30 minutes. Drain the softened dates. Combine dates, 1 cup walnut pieces, and 1 teaspoon honey in a food processor. Pulse until mixture is finely ground. Use in place of meat filling. Steam the dumplings using corn husks, banana leaves, or bamboo leaves to wrap.

Prepare the Rice

- Glutinous rice, or sticky rice, must be soaked 4 to 6 hours or overnight before cooking.

- Place 2 cups glutinous rice in a bowl with enough water to cover by a few inches. Soak 4 to 6 hours, then drain.

- Place the wet rice in a covered, heat-safe bowl. Place on a steaming rack in a wok over simmering water.

- Steam the rice 30 to 40 minutes or until tender. Chill before using in this recipe.

Wrap the Dumplings

- Blanch cabbage leaves just until flexible. (If using corn husks or other dried leaves, soak in warm water.)

- Rinse the leaves in cold water and shake off excess liquid.

- Place a triangle-shaped dumpling at one end of the cabbage leaf and fold the cabbage tightly over the dumpling, moving from one side to the other like you're folding a flag.

- Tie the wrapped dumpling with kitchen twine and steam 20 minutes.

LONG LIFE NOODLES

Long noodles mean longevity—in life, in marriage, in happiness

No Chinese birthday or New Year celebration would be complete without a dish of noodles, boiled straight from the package or straight from the pulling table, uncut. Noodles symbolize long life, which can be interpreted as good luck. Hand-pulled noodles, once common only in China, are now available in noodle shops around the world. These are especially valued because the dough is turned and pulled, folded and twisted into long, long strands of fresh wheat noodles.

The noodles are then dropped into boiling broth, where they cook quickly. Vegetables, meats, and seasonings are then added to the broth to make a delicious dinner course or whole meal.

Whether you live in an area where you can buy hand-pulled noodles, or just rely on dried noodles from the supermarket, this recipe will make you feel lucky.

Yield: Serves 4–6

Ingredients

1 pound Chinese egg noodles

8 cups chicken broth

$1/3$ cup soy sauce

2 tablespoons rice wine

1 teaspoon sesame oil

1 cup shredded cooked chicken

$1/2$ cup minced Smithfield-type ham

1 tablespoon cornstarch dissolved in 2 tablespoons cold water

2 eggs

Pepper or hot chile oil to taste

2 green onions, trimmed and shredded

Long Life Noodles

- Cook unbroken noodles in boiling water for 3 to 5 minutes or until tender. Drain and rinse.

- In a wok or soup pot, combine broth, soy sauce, wine, and oil. Bring to a boil. Reduce heat to medium; stir in chicken and ham. Simmer 10 minutes.

- Return to a boil. Stir in dissolved cornstarch. Reduce heat to simmer. Add eggs. Add pepper or chile oil.

- Place noodles in a serving bowl. Ladle broth over noodles and garnish with green onions. Serve immediately.

•••• RECIPE VARIATIONS ••••

Long Life Noodles II: Add 1½ cups coarsely chopped bok choy to the broth just as it begins to boil. Substitute shredded pork for the chicken. Follow the recipe as directed, omitting the eggs.

Vegetarian Long Life Noodles: Substitute vegetable broth for the chicken broth and 1 cup diced firm tofu for the chicken. Omit the ham and add ½ cup shredded daikon radish.

Mince the Ham

- In Chinese cooking, as in many cuisines, ham is used as a condiment or flavoring.

- China's prized Yunnan-style ham is dry cured and salty, much like American Smithfield or country-style ham.

- To get the most impact from the ham, a lean slice or piece should be trimmed of fat, then finely minced before being stirred into the soup.

- If you don't have time to mince the ham by hand (which is preferred), you can chop a few pieces in a food processor.

Add the Eggs

- The eggs in this recipe should create smooth ribbons moving in and around the noodles.

- Beat the eggs with 1 tablespoon water until light and fluffy.

- Stir the simmering broth. As you stir with one hand, slowly pour the eggs into broth in an even stream.

- As the eggs cook, ribbons should appear in the soup. Give the soup one last stir, add pepper or chile oil, and serve.

EASY MOON CAKES

The Mid-Autumn Festival brings out moon watchers—and delicious moon cakes

The Mid-Autumn Festival pays homage to the Goddess of Immortality, also known as the Moon Goddess. In her honor—and some say to commemorate a political uprising—the Chinese have been eating moon cakes for at least 1,500 years.

Moon cakes are actually filled pastries, and almost every region of the country has a preferred style. Some have flaky shells, others are chewy, and still others resemble a sweet piecrust. Traditional fillings include red bean paste, lotus seed paste, sweet taro paste, dates, and nuts. Pastry shops often make the cakes in molds that imprint elaborate floral designs. At home you could use a cookie stamp.

Yield: Serves 18

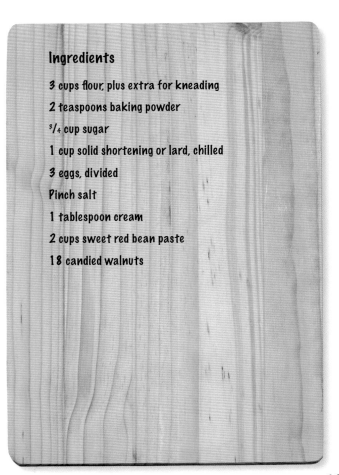

Ingredients

3 cups flour, plus extra for kneading

2 teaspoons baking powder

³/₄ cup sugar

1 cup solid shortening or lard, chilled

3 eggs, divided

Pinch salt

1 tablespoon cream

2 cups sweet red bean paste

18 candied walnuts

Easy Moon Cakes

- Combine flour, baking powder, and sugar in a bowl. Whisk to combine, breaking up lumps. Cut in shortening.

- Whisk together 2 eggs, salt, and cream. Add to flour mixture and stir until a sticky dough forms. Place dough on a floured surface and knead until pliable.

- Divide dough in half and roll into two tubes. Slice each into 18 pieces. Assemble 18 moon cakes.

- Place cakes on a baking sheet lined with nonstick foil. Bake at 350°F until golden, about 30 minutes.

• • • • RECIPE VARIATIONS • • • •

Yam-Filled Moon Cakes: Prepare moon cake dough as directed. Combine 1¾ cups mashed cooked sweet potatoes, ⅓ cup brown sugar, 1 teaspoon grated orange zest, and 1 egg. Substitute the sweet potato mixture for the red bean paste.

Almond-Filled Moon Cakes: Prepare moon cake dough as directed. Combine 1½ cups almond paste with ½ cup sugar, 2 eggs, and 2 tablespoons cream or coconut milk. Mix until smooth; refrigerate until chilled. Use almond paste mixture in place of red bean paste.

Combine Flour and Shortening

- Combine dry ingredients in a bowl. Whisk to combine and break up any lumps.

- Add cold shortening all at once. Using a pastry blender or two knives, cut into the shortening, gradually combining it with the dry ingredients.

- Keep working on the mixture, using short, quick strokes, until no large clumps of shortening remain.

- When the mixture resembles coarse meal, add egg mixture as directed.

Assemble Moon Cakes

- Cover dough with a damp towel to prevent drying. Remove one piece and place on a lightly floured surface.

- Press dough into a flat circle. Place a ball of bean paste and a walnut at the center.

- Press another slice of dough into a circle. Place the second circle on top of the first. Press the edges of the circles together.

- Beat remaining egg with 1 teaspoon water. Brush the tops of the cakes with the egg wash; place on baking sheet.

BEEF HOT POT

Dramatic, delicious, and low-fat—what more could you ask of a dinner party entree?

Nomadic tribes of northern China get credit for inventing the hot pot. By cooking the "meat of the day" in an iron caldron of water over a campfire, these culinary pioneers enjoyed an easy, moveable feast. The trick to a successful hot pot meal is to keep the broth simmering and to use very thin slices of meat. Thinly sliced meats cook quickly without drying out

and without lowering the temperature of the broth.

The classic hot pot vessel is a cast-iron ring with a chimney rising through the center. Hot coals or solid fuel in the base of the chimney keeps the water in the ring simmering. However, any fondue pot with a good heat source can be used.
Yield: Serves 6

Ingredients

1 1/2 pounds flank steak

1/2 cup soy sauce, divided

1 tablespoon rice wine vinegar

1 tablespoon dark sesame oil

1/2 teaspoon sugar

1 red bell pepper, cored and cut into strips

1 yellow bell pepper, cored and cut into strips

1 pound white mushrooms, cleaned and halved

2 cups green beans, trimmed

6 green onions, trimmed

6 cups beef broth

4 slices ginger root

Hoisin sauce

Hot chile paste

Sesame paste

Beef Hot Pot

- Freeze beef until firm, but not frozen—about 30 minutes. Cut across the grain into paper-thin slices.

- Combine beef with ¼ cup soy sauce, vinegar, sesame oil, and sugar. Cover, and refrigerate 30 minutes.

- Arrange vegetables and

beef on platters. In a saucepan, combine broth with remaining soy sauce and ginger. Bring to a boil, reduce heat, and simmer 10 minutes.

- Pour broth into hot pot. Place bowls of hoisin sauce and chile paste on the table, along with platters.

• • • • RECIPE VARIATIONS • • • •

Venison Hot Pot: Substitute 1½ pounds marinated venison steak for the flank steak.

Beef Tenderloin Hot Pot: Substitute 1½ pounds filet mignon for the flank steak. Replace green beans with vertically halved baby zucchini.

Arrange Raw Ingredients

- Arrange hot pot ingredients on your table in a manner that is both attractive and safe.

- Always keep raw meats and juices separate from vegetables. Divide sliced beef between two or more plates within easy reach.

- Arrange vegetables on platters.

- Each diner should have a plate for cooked meat and vegetables, individual bowls of dipping sauces, as well as long chopsticks or forks for cooking beef and vegetables and separate utensils for eating.

Prepare the Broth

- A rich broth cooks and flavors the ingredients.

- In a stockpot, combine a defatted broth made from beef and roasted beef bones with soy sauce and ginger.

- Bring to a rolling boil, then reduce heat and simmer 10 minutes. Carefully ladle the hot broth into the heated fondue or hot pot.

- Starting with a broth that is already hot ensures that diners can begin cooking immediately. It also eliminates any risk of the beef remaining at room temperature too long.

MONGOLIAN LAMB HOT POT
Serve this hearty lamb dish at a cool-weather dinner party

In Northern and Western China, lamb is the preferred, and most common, red meat. This recipe combines lean lamb with bold flavors like vinegar, cabbage, and green onion.

The dish is also a complete meal, with cellophane noodles added to the broth at the end of hot pot cooking. The broth, additionally flavored by the dipped and cooked ingredients, becomes a flavorful noodle soup.

At family meals in China, diners will sometimes eat soup directly from the hot pot, using it as a communal soup dish. That's probably a little too much togetherness for most households, so ladling soup into bowls is recommended. If the cellophane noodles prove unwieldy, you can always cut them with kitchen shears before adding them to the soup.
Yield: Serves 8

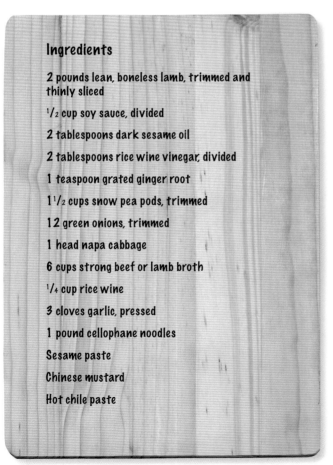

Ingredients

2 pounds lean, boneless lamb, trimmed and thinly sliced

$^1/_2$ cup soy sauce, divided

2 tablespoons dark sesame oil

2 tablespoons rice wine vinegar, divided

1 teaspoon grated ginger root

$1^1/_2$ cups snow pea pods, trimmed

12 green onions, trimmed

1 head napa cabbage

6 cups strong beef or lamb broth

$^1/_4$ cup rice wine

3 cloves garlic, pressed

1 pound cellophane noodles

Sesame paste

Chinese mustard

Hot chile paste

Mongolian Lamb Hot Pot

- Place lamb in a bowl with ¼ cup soy sauce, sesame oil, 1 tablespoon vinegar, and grated ginger. Cover and refrigerate 30 minutes.

- Prepare vegetables. In a stockpot, combine broth, remaining soy sauce, remaining vinegar, wine, and garlic. Bring to a boil. Pour broth into hot pot.

- Arrange lamb slices on a platter. Place lamb, vegetables, and dipping sauces on the table.

- After guests cook lamb and vegetables, stir prepared cellophane noodles into the hot pot.

Beef Hot Pot with Noodles: Substitute sliced beef sirloin steak for the lamb.

Pork Hot Pot with Noodles: Substitute boneless pork tenderloin for the lamb. Make sure broth is always simmering hot and instruct diners to cook pork slices thoroughly before eating.

HOT POTS

Prepare Vegetables

- Arrange snow pea pods and green onions on one or two platters.

- On a cutting board, trim the stem end from a well-rinsed and drained napa cabbage and discard.

- Slice the cabbage in half vertically. Slice each half horizontally in 1-inch-thick slices.

- Add the slices to the veg-etable platter, being careful to hold the slices together.

Cook Noodles

- While diners are cooking lamb and vegetables in the broth, soak cellophane noodles in a bowl of hot water 10 minutes; drain.

- If needed, replenish the hot pot with more broth from the stockpot.

- Add softened cellophane noodles to the hot pot and stir with chopsticks until tender.

- Ladle noodles and broth into each diner's bowl.

195

SEAFOOD HOT POT

The aroma of cooking scallops, shrimp, and fish makes this seaside feast irresistible

Coastal residents know the scent of a shrimp boil can draw neighbors from around the block. This seafood hot pot works the same way, only on a more limited scale. Use only hyper-fresh, well-chilled fish and shellfish for dipping, and instruct diners to simmer their fresh catch in broth just until the flesh is opaque. Flavorful claw crabmeat creates a rich soup, ready

to be fortified with cellophane noodles. For a small gathering, consider giving each guest a small wire basket strainer for cooking the hot pot ingredients. This should make the process move a little quicker, and broken fish pieces won't fall to the bottom of the pot.

Yield: Serves 6–8

Ingredients

4 dried wood ear mushrooms

8 ounces sea scallops

8 ounces shrimp, peeled and deveined

8 ounces sliced fresh halibut or sea bass

8 ounces white mushrooms, halved

12 baby bok choy, trimmed and halved

6 cups chicken or shrimp broth

2 tablespoons soy sauce

2 tablespoons rice wine

3 slices ginger root

1 teaspoon lemon zest

1 teaspoon dark sesame oil

4 ounces shell-free claw crabmeat

12 ounces cellophane noodles

¹/₃ cup cilantro, minced

2 green minced onions

Rice wine vinegar

Soy sauce

Sesame oil

Seafood Hot Pot

- Soak wood ears in hot water 30 minutes; drain and finely chop. Prepare seafood; place on a platter. Place white mushrooms and bok choy on another platter.

- In a saucepan, bring broth, soy sauce, wine, ginger, and lemon zest to a boil. Reduce heat and simmer 10

minutes. Stir in sesame oil, wood ears, and crabmeat.

- Pour broth into hot pot. Allow guests to cook ingredients.

- Add softened noodles. Serve noodles and broth with cilantro and green onion.

Fish Ball Hot Pot: In place of raw fish and seafood, set out platters of fish, pork, and shrimp balls to drop in the hot pot. To make fish or shrimp balls, combine 8 ounces firm white fish or shrimp with 2 tablespoons brown sugar, 1 egg white, and ¼ cup arrowroot or cornstarch in a food processor with a bit of minced green onion or chives, salt, and pepper. Pulse until a smooth paste forms.

Refrigerate until firm. Shape into balls and poach in boiling water for 5 minutes.

Hot Pot with Egg Noodles: In place of cellophane noodles, drop 12 ounces slightly undercooked egg noodles into the hot broth. Serve broth and noodles as soon as the egg noodles are hot and tender.

Prepare Seafood

- Seafood, meat, and poultry should be thinly sliced or cut into small pieces so the ingredients can be easily held in the broth with chopsticks and quickly and evenly cooked.

- Before bringing ingredients to the table, slice scallops in half crosswise to create two even discs.

- Likewise, cut the shrimp in half lengthwise, making two pieces that are as long, but half as thick as a whole shrimp.

- Cut or slice the fish into small cubes, depending on their firmness and texture.

Cooking Times

- Seafood cooks quickly in a hot pot, as long as the broth remains simmering.

- Cook shrimp and scallops 20 to 30 seconds in the broth.

- Fish cubes may take 15 to 25 seconds. At 15 seconds, diced tuna will be rare in the center.

- Be careful to allow the broth to cook at a full simmer for a few minutes after the last bit of raw fish or seafood has been added and before ladling the broth into bowls.

CHICKEN, HAM, & SHRIMP HOT POT
Smokey, sweet, and tender elements give this meal universal appeal

The wonderful thing about cooking with a hot pot is it gives the opportunity to offer a variety of ingredients in one dish, without having everything meld into a stew.

Chicken, Ham, and Shrimp Hot Pot is a perfect example of this, with the distinctive flavors of each ingredient complementing one another and flavoring the broth. When preparing the ingredients, make sure the shrimp and chicken are of comparable thickness so both will cook evenly and in the

same amount of time. If necessary, slice the shrimp in half lengthwise. The ham, which brings the most intense flavor to the pot, should be presented in ultrathin slices. Finally, don't add much salt, if any, to the broth. Between the soy sauce and ham, the liquid should be salty enough.

Yield: Serves 8

Ingredients

3 dried wood ear mushrooms

1 pound boneless chicken, sliced

1/2 pound Smithfield ham, thinly sliced

1 pound large shrimp, peeled and deveined

1 pound white mushrooms, halved

1 bunch Chinese broccoli or broccoli rabe

6 leeks, trimmed and halved

6 cups strong chicken broth

2 tablespoons soy sauce

1 tablespoon rice wine

1 teaspoon rice wine vinegar

2 slices ginger root

Chicken, Ham, and Shrimp Hot Pot

- Place wood ear mushrooms in a bowl. Pour hot water over to cover. Let stand 30 minutes; thinly slice.

- Arrange chicken, ham, and shrimp on separate plates. Place white mushrooms, broccoli, and leeks on a platter.

- Combine chicken broth, soy sauce, wine, vinegar, and ginger in a saucepan. Add wood ear mushrooms. Bring to a boil, then simmer 10 minutes.

- Pour broth mixture into a hot pot. Surround with platters of ingredients. Add dipping sauces as desired.

Dumpling Hot Pot: In place of the chicken, ham, and shrimp, bring 32 boiled dumplings to the table, preferably in a variety of fillings. The dumplings can be heated in the broth and eaten with a selection of hoisin, ginger-soy, sweet-and-sour, and plum sauces.

Chicken, Ham, and Shrimp Hot Pot with Wontons: Prepare the hot pot as directed. Once the ingredients have been cooked in the broth, drop 12 to 16 boiled pork wontons in the broth. Simmer until hot, then serve the wontons and broth in soup bowls.

Avoiding Cross-Contamination

- The trickiest thing about hot pots is keeping raw animal products—which can harbor disease-causing bacteria—separate from foods that can be eaten raw and foods that have been cooked.

- Keep raw meats and seafoods separate and refrigerated until serving time.

- Arrange washed vegetables on a platter separate from animal products.

- Make sure diners have their own plates for cooked foods, as well as separate utensils for cooking and eating.

Equipment Focus

- Electric hot pots allow you to raise the temperature on the broth to maintain a safe level.

- If you use a canned-fuel-powered hot pot, the broth may not remain hot enough to kill bacteria.

- To solve the problem, reheat the broth on the stove during the meal, then return it to the pot.

- If you are using a hot pot with an open flame, be careful and always keep a fire extinguisher nearby.

CHRYSANTHEMUM HOT POT

Autumn gatherings often include this festive hot pot with something for everyone

Chrysanthemum hot pot is the best example of that principle, with its components reflecting the full harvest of land and sea. At the same time, the broth is delicate, not spicy, and, with a final flourish of flower petals, beautiful.

Chrysanthemum hot pot traditionally appears at autumn celebrations, and usually the petals thrown into the pot at the end of cooking are from fresh, white chrysanthemums. If you can find organically grown fresh chrysanthemums, by all means add them. Most cooks, however, will have an easier time locating dried chrysanthemum petals, readily available in shops that carry Asian teas.

Yield: Serves 8

Ingredients

8 cups strong chicken broth

1 teaspoon minced ginger root

1/2 teaspoon white pepper

8 ounces chicken breast

8 ounces boneless pork chops

8 ounces shrimp, peeled and deveined

12 shucked clams or oysters

2 cups snow pea pods

1 red bell pepper, cored and sliced

8 ounces shiitake mushrooms, halved

1 head napa cabbage, cut in 2-inch pieces

12 ounces cellophane noodles

Dried chrysanthemum petals

1 cup soy sauce

1/3 cup rice wine vinegar

2 teaspoons honey

2 tablespoons sesame oil

1 tablespoon sesame seeds

Chrysanthemum Hot Pot

- Place chicken broth, ginger, and pepper in a saucepan. Bring to a boil; reduce to simmer.

- Thinly slice chicken and pork. Cut shrimp in half. Place sliced ingredients on separate plates.

- Place clams or oysters in shallow bowls. Divide snow peas, bell pepper, mushrooms, and cabbage on two platters.

- Pour hot broth into one or two hot pots. Allow guests to cook ingredients; add remaining ingredients and prepare dipping sauce.

Chrysanthemum Hot Pot II: Add 4 ounces of rinsed, well-chilled chicken livers and 4 cleaned, sliced squid to the mix of dipping ingredients in the hot pot. Baby bok choy can be substituted for the cabbage.

Chrysanthemum Seafood Hot Pot: In place of the chicken and pork, substitute 8 ounces scallops and 8 ounces of either spiny lobster tail or sliced firm white fish.

Complete the Meal

- Soften cellophane noodles in warm water 10 minutes.

- After diners have cooked ingredients, add softened noodles to the hot pot or pots.

- Let noodles stand 10 minutes, then sprinkle the broth with chrysanthemum petals.

- Serve broth and noodles in bowls.

Make Dipping Sauce

- Hoisin sauce, shacha sauce, and plum sauce can be purchased ready-made, but some dips are better made fresh.

- To make a simple sesame-soy sauce, whisk together soy sauce, vinegar, honey, sesame oil, and sesame seeds.

- Variations on this sauce include the addition of grated fresh ginger root, hot chile paste, or minced green onions.

- Divide sauce into small dipping bowls, providing individual bowls for each diner.

VEGETARIAN HOT POT

Fresh corn gives this broth a sweet, aromatic flavor without the addition of meat

No one ever accused the Chinese of being a nation of squeamish diners. Part of the vast spectrum of flavors and condiments on the Chinese table comes from a historic willingness to experiment gastronomically with virtually any creature that walks, flies, swims, or slithers. However, the Chinese also have a long culinary history of transforming the bounties of the soil. Even households that don't practice vegetarianism nevertheless prepare meals built around meatless entrees. The fact that the Chinese eat so many different roots, vegetables, fruits, and legumes means a vegetarian meal in China is never boring.

Yield: Serves 6

Ingredients

4 dried wood ear mushrooms

6 cups water

1 cup freshly scraped corn kernels

4 dried hot chiles

1/2 cup soy sauce

1/3 cup rice wine

2 teaspoons sugar

1/4 cup rice wine vinegar

2 tablespoons dark sesame oil

2 eggs, beaten

1 pound firm tofu

1 pound white mushrooms

1 bunch Chinese broccoli or broccoli rabe

1 daikon radish, thinly sliced

6 green onions, trimmed

1 red bell pepper, cored and sliced

8 ounces cellophane noodles

1/4 cup minced cilantro

Vegetarian Hot Pot

- Combine wood ears, water, corn, chiles, soy sauce, wine, sugar, and vinegar in a saucepan. Bring to a boil over high heat. Reduce heat and simmer 10 minutes.

- Stir in sesame oil. Slowly add beaten eggs, stirring while pouring. Arrange tofu and vegetables on a platter.

- Pour broth into a hot pot. Let diners cook ingredients; add softened cellophane noodles to pot.

- Allow noodles to steep 5 to 10 minutes, then add cilantro. Serve noodles and broth in bowls. Pass extra soy sauce.

Tofu-Free Hot Pot: Not everyone loves tofu. If you would prefer a curd-less hot pot, consider substituting baby zucchini, sliced eggplant, or blanched small red potatoes in place of the tofu. If you use potatoes, they should be a waxy variety, kept whole or halved to keep from breaking in the pot.

Mixed Greens Hot Pot: Prepare the broth as directed. In place of the mushrooms, radish, tofu, and bell pepper, give each diner 2 cups of assorted greens, including spinach, watercress, mustard greens, and the broccoli or broccoli rabe. The greens should be cooked in the hot pot using individual basket strainers, rather than forks or chopsticks. Serve with chopped peanuts for garnish.

Prepare Broth

- Dried wood ear mushrooms will soften in the boiling broth and flavor the broth. However, they will still be crisp.

- For a softer texture, place dried mushrooms in a bowl of hot water before preparing broth. Soak 30 minutes.

- Strain the soaking liquid into the broth in the saucepan and chop mushrooms as desired.

- This broth is flavored with sweet, spicy, and tart elements—corn, soy sauce, chiles, vinegar. Experiment with proportions to your own taste.

Vegetarian Victuals

- Vegetarian Hot Pot includes ingredients most cooks can find in the local supermarket. Feel free to change the mix.

- In China you'd likely find blanched taro root and sliced lotus root among the hot pot veggies. You can also opt for flavored or smoked tofu rather than plain.

- The eggs in this dish give the broth body, but keep it from being a vegan entree.

- If you would prefer an egg-free broth, simply thicken with diluted cornstarch.

ROAST PORK BUNS

Steaming produces tender, beautifully glossy white breads

Steamed breads may be an acquired taste, but once acquired the taste quickly turns into a craving.

Properly made steamed roast pork buns are plump and moist, with the texture of well-made flour dumplings on the outside and a savory, dark filling inside.

Although pork is the traditional filling, these dim sum favorites can be filled with a wide range of chopped meats or vegetables. This recipe uses hoisin sauce, but some cooks prefer to add oyster sauce. (Although not a Chinese option, ready-to-eat chopped barbecue can substitute for the homemade filling.)

Steamed pork buns can be purchased from street vendors in China and from Chinese bakeries in some Western cities. But for most fans, indulging a love of steamed pork buns means finding a table-service Chinese restaurant that offers dim sum—or making the buns at home.

Yield: 12 buns

Ingredients

1 pound prepared bread dough

1 tablespoon dark sesame oil

1 tablespoon vegetable oil

2 cloves garlic, minced

1 green onion, minced

1/2 pound roast pork, finely chopped

3 tablespoons soy sauce

2 tablespoons hoisin sauce

1 teaspoon sugar

1 tablespoon cornstarch dissolved in 2 tablespoons cold water

Roast Pork Buns

- Shape dough into a ball and coat with sesame oil. Cover and let stand until doubled, about 1 hour.

- Place wok over high heat. Add vegetable oil. Stir-fry garlic, green onion, and pork 1 minute. Stir soy sauce, hoisin sauce, and sugar together; add to pork.

Add dissolved cornstarch.

- Allow filling to cool completely. Shape and fill buns. Cover; let rise 45 minutes.

- Place buns on foil disks in a steamer. Close and steam 10 to 12 minutes. Serve warm.

Baked Pork Buns: Prepare buns as directed. Brush tops with a mixture of 1 egg beaten with 1 tablespoon water. Place buns on a baking sheet lined with nonstick foil. Bake at 350°F for 20 minutes or until browned.

Pulled Pork Buns: Prepare buns as directed, but substitute ½ pound finely shredded barbecued pulled pork for the roast pork.

Fill the Buns

- Punch down dough. Place on a floured work surface and knead until dough is smooth and pliable.

- Divide dough into 12 pieces. Roll each piece into a 3-inch circle and fill with 2½ tablespoons pork mixture.

- Pull the sides of the dough up around the filling, gathering the dough to enclose the filling.

- Place each bun on a foil disk and steam as directed.

Freezing Buns

- Making pork buns for steaming is a labor-intensive task.

- Fortunately they can be made in advance and frozen up to 3 months.

- Prepare buns as directed and steam until done. Allow buns to cool completely.

- Place buns into a gallon-size resealable plastic bag and carefully press out excess air. Freeze. When ready to serve, thaw and steam to heat.

SHRIMP TOAST

The spread and bread become one in this dim sum favorite

The best shrimp toast is full of shrimp flavor, with a layer of shrimp completely fused to the bread, making you wonder how the two elements merged.

Getting this snack or appetizer to that point requires a bit of practice—but that practice is half the fun.

To give the filling a good platform, buy dense, homemade-style white bread for this recipe. The bread should be slightly stale. If the slices seem soft, place the bread in an oven at 250°F for a few minutes to remove any moisture. Also, make sure the oil is hot before adding the shrimp toast triangles. This will cook the toasts quickly and keep the bread from soaking up oil.

Feel free to vary the herbs and seasonings in the shrimp topping, adding a bit of cilantro or hot chile flakes. Just don't add anything that might make the filling more "wet."

Yield: Serves 6

KNACK CHINESE COOKING

Ingredients

$^{1}/_{2}$ **pound shrimp, peeled, deveined, and patted dry**

1 teaspoon butter

1 green onion, chopped

2 cloves garlic, chopped

$^{1}/_{3}$ **cup water chestnuts**

$^{1}/_{2}$ **teaspoon grated ginger root**

2 egg whites

$^{1}/_{2}$ **teaspoon rice wine vinegar**

$^{1}/_{2}$ **teaspoon salt**

$^{1}/_{2}$ **teaspoon white pepper**

2 teaspoons cornstarch

6 slices day-old white bread

Vegetable oil for frying

Shrimp Toast

- In a food processor, combine shrimp, butter, green onion, garlic, water chestnuts, ginger, egg whites, vinegar, salt, pepper, and cornstarch. Pulse to a paste.

- Cut bread slices in half or quarters, diagonally. Spread shrimp mixture over one side of each piece.

- Add oil to a wok to a depth of 2 inches. When oil is very hot, place bread shrimp side down in the oil.

- Fry 2 minutes; turn and fry 30 seconds. Remove to a paper towel–lined plate. Serve warm.

Lobster Toast: Substitute a peeled, half-pound lobster tail for the shrimp.

Shrimp Mousse Toast: In place of the filling, use 12 ounces of prepared shrimp mousse. Spread the mousse on one slice of stale bread and top with another slice. Cut the mousse sandwich diagonally into quarters and dip the quarters into two beaten eggs. Fry the sandwiches in hot oil and serve.

White Bread

- Don't try to make Shrimp Toast with air bread.

- Those squishy loaves that children favor just don't have enough heft to make a good dim sum offering.

- Instead, shop for hearty loaves of white bread with wide, substantial slices and a slightly dense texture.

- If you prefer to go whole grain, look for a multigrain or honey wheat.

Making Shrimp Paste

- One of the great things about food processors is the ability to finely mince or puree several ingredients together.

- This blends flavors while creating a mix with a uniform texture.

- To ensure that everything purees evenly, cut meats and vegetables into similar pieces and chop aromatics and herbs.

- When preparing shrimp paste, pulse the mixture in a few short bursts to keep from liquefying the shrimp.

CHICKEN POT STICKERS

Everybody loves these little two-bite–size dumplings

When most people think about Chinese dumplings, this is the dish they're conjuring. Pot stickers—with their juicy filling, tender wrappers, and crisp, pan-fried bottoms—bring together irresistible tastes and textures. They're also fun to dip, especially in soy sauce laced with vinegar and hot chile peppers or minced ginger.

These pot stickers are made the quick and easy way with ready-to-use wonton wrappers for the dough. However, we do offer the recipe for the traditional flour and water wrapper. Also, there's some debate about whether pot stickers really need to be steamed before frying. The answer to that is, no, they do not. However, if you go straight to pan-frying after filling, it's important to keep the wok on low enough that the filling can cook completely while the pot stickers become browned but not burnt.

Yield: Serves 4–6

Ingredients

8 ounces boneless chicken thighs, ground

1 tablespoon soy sauce

1 teaspoon dark sesame oil

4 garlic chives or chives, chopped

1/2 cup sliced mushrooms

1/2 teaspoon coarse salt

1/4 teaspoon five-spice powder

24 small wonton wrappers

1 teaspoon cornstarch

3 tablespoons vegetable oil

Chicken Pot Stickers

- Combine chicken, soy sauce, and sesame oil. Place chives, mushrooms, and salt in a food processor. Pulse until finely chopped, but not pureed.

- Place mushroom mixture in a strainer and press out excess liquid.

- Mix chicken with mushroom mixture and five-spice powder. Freeze 20 minutes. Fill wontons and steam.

- Place a skillet over high heat; add vegetable oil. Fry dumplings, seam side up, 2 to 3 minutes, until bottoms are browned. Serve with dipping sauces.

208

Pork Pot Stickers: Replace the ground chicken in the filling with ground or minced pork.

Pot Stickers with Handmade Dough: Prepare dumpling filling as directed. In a large bowl, whisk 2 cups of flour and a pinch of salt; break up lumps. Slowly add 1 cup boiling water to the flour and stir until mixture pulls from the sides of the bowl. Place the dough on a floured surface and knead until no longer sticky. Divide dough in half and roll each into a cylinder. Slice cylinders crosswise into 12 pieces. Roll each piece into a thin circle. Fill circles with chicken filling and proceed with recipe as directed.

Fill Pot Stickers

- Remove chicken filling from freezer.

- Lay a wonton wrapper on a work surface. Place a teaspoon of filling at the center of the wrapper.

- Fold dough over filling and trim if necessary to create a crescent shape.

- Dissolve cornstarch in 1 tablespoon water. Brush a small amount of cornstarch mixture over the edges of the wrapper to seal.

Steam Dumplings

- Steaming before pan-frying ensures dumplings will be completely cooked through.

- Place dumplings on a plate, seam side up.

- Place the plate in a steamer basket, close, and steam 5 minutes.

- Remove dumplings from the steamer and let stand 2 to 3 minutes before pan-frying in hot oil.

DIM SUM DISHES

STEAMED SHRIMP DUMPLINGS
Perfect little pouches of seasoned shrimp make an irresistible snack

Dumplings, in all shapes and with all sorts of wrappers and fillings, are a mainstay of the Chinese dim sum experience. If you think about it, they're a perfect choice for a brunch or teatime meal made up of small plates. Each dumpling is a self-contained, balanced dish made up of protein, starch, and seasonings.

The trick to making excellent steamed dumplings is to remember that less is more. Don't make the fillings too saucy,

don't try to fill the wrappers too generously, and don't overcook the dumplings. You want the delicate steamed wrappers to hold together and the fillings to cook quickly in the moist steam heat.

Always provide dipping sauces for dumplings. A simple mix of rice wine vinegar, soy sauce, and hot chile flakes will do nicely.

Yield: Serves 4–5

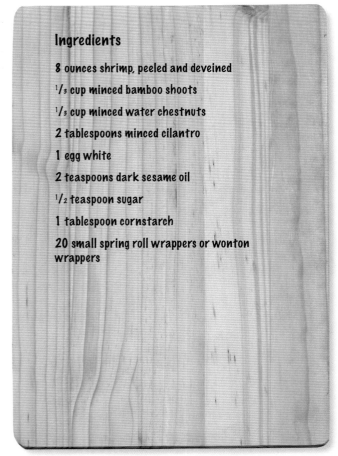

Ingredients

8 ounces shrimp, peeled and deveined

$^1/_3$ cup minced bamboo shoots

$^1/_3$ cup minced water chestnuts

2 tablespoons minced cilantro

1 egg white

2 teaspoons dark sesame oil

$^1/_2$ teaspoon sugar

1 tablespoon cornstarch

20 small spring roll wrappers or wonton wrappers

Steamed Shrimp Dumplings

- Mince shrimp; place in a strainer to drain as much liquid as possible. In a bowl, combine shrimp, bamboo shoots, water chestnuts, cilantro, and egg white. Mix with hands until well blended.

- Stir in sesame oil and sugar. Sprinkle cornstarch over

mixture and stir to distribute.

- Cover shrimp filling and freeze 20 minutes. Fill wrappers.

- Place dumplings in a steamer and steam 6 minutes, or until wrappers turn translucent. Serve with dipping sauces.

Steamed Scallop Dumplings: Substitute 8 ounces sea scallops for the shrimp.

Steamed Pork Dumplings: Substitute 8 ounces ground pork for the shrimp.

Steamed Salmon Dumplings: Mince together 6 ounces fresh salmon and 2 ounces smoked salmon. Use in place of the shrimp.

Rice Paper Wrappers

- Some cooks prefer to make these dumplings with rice paper wrappers for a more delicate appearance.

- Rice paper wrappers are ultrathin, brittle, and translucent circles made with rice flour, salt, and water. They must be softened before use.

- To soften, place one wrapper in a bowl of warm water and let stand 20 to 30 seconds. Remove to a damp, lint-free kitchen towel and fill as desired, gathering the sides to form a pouch.

- Repeat with remaining wraps and filling.

Fill Wrappers

- Place a wrapper on a work surface lightly sprinkled with cornstarch.

- Scoop a teaspoon of cold shrimp filling and place in the middle of the wrapper.

- Pull the four corners of the wrapper up and press together, forming a pouch.

- If you desire a decorative touch, blanched green onion strips can be used to "tie" the pouches closed.

MEATBALLS

East meets West in these popular and versatile snack bites

Chinese meatballs resemble dumpling fillings—a finely ground and tightly packed paste of pork and shrimp or fish, seasoned with green onion and other aromatics. After a quick stir-fry to help the shaped balls hold together, Chinese cooks usually steam or simmer the little morsels until cooked.

Western meatballs are coarse and meaty, with bread or bread crumbs as fillers and an exterior well browned in oil before being spooned into a heavy sauce.

This recipe merges the two concepts a bit. We've omitted any seafood from the meatball mixture and kept the Western technique of frying the meatballs until fully cooked. However, the fine texture and seasoning of these meatballs is all Chinese. Serve them with sweet-and-sour sauce or hoisin sauce.

Yield: Serves 6

Ingredients

8 ounces ground beef

8 ounces ground pork

1 green onion, chopped

$1/4$ teaspoon grated ginger root

2 tablespoons ice water

1 tablespoon soy sauce

1 teaspoon sesame oil

2 egg whites

2 tablespoons cornstarch

Salt and pepper to taste

Sweet-and-sour sauce

Hoisin sauce

Meatballs

- Combine beef, pork, green onion, and ginger in a food processor. Add ice water and pulse until meat resembles a fine paste.

- Combine meat mixture with soy sauce, sesame oil, and egg whites. Mix well, then mix in cornstarch, salt, and pepper. Mix again.

- With wet hands, form mixture into 20 small meatballs. In a nonstick skillet or wok, fry meatballs over medium-high heat until brown, about 10 minutes.

- Drain meatballs on paper towels and serve with dipping sauces.

Salmon and Scallop Balls: Substitute 12 ounces raw salmon and 4 ounces finely minced scallops for the pork and beef. Place the salmon in a food processor with green onion and ginger and reduce ice water to 1 tablespoon. After preparing salmon paste, stir in finely minced scallops and prepare balls as directed. If balls seem too moist, coat with a small amount of bread crumbs.

Meatballs with Lamb: Substitute 8 ounces ground lamb for the pork.

Processing Meats

- Already-ground meats purchased from most supermarkets are gauged at a "medium" grind.

- This is perfect for most home uses, particularly hamburgers and meat sauces. However, it makes very coarse meatballs and meat fillings.

- A food processor with a metal blade can remedy this problem by regrinding the meat into a fine, smooth paste.

- Adding ice water to the mix keeps the meat moist and firm, while dissipating any heat buildup from processing.

Shaping Meatballs

- The density or tenderness of meatballs depends a lot on how deftly they're shaped and handled.

- Always make sure the meat mixture is very cold before you begin working and keep your hands slightly wet.

- Shape meatballs lightly and quickly, to avoid toughening the meatballs or transferring the heat from your hands to the meat.

- Gently roll meat into a sphere between your palms. Use just enough pressure to mold the mixture evenly.

DIM SUM DISHES

MARBLED TEA EGGS
Tea and spices create boiled eggs that are both beautiful and tasty

Who knew that twice-cooked eggs could become works of art? Marbled tea eggs are a dim sum favorite, but they look almost too good to eat.

A broth of tea, soy sauce, and spices infuses cracked (but not peeled) hard-boiled eggs with flavor and a lovely variegated pattern. Think of it as tie-dyeing for boiled eggs. The hour-long cooking time also firms the egg whites, making them seem preserved by the broth.

Always serve marbled tea eggs cold so the smooth texture and slightly salty flavor come through.

Yield: Serves 6

Ingredients

6 hard-boiled eggs

¹/₂ cup soy sauce

3 tablespoons loose black tea

3 star anise

2 slices ginger root

1 cinnamon stick

1 teaspoon sugar

4 Szechwan peppercorns

Marbled Tea Eggs

- Crack the eggshells all over, but don't peel. Fill a large saucepan two-thirds full with water. Add soy sauce, tea, star anise, ginger root, cinnamon, sugar, and peppercorns.

- Bring mixture to a boil. Remove from heat and let stand 5 minutes.

- Add eggs to saucepan. Place over high heat and bring to a boil. Reduce heat to medium.

- Allow eggs to simmer 1 hour. Remove from heat and let eggs and liquid cool completely. Refrigerate overnight. Carefully peel eggs and serve.

Quail Tea Eggs: Substitute 12 quail eggs for the 6 eggs in the recipe. Prepare as directed, but halve the cooking times.

Blushed Eggs: In place of the tea and soy sauce, add 2 peeled and diced red beets and 2 teaspoons salt to the simmering water. Cook as directed.

Pickled Blushed Eggs: In place of the tea and soy sauce, add 1 jar of pickled beets to the simmering water. Cook as directed.

Crack the Eggs

- To make hard-boiled eggs, use raw eggs purchased a couple of days earlier. Allow them to reach room temperature, then place in a pot of cold water to cover.

- Bring water to a boil over high heat. Reduce heat to medium; simmer eggs 10 minutes.

- Remove from heat and let eggs stand in the water until cool enough to handle.

- Carefully crack eggs all over, using quick, light strokes. The side of a spoon works well. The eggshells should hold together and remain attached.

About Black Tea

- Black tea refers to leaves of the *Camellia sinensis* plant that have been allowed to dry and oxidize.

- Although in China green tea is the sipping tea of choice, most Western tea is either a single source or blend of black teas.

- For this recipe, you might add Lapsang Souchong, a smoky-flavored Chinese black tea, or a citrusy Ceylon black tea. Or, you can just pop open a few tea bags.

- Don't use your last few tablespoons of an expensive black tea in this recipe.

EGG CUSTARD TARTS

Serve creamy, rich custard tarts with a few berries for a beautiful end to a meal

Custard has soothing qualities, whether slightly sweetened and coddled in a water bath or elaborately flavored and seared with a cracked sugar crust for crème brûlée.

Portuguese traders introduced the Chinese to the wonders of egg custard, and the Chinese promptly created egg custard tarts, a delectable sweet offered at dim sum services and banquets. Usually Chinese cooks prefer to serve egg custard tarts plain or ever-so-faintly scented with vanilla. This recipe takes liberties by adding cinnamon, cloves, ginger, and nutmeg to the silky custard. For those who prefer a less spicy dessert, we offer vanilla tarts as a variation.

Yield: Serves 16

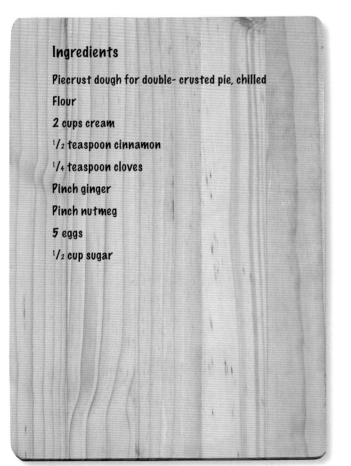

Ingredients

Piecrust dough for double- crusted pie, chilled

Flour

2 cups cream

$^1/_2$ teaspoon cinnamon

$^1/_4$ teaspoon cloves

Pinch ginger

Pinch nutmeg

5 eggs

$^1/_2$ cup sugar

Egg Custard Tarts

- Roll piecrust to about ¼-inch thick. Cut into 16 2-inch circles; press into tartlet pans.

- In a saucepan, combine cream, cinnamon, cloves, ginger, and nutmeg. Bring to a boil over medium-high heat, stirring constantly. Reduce heat to medium.

- In a bowl, beat eggs and sugar until light. Pour a little hot cream into eggs, beating constantly. Pour egg mixture into cream and whisk quickly. Remove from heat.

- Pour filling into crusts. Bake at 350°F 20 minutes. Cool to room temperature; serve.

Vanilla Egg Custard Tarts: Omit cinnamon, cloves, ginger, and nutmeg. Stir 1 teaspoon vanilla into the cooked custard, then follow recipe as directed.

Mango Custard Tarts: Omit cinnamon, cloves, ginger, and nutmeg. Stir vanilla into the cooked custard. Add 1 tablespoon chopped fresh mango to each crust-lined tart cup. Pour custard over the mango and bake as directed.

Prepare the Crust

Temper the Eggs

- Good refrigerated piecrusts are available at most supermarkets. Packages usually hold two pastry circles that can accommodate a 9- to 10-inch pie or tart.

- Use refrigerated crust or your favorite recipe. Either way, roll crusts as thin as possible without breaking the dough.

- Flour a 1½- or 2-inch cookie cutter and cut out 16 circles. You may need to reroll leftover dough scraps.

- Press the circles into mini tart pans (preferably non-stick), covering the bottom and sides.

- It only takes a bit of heat to begin cooking—or curdling—raw eggs.

- To keep from creating scrambled eggs, temper the eggs before adding them to the scalding milk.

- Add a ladle full of simmering cream to the eggs and sugar, while actively beating the eggs and sugar.

- Quickly pour the warmed and diluted egg mixture into the simmering cream, whisking constantly until the eggs and sugar have dispersed smoothly in the cream.

FRUITS & SWEETS

FRUIT WITH GINGER SYRUP

Ginger moves from savory to sweet in this supersimple dessert

The Chinese embrace the refreshing, naturally sweet goodness of fruit. Elaborate desserts may turn up at festival and holiday celebrations, but at family meals, dessert is more likely to be a wedge of melon or a few orange slices. This dish adds an aromatic flourish to a tropical fruit salad with a ginger-spiked simple syrup. Cooking sugar and water together turns the sugar into a liquid, which can be flavored in a variety of ways. If you aren't in the mood for ginger, try va-

nilla beans, cinnamon sticks, or mint leaves to enhance your dish. Of course if you can't imagine ending a meal without cake, this gingered-fruit mixture makes an excellent topping for sponge cake, pound cake, or even bread pudding.

Yield: Serves 8

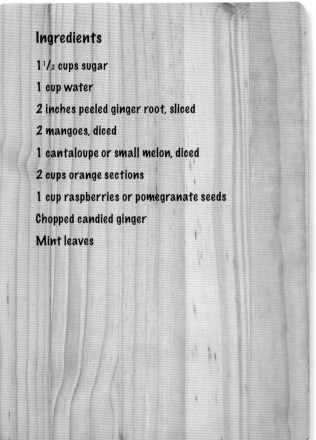

Ingredients

1¹/₂ cups sugar

1 cup water

2 inches peeled ginger root, sliced

2 mangoes, diced

1 cantaloupe or small melon, diced

2 cups orange sections

1 cup raspberries or pomegranate seeds

Chopped candied ginger

Mint leaves

Fruit with Ginger Syrup

- Place sugar and water in a saucepan. Bring to a boil over medium-high heat, stirring constantly. Cook until sugar is completely dissolved.

- Reduce heat to medium. Add ginger; simmer 5 minutes. Remove from heat and let cool completely. Strain

syrup into a bowl, cover, and refrigerate.

- Combine fruits in a large bowl. Drizzle syrup over the fruits and gently toss to combine.

- Spoon fruit into individual dishes. Garnish with candied ginger and mint leaves.

Fruit with Ginger Syrup II: Replace mango, melon, and oranges with 2 cups each peaches, nectarines, and plums. Substitute ⅓ cup white wine for ⅓ cup of the water in the syrup mixture. Prepare recipe as directed.

Fruit with Ginger-Kumquat Syrup: Finely chop 4 kumquats in a food processor. Add to sugar syrup with ginger and prepare as directed. Strain sugar syrup well before refrigerating. Add to fruits as desired.

Make Simple Syrup

- Simple syrup can be used for everything from flavoring fruit to sweetening lemonade or ice tea.

- When heated, sugar becomes a liquid. Keeping sugar over high heat for long periods causes it to caramelize, solidify when cooled, and eventually burn.

- Adding water to the sugar while heating keeps the sugar from dissolving. This results in a sweetener that has more body and versatility than sugar water alone.

- Simple syrups can be flavored with fruits, herbs, or spices. Always strain to prevent cloudiness.

Dicing Mango

- Mangoes have a hard, irregular-shaped seed. To cut a mango into clean pieces, hold the fruit narrow side down on a cutting board.

- Make a straight slice about ⅓ inch from the center on each side.

- Score the flesh of each side in a cross-hatch pattern, cutting to the peel but not through it.

- Grab the peel at the top and bottom and turn it back. The diced fruit will protrude, ready to be sliced from the peel.

FRUITS & SWEETS

STEAMED PEARS

This dessert is simplicity itself, but still worthy of your favorite guests

Crisp, crunchy Asian pears steam into a luscious, fragrant dessert. Lemon-spiked honey enhances the flavor of the dish, while almonds add a little bite to the mix.

Although pears are especially well suited to steaming, any tree fruit can be cooked in this simple manner. In China, steamed fruit is a dessert in itself, but Westerners may want to add a dollop of lightly sweetened cream or a drizzle of chocolate sauce to the cooked fruit.

Yield: Serves 6

Ingredients

3 Asian pears

1/3 cup honey

1 tablespoon hot water

1 teaspoon lemon juice

1/2 cup slivered almonds

Steamed Pears

- Peel and core pears. Cut into quarters and place in a shallow, heat-safe bowl.

- Combine honey, water, and lemon juice. Brush over the pears.

- Place a steaming rack inside a wok and fill with water to just below the rack. Bring water to a boil over high heat, then reduce heat to medium.

- Place plate on the steaming rack; cover and steam 20 minutes. Spoon pear quarters onto a serving plate, sprinkle with almonds, and serve.

Steamed Apples with Walnuts: Substitute 3 Rome or Gala apples for the Asian pears. In place of the slivered almonds, sprinkle the fruit with chopped candied walnuts.

Steamed Asian Pears with Stilton Cheese: Sprinkle ½ cup crumbled Stilton cheese over the warm pears before serving.

A Touch of Honey

- Honey reflects the flavors of the flowers and trees from which the bees harvested the nectar.

- There are almost-clear mild-flavored honeys and dark molasses–like honeys, as well as honey blends, unfiltered honey, and pasteurized honey.

- China is the world's largest producer of honey, mostly common clover varieties. However, China also produces some of the world's finest pearl-white, unfiltered honey and delicate Acacia honey.

- Specialty food stores and Asian markets carry these.

Steaming Fruit

- Steaming brings out the full flavors of fruit, while turning the flesh into a soft, luscious treat.

- Almost any tree fruit can be steamed, as long as you reduce the cooking time for "wet" fruits like peaches, plums, and nectarines.

- Start with fruit that's ripe but still firm. Cut into uniform pieces; for small fruits, simply core and steam whole. Don't overcook.

- Add a light syrup while steaming, or add a drizzle of sweetened berry puree or caramel before serving.

SWEET RICE BALLS

Rice flour gives these unusual little bonbons a chewy texture

In China virtually anything starchy can be transformed into flour, and all flours are likely to turn up in noodles and dumplings somewhere.

Glutinous rice flour, which cooks into goods with a chewy, moist texture, is Asia's favorite flour for desserts and steamed breads. Doughs made with glutinous rice flour are sometimes dyed with food coloring or colorful ingredients to create green or red-colored desserts. Although regular rice flour can be used to create cut noodles and noodle sheets, rice flour cannot be used in recipes that call for glutinous rice flour. This recipe calls for a coconut coating, but purists might prefer to go with a light dusting of confectioner's sugar instead.

Yield: Serves 6

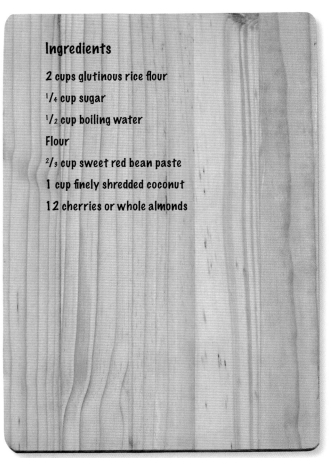

Ingredients

2 cups glutinous rice flour

1/4 cup sugar

1/2 cup boiling water

Flour

2/3 cup sweet red bean paste

1 cup finely shredded coconut

12 cherries or whole almonds

Sweet Rice Balls

- Mix rice flour and sugar in a bowl. Make a well in the center. Pour in boiling water and stir until a soft dough forms.

- Form the dough into a ball. Place on a floured surface and knead until pliable. Shape and fill the dough.

- Place balls in a steamer basket. Place in a wok with water just below the basket.

- Steam balls over simmering water 12 minutes. Coat each with coconut; top with a cherry or almond.

Quick-Fix Rice Balls: Mix cooked glutinous rice—not rice flour—with enough condensed milk to sweeten the rice and hold it together. Shape the rice into balls and roll in shredded coconut, chopped dates, sesame seeds, or crushed nuts.

Candy-Filled Rice Balls: This variation isn't exactly Chinese, but it is yummy. Prepare rice balls as directed, with glutinous rice flour dough. Substitute 12 caramel candies for the red bean paste. Press one caramel square into the center of each rice ball and steam. Roll in coconut.

Shape and Fill Dough

- Glutinous rice flour dough should be the consistency of children's modeling clay—soft but not sticky.

- First, adjust the dough as needed. More liquid will make the dough softer; more flour will make it less sticky.

- Knead dough; roll it into a tube. Slice the tube crosswise into 12 equal pieces.

- Roll each piece into a ball, flatten into a circle, and press the red bean paste into the circle. Roll the dough into a ball again, encasing bean paste.

Coat the Rice Balls

- Pour coconut onto a plate or shallow bowl.

- With a slotted spoon, remove the rice balls from the steamer and place on a plate.

- While the balls are still hot, roll in coconut until well coated. If balls are too

hot to touch, use spoons or chopsticks to roll them around.

- Place coconut-covered balls on a serving plate and top with a cherry or almond.

FRUITS & SWEETS

EIGHT PRECIOUS PUDDING

This banquet dessert turns homey rice pudding into a haute delight

Eight precious pudding is sometimes called eight treasures pudding, referring to the eight candied fruits and almonds that stud the steamed dessert. To make the name accurate, make sure the mix of candied fruits you buy has at least five different fruits. Combined with the cherries, dates, and almonds, you'll have your eight treasures. If you're not a fan of candied fruit, substitute finely chopped dried fruits—pineapples, apricots, peaches, figs, pears—to your pudding.

Glutinous rice contains large amounts of a particular starch that renders the cooked grains sticky. Sticky rice alone isn't sweet, but the thick texture lends itself nicely to dessert preparations.

Yield: Serves 4–6

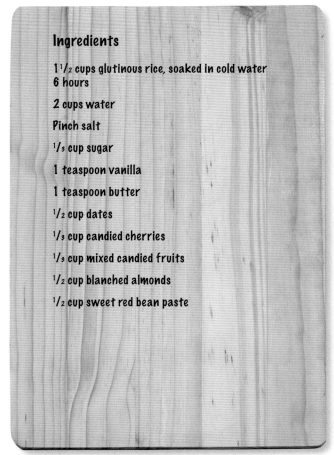

Ingredients

1½ cups glutinous rice, soaked in cold water 6 hours

2 cups water

Pinch salt

⅓ cup sugar

1 teaspoon vanilla

1 teaspoon butter

½ cup dates

⅓ cup candied cherries

⅓ cup mixed candied fruits

½ cup blanched almonds

½ cup sweet red bean paste

Eight Precious Pudding

- Drain rice. Combine rice, water, salt, sugar, and vanilla in a saucepan. Bring to a boil. Reduce heat to medium-low. Cover and cook 15 minutes.

- Drain and chop dates. Butter a deep, medium bowl. Arrange fruit and almonds around side of bowl.

- Layer half the rice into the bowl. Place bean paste in a flat disk at the center of the rice. Spoon in remaining rice.

- Cover bowl tightly. Place on a steamer rack over simmering water; cover and steam 1 hour. Unmold and serve in wedges.

Cherry-Almond Pudding: Substitute dried cherries for the dates and increase candied cherries to ⅔ cup. Omit mixed candied fruits. Sweetened almond paste can be substituted for the red bean paste.

Black Sticky Rice Pudding: Soak 1½ cups black glutinous rice in cold water for 6 hours or overnight. Combine the rice with 2 cups water and 1½ cups coconut milk, plus salt, sugar, and vanilla. Cook for 45 minutes to 1 hour or until rice is tender.

Mango Rice Pudding: Arrange fresh mango slices around the bowl in place of candied fruits, dates, and cherries.

Prepare the Bowl

- Select a heat-safe ceramic bowl that is narrower at the base than at the top. The bowl should be able to fit into a wok or on a rack with a little room around the sides.

- Generously coat the bowl with butter.

- Center a cherry at the bottom of the bowl. Press fruits and almonds into the butter inside the bowl.

- Add rice to the bowl, allowing the mass to press against the fruits and almonds. Place red bean paste in the center.

Unmold the Pudding

- Carefully remove the pudding bowl from the steamer. Wipe any water from the outside of the bowl.

- Uncover the bowl and slide a knife between the pudding and the sides of the bowl. Push the knife straight down in three or four places.

- Carefully run the knife all around the edge of the pudding to loosen.

- Place a serving plate over the top of the pudding. Flip the plate over and tap the bottom of the bowl. The pudding should drop onto the platter.

ALMOND COOKIES

Keep tins of these delicious cookies on hand for a teatime treat

Bake shops in China sell simple, melt-in-your-mouth almond cookies. But these addictive little morsels really have been embraced by Chinese food lovers in the West. Home cooks, in particular, love to pass a plate of almond cookies with Chinese teas or after a dinner party featuring a Chinese-inspired entree. Serve these delicately flavored Almond Cookies alone, or as an accompaniment to fruit or sorbet. The cookies keep very well in airtight tins, and the dough can be frozen for a

quick cookie-fix.

If you think your arteries can handle it, substitute lard for all or part of the butter. Lard gives these basic cookies a rich shortbread-like texture that's irresistible.

Yield: Makes 24 cookies

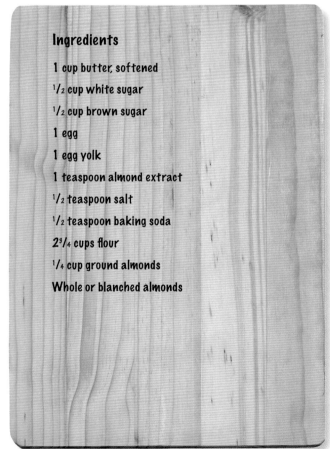

Ingredients

1 cup butter, softened

$^1/_2$ cup white sugar

$^1/_2$ cup brown sugar

1 egg

1 egg yolk

1 teaspoon almond extract

$^1/_2$ teaspoon salt

$^1/_2$ teaspoon baking soda

$2^3/_4$ cups flour

$^1/_4$ cup ground almonds

Whole or blanched almonds

Almond Cookies

- Combine butter and sugars in a bowl; beat until creamy.

- Add egg, egg yolk, and almond extract. Beat until fluffy. Combine salt, baking soda, flour, and ground almonds. Whisk to break up any lumps.

- Add flour mixture to butter mixture. Beat on medium until batter is smooth. Cover and refrigerate dough 30 minutes.

- With floured hands, shape dough into small balls and place on prepared baking sheet. Place an almond in the center of each cookie. Bake at 325°F 15 minutes.

Pecan Cookies: Substitute ground pecans for the ground almonds and almond halves for the slivered almonds. Almond extract or vanilla extract can be used for flavoring.

Chocolate Almond Cookies: Add ⅓ cup cocoa powder to dry ingredients and reduce the flour to 2½ cups.

Combine Ingredients

- Achieving proper dough consistency begins with softened but cool butter.

- Add sugars and beat on low until mixture is blended. Turn mixer to medium and cream sugar and butter until fluffy.

- Turn speed to low and add eggs and flavoring. Only after liquid ingredients are beaten into a light, creamy base should the dry ingredients be added.

- Add dry ingredients to butter mixture one scoop at a time. Beat on low after each addition. Beat on medium to finish.

Prepare the Pan

- Cooks debate whether a cookie sheet should be greased.

- Greased cookie sheets have a "frying" effect on the dough and can burn cookies. The grease also allows dough to spread and flatten as it bakes.

- Baking sheets develop scratches or stains over time and those spots can cause dough to stick.

- The best way to avoid stuck or overcooked cookies is to line your baking sheets with nonstick foil or silicon liners.

FRUITS & SWEETS

227

EQUIPMENT

You can start your Chinese cooking odyssey without special equipment. But before long, you'll start yearning for a new wok, a hot pot, and other specialized gear. When that happens, here are a few places to turn.

Web Sites

Chefs Catalog

www.chefscatalog.com
Find a variety of woks, hot pots, cleavers, cutting boards, and other equipment at this high-end online emporium.

Cooking.com

www.cooking.com
Buy a metal tub boasting a logo from your alma mater to ice Chinese beer. Then move on to one of the best selections of woks on the Web.

Gourmet Sleuth

www.gourmetsleuth.com
Chinese clay pots, mortar and pestle sets, hot pots, and more can be found on this fun site. Take time to browse the recipes.

Mrs. Lin's Kitchen

www.mrslinskitchen.com
This site offers equipment for both Chinese and Japanese cooking. Check out the beautiful chopsticks and tea sets.

Catalogs

Chefs Catalog

www.chefscatalog.com
This great Web site also sends out full-color catalogs that feature seasonal specials and markdowns. Order a catalog from the site or call (800) 338-3232.

Sur La Table

www.surlatable.com
Beautiful table settings and serving pieces are the hallmark of this kitchen store, catalog, and Web site. However, browse the cata-

log and you'll find wonderful wok spatulas and bamboo tongs, as well as woks and cleavers.

Williams-Sonoma
www.williams-sonoma.com
If you live near a Williams-Sonoma store, you've gotten a taste of the broad range of kitchen niceties available. The catalog offers more products without the trip. Check out the Shun knives, the hot pepper corers, and other gadgets. (877) 812-6235

Stores

Bed, Bath and Beyond
www.bedbathandbeyond.com
Walk into one of the 900-plus locations of this chain and find woks ranging in price from $15 to $300, as well as all the tools and table accessories you might desire.

Fante's
www.fantes.com
1006 South 9th Street
Philadelphia, PA
(800) 443-2683
For 100-plus years, Fante's has reigned as South Philadelphia's source for quality cookware and culinary guidance. Shop for woks, steamers, and tools, and don't miss the stunning hammered-copper hot pot.

Target
www.target.com
Go to the Web site to find the location of a Target near you. These ubiquitous stores offer a good selection of rice cookers, as well as electric hot pots, woks, and gadgets at reasonable prices.

The Wok Shop
www.wokshop.com
718 Grant Avenue
San Francisco, CA
(415) 989-3797
If you're visiting or live near San Francisco, drop in to this 35-year-old landmark. You'll find a staggering array of Chinese kitchen tools and equipment, as well as opportunities for cooking classes and tours.

INGREDIENTS

Strolling through a market in China will open your eyes to ingredients you've never seen, as well as things you never expected to see as ingredients. Even if you're cooking on the other side of the globe, you can find many Chinese specialties at your supermarket, a local Asian grocery, or by ordering from one of these vendors.

Wholesale

Frieda's Inc.

www.friedas.com

Frieda's products are widely distributed in store produce departments, but the Web site offers a consumer ordering option as well. Find wraps, bitter melon, Chinese broccoli, Asian pears, and fresh lychees, among other delights.

Generation Tea

www.generationtea.com

This company specializes in fine teas from China and offers both wholesale programs and direct-to-consumer sales from their Web site. In addition to favorites like jasmine tea, oolong tea, and black teas, the company sells rare vintage teas, tea extracts, and a lovely white tea soap.

Melissa's Produce

www.melissas.com

Melissa's distributes fresh and dried Chinese mushrooms, organic baby bok choy, Chinese long beans, and banana leaves, among other hard-to-find items. Check the Web site for availability and retailers that carry Melissa's products.

Specialty Stores

Asian Food Grocer

www.asianfoodgrocer.com

Chinese beverages, candies, pickles, noodles, and other staples can be ordered from this pan-Asian virtual grocery.

Ethnic Grocer

www.ethnicgrocer.com

Stock the pantry with Chinese seasonings and staples—rice, dried mushrooms, sauces—from this online global food resource.

Oriental Super-Mart

www.orientalsuper-mart.com

Located in Miami, this large Asian store offers, among 2,000 other products, a good selection of glutinous rice, including black sweet rice. Lee Kum Kee, Panda, and other favorite brands of Chinese sauces and marinades can be ordered online.

United Noodles

www.unitednoodles.com

If you're in Minneapolis, be sure to drop by for a take-out package of fresh Chinese roast pork or roast duck. Also peruse the extensive produce aisle. If you're out of town, you can still order dried spices, sauces, noodles, and mushrooms.

Farmers' Markets

Chinatown Produce Stands
Forsyth Street between Canal and Division Streets, NY. Open daily. This isn't a farmers' market per se, but a collection of produce stands in the middle of Chinatown. Look for exotic fruits and vegetables at great prices, but shop carefully since some items may be overripe.

Dekalb Farmers Market
3000 Ponce de Leon Ave., Decatur, GA. Open daily.
www.dekalbfarmersmarket.com
Get a map before browsing this 140,000-square-foot indoor market outside Atlanta. In addition to fresh Asian produce and a huge selection of fresh and dried peppers, the Dekalb market also produces and bottles many sauces and condiments in-house.

The French Market
Decatur Street in the French Quarter, New Orleans, LA. Open daily.
www.frenchmarket.org
It's easy to get distracted by the art and confectioner shops, the kitschy flea market, and Café du Monde. But keep walking until you reach the farmers' market for locally grown produce, including Asian vegetables.

The Hayward Farmers Market
City Hall Plaza, Hayward, CA. Saturday 9 a.m. to 1 p.m.
www.marinfarmersmarkets.org
This Marin County farmers' market offers a cornucopia of fresh produce, including abundant displays from local Asian farmers.

Union Square Greenmarket
17th and Broadway, NY. Open Monday through Friday and Saturday
www.cennyc.org
The flagship of several Greenmarkets in NYC, this outdoor produce and gourmet foods market supports regional New York growers.

KITCHEN READING

The more exposure you have to Chinese food history, recipes, and techniques, the more comfortable you'll be experimenting with your own creations. Of course books and magazines can offer refresher courses in basic kitchen skills as well. Here are a few tomes and periodicals to peruse.

Books

The Breath of a Wok: Unlocking the Spirit of Chinese Wok Cooking Through Recipes and Lore by Grace Young and Alan Richardson (Simon and Schuster)
This book has quickly become a culinary classic. It's beautifully written and illustrated, with recipes for many Chinese restaurant favorites. However, the book is strongest in its almost-scholarly discussions about the history, manufacture, value, and use of the wok.

The Fortune Cookie Chronicles: Adventures in the World of Chinese Food by Jennifer 8 Lee (Twelve)
This lively read is ostensibly about the all-American Chinese dessert: the fortune cookie. But it actually explores immigration, assimilation, and the culture of food.

Martin Yan's China by Martin Yan (Chronicle Books)
The companion book to the PBS series *Martin Yan's China* is filled with stunning photos, a wealth of information about the history and culture of China, and some great recipes. Order it from his Web site and get a companion DVD free.

Magazines

Cook's Illustrated
www.cooksillustrated.com
This advertising-free bimonthly offers the best step-by-step cooking instructions and illustrations around. Plus, the no-nonsense test-kitchen cooks share the good, bad, and ugly about dishes. Subscribe on the Web site.

Flavor and Fortune: Dedicated to the Art and Science of Chinese Cuisine
www.flavorandfortune.com
This nonprofit quarterly is dedicated to promoting dialog among professionals and lay cooks about everything related to Chinese cuisine. Subscribe on the Web site.

Saveur
www.saveur.com
Big, beautiful food magazine with a fine techniques section. Subscribe online for nine issues a year.

KITCHEN VIEWING

Laptops have made it easy to pull up an online video or pop a DVD into the disk drive for an as-you-go cooking lesson in the kitchen. Here are a few products and sites worth watching.

DVDs and Videos

Go Cooking Videos
www.gocookingvideos.com
This free site is supported by Web ads. It's an amalgamation of cooking videos—many amateur—that appear on YouTube and other sites.

Howcast
www.howcast.com
Great free instructional videos on a variety of topics. Use the search feature to find the well-populated Asian cooking section.

New Asian Cuisine/Rouxbe
www.nac.rouxbe.com
This partnership offers an online subscription that allows access to step-by-step recipe videos and an online cooking school. Go to the Web site to sign up for a free trial membership.

Wok Fusion
www.wokfusion.com
This site offers DVD-based Chinese cooking courses and down-loadable e-cookbooks. Order online from the Web site.

Yan Can Cook
www.yancancook.com
Venerable Chinese chef Martin Yan offers beautifully produced videos of several recipes on his primary Web site.

RESOURCES

GREAT LINKS

Once you get comfortable with—and learn to love—your own Chinese dishes, you'll want to expand your repertoire. Here are some Web sites that can inspire, instruct, or simply entertain.

Web Sites

About.com
www.about.com
Canada-based cookbook author and caterer Rhonda Parkinson does a great job as About's guide to Chinese food. Her discussions will pique your interest, and her recipes are clear and easy to follow.

Appetite for China
www.appetiteforchina.com
Food and travel writer Diana Kuan chronicles her pursuit of Chinese cuisine as prepared around the globe. Her bonafides are excellent: She grew up in Puerto Rico, the daughter of a Chinese restaurant family.

Jacqueline Church
http://jacquelinechurch.com
Prolific, funny, and passionate food writer Jacqueline Church blogs about a wide range of food and libation topics. However, her discourses on fresh produce and sustainable dining are not to be missed.

Red Cook: Adventures from a Chinese Home Kitchen
www.redcook.net
New York–based private chef and writer Kian Lam Kho's home site offers captivating blog entries, instruction, and photos that will make you want to cook—or at the very least eat—authentic Chinese cuisine.

METRIC CONVERSION TABLES

Approximate U.S. Metric Equivalents

Liquid Ingredients

U.S. MEASURES	METRIC	U.S. MEASURES	METRIC
¼ TSP.	1.23 ML	2 TBSP.	29.57 ML
½ TSP.	2.36 ML	3 TBSP.	44.36 ML
¾ TSP.	3.70 ML	¼ CUP	59.15 ML
1 TSP.	4.93 ML	½ CUP	118.30 ML
1¼ TSP.	6.16 ML	1 CUP	236.59 ML
1½ TSP.	7.39 ML	2 CUPS OR 1 PT.	473.18 ML
1¾ TSP.	8.63 ML	3 CUPS	709.77 ML
2 TSP.	9.86 ML	4 CUPS OR 1 QT.	946.36 ML
1 TBSP.	14.79 ML	4 QTS. OR 1 GAL.	3.79 L

Dry Ingredients

U.S. MEASURES	METRIC	U.S. MEASURES		METRIC
1⁄16 OZ.	2 (1.8) G	2⅘ OZ.		80 G
⅛ OZ.	3½ (3.5) G	3 OZ.		85 (84.9) G
¼ OZ.	7 (7.1) G	3½ OZ.		100 G
½ OZ.	15 (14.2) G	4 OZ.		115 (113.2) G
¾ OZ.	21 (21.3) G	4½ OZ.		125 G
⅞ OZ.	25 G	5¼ OZ.		150 G
1 OZ.	30 (28.3) G	8⅞ OZ.		250 G
1¾ OZ.	50 G	16 OZ.	1 LB.	454 G
2 OZ.	60 (56.6) G	17⅗ OZ.	1 LIVRE	500 G

GLOSSARY

Chinese ingredients may appear in markets under various names, depending on whether proprietors go with the pinyin (Chinese written in Western characters) name of a vegetable or sauce, or an English name. Here are a few definitions that might help.

Chinese Kitchen Definitions

Baby Bok Choy: Sometimes called Shanghai cabbage, this green is a smaller, sweeter cultivar of full-size bok choy.

Bamboo Shoots: Canned bamboo shoots can be found everywhere. Fresh shoots—the cone-shaped sprouts of new bamboo stalks—can sometimes be found at specialty stores. Aficionados say winter shoots are more tender than spring shoots.

Bitter Melon: A knobby cucumber-shaped gourd that can be used like eggplant or zucchini in recipes. Blanch before cooking to reduce bitterness.

Black Bean Paste: Made from fermented soy beans mixed with flour and seasonings. Black bean sauce can be made from the paste, or from whole, salted fermented black beans.

Chinese Cabbage: In some Western supermarkets bok choy is called Chinese cabbage. The term more accurately refers to one of many long, compact cabbage varieties, such as napa cabbage.

Chinese Green Beans: Also called yard-long beans, these tropical relatives of the cowpea grow to about 18 inches long. They can be prepared in the same manner as green beans, or dry-fried in a wok, then allowed to soak up added sauces and flavorings.

Chinese Sausages: These thin, dried sausages resemble pepperoni in texture and have a pronounced salty-sweet flavor. Most are made with pork, although some include liver in the mix. Find these at Chinese grocery stores.

Choy Sum: A small, tender bok choy relative with green stalks, dark green leaves, and small, edible flowers that hint at the taste of mustard greens. Also called flowering cabbage.

Cilantro: The fresh leaves of the coriander plant can be an acquired taste. Frequently used in Asian, Mexican, and some Caribbean cuisines, cilantro is sometimes called Chinese parsley. Most supermarkets carry fresh cilantro, or you can grow your own.

Daikon Radish: Looking more like a white parsnip than a radish, this crisp, mild-flavored root can be used raw in salads or sliced into stir-fries and soups.

Enoki Mushrooms: Very thin, long, pale mushrooms that can be found in stir-fries, soups, and salads. These delicate mushrooms can be found in supermarkets, but should be used quickly. Also known as golden mushrooms.

Five-Spice Powder: This classic spice may contain a variety of ingredients, with star anise, fennel, cloves, and cinnamon being common. Mouth-numbing Szechwan peppercorns should be a primary ingredient; however, some Western blends substitute black or red pepper.

Garlic Chives: These flat-leafed chives carry a mild garlic flavor and are a favorite in soups. Both the green, strappy leaves and the herb blossoms can be used in cooking.

Ginger Root: With garlic and green onions, ginger root stars in the Chinese seasoning trinity. Buy firm, unblemished "hands" of this knobby root and store loosely wrapped in the refrigerator. Ginger is too fibrous to munch in large pieces. Invest in a fine-planed ginger grater to shred the aromatic root for recipes.

Lychees: Lychees or lychee nuts aren't nuts at all, but rather a tropical fruit that grows in clusters on small evergreen trees. The fruit has a rough, red skin and a large inner brown seed. In between, the translucent, creamy-colored flesh is moist, sweet, and fragrant. Fresh lychees can be found in some Asian markets, and canned lychees are in supermarkets everywhere.

Pickled Vegetables: Chinese cooks pickle all manner of vegetables, then use the pickles in various dishes. Szechwan province is famous for spicy pickled vegetables that usually include turnips and cabbage in a salty brine packed with chiles and Szechwan peppercorns.

Tiger Lily Buds: These dried, unopened lily flowers add texture and a warm, earthy flavor to soups and stir-fries. The long, thin, rehydrated buds, sometimes called golden needles, are featured in hot and sour soup.

Wood Ear Mushrooms: Also called tree ears (or incorrectly, cloud ears), this fungus grows on the sides of certain tree trunks. Wood ears are highly perishable and generally are available dried. Rehydrated in hot water, the mushrooms can increase in size fivefold.

INDEX

239

243

INDEX